From
Christine, zo...

TO: _____

FROM: _____

DATE: _____

beloved

365 DEVOTIONS FOR YOUNG WOMEN

WRITTEN BY LINDSAY A. FRANKLIN

ZONDERVAN

ZONDERVAN

Beloved
Copyright © 2018 by Zondervan

This title is also available as a Zondervan ebook.

Requests for information should be addressed to:
Zondervan, *3900 Sparks Dr. SE, Grand Rapids, Michigan 49546*

ISBN 978-0-310-76277-5

Published in association with the Books & Such Literary Management, 52 Mission Circle, Suite 122, PMB 170, Santa Rosa, California 95409-5370, www.booksandsuch.com

Contributor: Lindsay A. Franklin
Interior design: Denise Froehlich

Printed in China

18 19 20 21 22 /DSC/ 10 9 8 7 6 5 4 3 2 1

introduction

It's hard to be a young woman sometimes. We're bombarded by lots of different messages about who we're supposed to be—and often, those messages contradict each other. So, what's the right path? Who do we listen to? Which messages should be filtered out and which should be embraced?

If we're followers of Jesus, we look to God's Word for answers. What does God think about the issues we face? What does he say about who we're supposed to be and how we're supposed to act? What does it mean to be a godly woman, anyway?

We can find a lot of wisdom about this in Proverbs 31. But is that all the Bible has to say about being a girl? Maybe you feel like your entire identity as a woman can't fit into a proverb. Welcome to the club, sister. Few of us feel like we can be summed up in a small sound bite.

Thankfully, the Bible has *so much more* to say about the unique challenges—the heartaches and the high points—of being female. There are dozens of women in the Bible, some named but many unnamed. We're going to take a look at about sixty of them. Through their stories, we'll discover role models and cautionary tales, tragedies and triumphs. And guess what? The stories of these ancient women are surprisingly relevant to our lives today.

Your identity as a woman matters to God, beloved daughter. So, let's see what he has to say about it.

day 1

"You are altogether beautiful, my darling; there is no flaw in you."
—SONG OF SONGS 4:7

Some people think that the Bible is a "guys' book." A book written by men, about men, for men. That girls and women have little or no role in God's interaction with humankind. That we're afterthoughts.

What a strange misconception. The truth is God not only protected, upheld, and valued women in ways far beyond most cultures in the eras when the Bible was written, but he also saw fit to include many three-dimensional portraits of historical women in his Word. Our female examples in the Bible rarely fall into the two stereotypes so often foisted upon women—virtuous angels or wicked seductresses. No, most women of the Bible are drawn in real, human shades of gray—sometimes displaying good qualities, sometimes displaying negative qualities, filled with wisdom as well as bad choices, walking in faith and stumbling in darkness. Just like the men of the Bible. *Just like us.*

Girls and women are not God's afterthoughts. We're his daughters. Valued. Adored. Cherished. Beloved.

day 2

"The LORD God said, 'It is not good for the man to be alone. I will make a helper suitable for him.' ... So the LORD God caused the man to fall into a deep sleep; and while he was sleeping, he took one of the man's ribs and then closed up the place with flesh. Then the LORD God made a woman from the rib he had taken out of the man, and he brought her to the man."

–GENESIS 2:18, 21–22

These few lines from Genesis have sparked a lot of debate in the millennia since they were written. Are they proof of women's inferiority to men? Are they proof that women were created to serve men? Are they proof that a woman's worth depends entirely on what she has to offer a man?

When we look closer, we can see something beautiful here. We see that God was not creating an accessory for Adam—something pretty to dangle from Adam's arm like a piece of jewelry. God was a creating a missing piece for Adam. Mankind, God's highest and most treasured creation, was not complete without women.

We are not mere accessories, ladies, and we never have been. We are the final piece of creation, formed in a way unique from every other creature God made.

day 3

"A wife of noble character who can find? She is worth far more than rubies."
—PROVERBS 31:10

If you ask a hundred people what the "ideal woman" is like, you're likely to get a hundred different answers. Depending on the worldview, culture, and personality of the person you're asking, you could hear anything from "meek and mild" to "independent and assertive." But what does God have to say on the matter?

There probably isn't one "ideal woman" from God's perspective either. He has made us wonderfully diverse with varying strengths, weaknesses, and interests, just like men. But when we read about the "Wife of Noble Character" in Proverbs 31, we can begin to see some of the qualities that are biblical ideals for femininity. No matter our personality or our interests, whether or not we'll be someone's wife, these qualities are worthy ones for all women who seek to serve God.

So, what does God's ideal woman look like? Is she a superheroine or a regular girl? Is she tough or tender? The answer to all those questions is . . . yes, she is. She is all these things, and more.

day 4

"She is clothed with strength and dignity; she can laugh at the days to come."

–PROVERBS 31:25

Strength. The Wife of Noble Character is a pillar. She doesn't crumble. She exudes confidence because she is capable and respected. She's straight-up strong, and there's no denying it.

This sounds like all of us, one hundred percent of the time, right? Ahem. Yeah, probably not. Sometimes we're not oozing confidence. Sometimes we're the awkward girl in the back of the room hoping no one will notice us. Sometimes we're the girl who feels overwhelmed by her responsibilities and who would very much like to crumble.

That's okay. An ideal is something to shoot for. If we can grasp how God sees us—as beloved daughters, equipped to do everything he has set before us—then we can begin to grow in strength and confidence. We can nurture this godly ideal that lives somewhere inside each of God's daughters. Embrace your strength. It's there already, waiting for you to grow into it.

day 5

"Her husband has full confidence in her and lacks nothing of value. She brings him good, not harm, all the days of her life."

–PROVERBS 31:11–12

Enriching. That probably seems like a strange word to add to our "ideal woman" picture. Maybe the idea of enriching brings to mind food that has vitamins added to it. So, are we supposed to be like the vitamin D in milk?

Yes, kind of. The word "enrich" means to add to—to make better or to increase. A godly woman enriches the lives of those around her. We can be an enricher wherever we are—at home with our parents, at school, in the workplace, with our friends. Take a moment to think about that. What do you bring to the lives of those around you? Do you add joy, stability, strength, kindness, compassion, humor, love?

Think of one or two ways you can focus on enriching those around you. You'll bless them, no doubt, but you'll find yourself equally blessed.

day 6

"She speaks with wisdom, and faithful instruction is on her tongue. She watches over the affairs of her household and does not eat the bread of idleness."

—PROVERBS 31:26–27

In some ways, Proverbs 31 sounds like an ancient woman's daily to-do list. And goodness, did she get a lot done! We lead equally busy lives in modern times, though our to-do items probably look very different from those in Proverbs.

Two things carry through the ages, though: productivity and clear-mindedness. This ideal woman goes about her daily affairs with wisdom. She makes good decisions and plans for the future. She doesn't waste a bunch of time. She understands the value of hard work.

If you're shrinking away from these qualities thinking, "I will never fit that ideal!" don't worry. It can sound daunting, especially in this day and age when we have so much going on, whether that's school, sports, music, art, friends, or even catching up on your latest Netflix guilty pleasure. It's okay to relax and have fun, but the point of this verse is that the great girls and women of God work hard to make the most of their lives here on Earth. What are a few ways you can use *your* time wisely?

day 7

"Adam named his wife Eve, because she would become the mother of all the living."
—GENESIS 3:20

What better place to begin our look at the triumphs and trials of biblical women than with Eve, the first woman? Eve's name is derived from the Hebrew word "to breathe" or the related word "to live." How cool is that? Breath and life, two words that bring to mind "vitality," and that's what Eve was. With Adam, she began human life.

Eve's story, more than perhaps any other biblical woman, represents the highest of highs and the lowest of lows. She alone of all women lived without sin for a while. Eve experienced the fullness of God's favor and his blessing. She was female kind as we were created to be. And only in understanding that can we fully appreciate the great tragedy of Eve's mistake.

Eve was deceived into disobeying God's one command (Genesis 3:5–6). She broke a rule that probably felt so small at the time—a mere tiptoe away from the Father and toward her own desires. Just one bite. But that tiptoe sparked catastrophic results. In Eve, we have both our first role model and our saddest cautionary tale. Using Eve's mistake as a warning, we can grow in obedience to God's commands, big and small.

----

day 8

"So God created mankind in his own image, in the image of God he created them; male and female he created them."

–GENESIS 1:27

In English, we always refer to God using the masculine pronoun "he." When Jesus was born in a human body, it was a male body. God is our Father, and men were made first. These facts—all true!—have been used for centuries to justify lessening the dignity of women. But is that what's in God's heart? Does God believe his male creation is a better reflection of himself, superior to his female creation?

Look at this verse in the very first chapter of the Bible, speaking of Adam and Eve. Male *and female*, human beings were created in God's image. That means women are every bit as much a reflection of God as men are. God is bigger than either gender and more complete than both. Men and women each reflect different aspects of God's character, and mankind wasn't done until womankind was added into the mix.

Don't ever feel less-than-beloved because you're a woman. We are all created in God's image.

day 9

"The man said, 'This is now bone of my bones and flesh of my flesh; she shall be called "woman," for she was taken out of man.'"

–GENESIS 2:23

Eve is someone who has been defined by her mistakes for thousands of years. Literally thousands. Can you imagine? Can you imagine if your worst mistake, the offense you committed that you were *most* ashamed of, echoed through millennia and became one of the single most important moments in redemptive history?

Yikes. We may worry that our biggest mistakes get publicized on social media and go viral. That would be bad enough. But being known as "that girl who started the whole sin thing" for all of written history is infinitely worse. And yet that's not the whole of who Eve was. Remember how we talked about womankind being the missing piece of the creation puzzle? God fitted that perfect piece through Eve. She was *that* before she was "the sin girl."

You are not defined by your mistakes, either, no matter how much it feels that way sometimes. God saw Eve as the complete person she was. She suffered consequences, absolutely, but God also blessed and cared for her. We don't have to let our mistakes become our identity.

day 10

"That is why a man leaves his father and mother and is united to his wife, and they become one flesh."

–GENESIS 2:24

Not everyone has a desire to get married, which is perfectly okay. Paul writes about the benefits of the single life, focused on serving God, in 1 Corinthians 7. Singleness—both as a long-term lifestyle and as a shorter season before marriage—can be a wonderful, God-honoring, God-serving time in our lives.

But if you *do* have the desire to be married someday, consider praying for your future spouse, starting right now. You're never too young to start praying for the character of the person to whom you'll be joined for the rest of your life. That's a very big deal!

Even if you're years away from considering marriage, the same principle applies to dating and choosing a good boyfriend. How do we discern between a good, godly partner and one who is merely attractive? It's important that we consistently ask God for wisdom in this area because sometimes emotions make our discernment fuzzy. Relationships with the opposite sex can be confusing, but God wants to help guide us toward good choices that honor him. We just need to ask and follow his leading!

day 11

"Adam and his wife were both naked, and they felt no shame."

–GENESIS 2:25

The last time you walked around naked in front of anyone you're not related to, you were probably young enough to be wearing diapers. In fact, many of us have had actual nightmares about showing up in a public place after somehow forgetting to throw on our pants. It would probably be on almost everyone's list of top ten most embarrassing things that could happen, ever in the history of all things.

And yet, our embarrassment about our nakedness and our desire to show some degree of modesty is a result of sin. Before sin, Adam and Eve felt no shame about their bodies. There was no worry about lustful looks or scandalized stares. They were naked and they felt no shame. That tells us our bodies are beautiful things and not in themselves shameful.

Still . . . don't walk down the street naked, or anything close to it. (Seriously, you could get arrested.) Instead, consider growing in appreciation of the wonderful body God created for you. Speak positively about your body. Avoid nitpicking your physical appearance. Understand that your body is not a shameful, sinful thing. It was created as a thing of beauty.

day 12

"'You will not certainly die,' the serpent said to the woman. 'For God knows that when you eat from it your eyes will be opened, and you will be like God, knowing good and evil.'"

–GENESIS 3:4–5

Oh, Eve. The fateful words of the serpent live on in infamy, and each time we read them, we may have the desire to shout at her, "Don't do it!" We know the end of the story. We feel the effects of Eve's actions each day as we battle against our own selfish desires.

Even though most of our struggle with obedience to God might come from within, battling our own impulses or wrong choices, we're not totally unlike Eve. Chances are you don't have a literal serpent squirming through your garden trying to lead you astray, but what about a metaphorical serpent?

Perhaps it's someone in your life you know is a negative influence, constantly tugging you away from God. Perhaps it's a worldview which says there is no God, and everywhere you turn, you're confronted by that serpent asking you, "Did God *really* say . . ." We can learn from Eve's mistake. We know how it turns out when we give in to the serpent. Return to God's Word to reaffirm all you know to be true and battle against those deceptive whispers.

_____

_____

_____

_____

day 13

"And he said, 'Who told you that you were naked? Have you eaten from the tree that I commanded you not to eat from?' The man said, 'The woman you put here with me—she gave me some fruit from the tree, and I ate it.' Then the Lord God said to the woman, 'What is this you have done?' The woman said, 'The serpent deceived me, and I ate.'"

—GENESIS 3:11–13

It took about three seconds from the time we first sinned to the time we first shifted the blame to someone else. And let's be real—that struggle continues today in full force. Small children don't need to be taught to try to blame someone else for their wrongdoing. We have a natural, if sinful, instinct to try to wriggle out of trouble.

But accepting blame when we've messed up is important. Really important. It goes so much deeper than just being willing to face our consequences or making sure someone else doesn't have to face the repercussions of our actions. These things matter, of course, but they matter in a worldly sense.

Accepting responsibility is *spiritually* important because it's the first step toward repentance. If we're busy trying to convince others (or ourselves) that we did nothing wrong—that the serpent made us do it—then we can't turn away from that wrongdoing. We can't apologize to God or anyone else we've hurt. We can't walk away from that mistake and commit to never do it again. Accepting responsibility is the start; true repentance is the goal.

_____

_____

_____

_____

19

day 14

"[Eve] became pregnant and gave birth to Cain. She said, 'With the help of the LORD I have brought forth a man.'"

–GENESIS 4:1

It's stated so simply: Eve gave birth to Cain. That's it. But can you imagine what that first childbirth experience was like? There were no prenatal classes. No tour of the hospital beforehand so Adam and Eve would feel comfortable and relaxed when the time came. No experienced midwife who had delivered a hundred babies before and knew exactly what to do for Eve. Just *hello, labor*. Then, *hello, baby*. Motherhood is a beautiful thing, but it can also be scary. We can imagine it was doubly scary for Eve.

Have you ever faced anything like that? Something that was a great, big unknown at the start but ended up being beautiful? Sometimes the scariest things in life turn out that way. Sometimes the biggest leaps God asks us to make are the ones with the greatest rewards.

Is there an area of your life where you're holding back right now because you're scared? Pray about it. See if this is something God really wants you to do. If so, draw strength from the example of our first mother and take the leap!

---

day 15

"But I will establish my covenant with you, and you will enter the ark—you and your sons and your wife and your sons' wives with you."

–GENESIS 6:18

Okay, so it's not the most glamourous mention in the Bible. In fact, it's easy to skip over. Noah's wife doesn't get a detailed, three-dimensional rendering the way many of our other biblical women do. We don't even get her name. While Noah is the star of the story about the flood, it's important to remember that his wife was alongside him the whole time. So, in many ways, Noah's story is her story too.

There's an old saying: "Behind every great man is a great woman." That was probably true in Noah's case because he would have needed a lot of support to complete the task God had given to him! Many of our biblical women don't get to bask in the spotlight, but we know they were there. We know they were important, if less visible, parts of the story.

Noah's story is the story of his whole family. They were all along for the ride, rescued from destruction by God's mighty hand. And through reading Scripture, we get to be along for the ride too.

day 16

"But Noah found favor in the eyes of the Lord."

–GENESIS 6:8

Sometimes it feels like our culture has reached the depths of depravity, the ends of corruption, and that it's impossible to try to please God while living in such an environment. But Old Testament stories show us that mankind has taken massive cultural detours many, many times throughout history. Our modern culture isn't the worst ever, and it's likely to get worse still before Jesus returns.

Sorry to be a bummer. But the good news is that we have many strong examples in the Bible of those who stood out in their ungodly cultures—those who stood out in the best way possible. Standing out isn't always what we're inclined to do. Particularly if you're shy, you may be happy to hang back, blend in, and not do anything to make yourself noticeable.

But sometimes we *have* to stand out. When the tide around us has turned away from God, we *should* look different than everyone else, just as Noah and his family did during the days before the flood. We are called to be lights in the midst of a dark world.

day 17

"'So make yourself an ark. . . . I am going to bring floodwaters on the earth to destroy all life under the heavens, every creature that has the breath of life in it. Everything on earth will perish.' . . . Noah did everything just as God commanded him."

–GENESIS 6:14A, 17, 22

Imagine you're hanging out in your room and suddenly God speaks to you: "Beloved daughter, I want you to build a spaceship in your front yard. I'm going to destroy the earth with fire. Everything will die, but you have found favor with me so you'll live by escaping to space for a while. Bring animals. Here are the blueprints, now get building." That is, perhaps, a modern-day version of the message Noah got from God.

What proof did Noah have that God would follow through on his word? Did Noah worry about looking like a fool? And just how insane did Noah's neighbors think he was as he built this massive ark?

We don't know the answers to all those questions, but we do know Noah acted on faith. He had no proof, except God's promise, that God would flood the earth. And Noah probably spent years devoted to following God's command to build. Can you imagine dedicating so much of your life to what sounded like a crazy request to everyone else? We are asked to trust in much smaller ways, and it's still tough to trust God when we seem to be the only ones doing so. But if Noah can build his ark, we can faithfully trust God's Word too.

day 18

"And Noah and his sons and his wife and his sons' wives entered the ark to escape the waters of the flood."

–GENESIS 7:7

Do you ever feel like you're drowning? Life circumstances can be overwhelming. Maybe your family life isn't perfect right now (or maybe it's always far from perfect). Maybe school has been intense and full of pressure lately. Maybe you're dealing with friction in some of your relationships with your friends. Or maybe you find yourself questioning what should be the foundation of our lives—your relationship with God.

Any of these things—plus about a million others—can feel like a mini-flood. And when the floodwaters rise, sinking becomes a real possibility. Sometimes it seems like we won't withstand the onslaught.

But God is like our ark. Our safe place. Our shelter from the storm. Even if your flood is rooted in questioning your relationship with God, and perhaps *especially* so, God is the shelter to which you can run. In God's presence, we find the safety to be vulnerable, the love that allows us to be ourselves, and the guiding hand that pushes us toward growth. God is our ark above the floods of life.

---

day 19

"He took his wife Sarai, his nephew Lot, all the possessions they had accumulated and the people they had acquired in Harran, and they set out for the land of Canaan, and they arrived there."

—GENESIS 12:5

If Abraham is the father of God's people, then Sarah must be our mother. Of course, when we first meet Sarah in Genesis 12, she's called Sarai and Abraham is still Abram. God is just beginning to intersect with their lives in a very dynamic, special way.

And that's really what Abraham and Sarah's story is all about—the wild, divine intersection of God and his human creations. God makes this couple promises that seem unbelievable—then he follows through. God directs them to move several times. God changes both their names. He blesses them, speaks with them, meets with them. In Abraham, we see one of the clearest examples of God taking a faithful person by the hand and guiding his steps.

And Sarah was a part of it all, sometimes displaying the same sort of faith her husband is remembered for, and other times showing us examples of how *not* to respond to our major life events. Sarah is real and human, and we can learn a lot from reading her story.

day 20

"As he was about to enter Egypt, he said to his wife Sarai, 'I know what a beautiful woman you are. When the Egyptians see you, they will say, "This is his wife." Then they will kill me but will let you live. Say you are my sister, so that I will be treated well for your sake and my life will be spared because of you.'"

–GENESIS 12:11–13

Abram's fear for his life on account of his beautiful wife is unfortunate. It led to Pharaoh bringing Sarai to his palace as a wife, which then led to plagues being sent to the Egyptians. Yikes. What a mess.

This isn't the only time Sarai and Abram found themselves in a sticky situation. Can you guess the common denominator in all these situations? Despite having a close, personal relationship with God, it doesn't appear that either Sarai or Abram asked God how to handle the "beautiful wife" situation or any of the other situations that turned sticky. Perhaps Abram's fears were justified, and they were in real danger, but what if he and Sarai had just asked God for protection?

It's very tempting to give in to fear rather than lean on God or ask for help. But God doesn't want us to live in a state of fear; he wants us to be bold (2 Timothy 1:7). Are there areas in your life where you're leaning on your own strength and haven't asked God to help you? Can you release your fear, let go of control, and ask God to meet you where you're at? You may be surprised by his response!

----

day 21

"Now Sarai, Abram's wife, had borne him no children. But she had an Egyptian slave named Hagar."

—GENESIS 16:1

Each of our stories is intertwined with the stories of many other people. Our parents, our siblings, our friends, our neighbors, our coworkers. At some points, our stories become so deeply connected with others', it's impossible to tell one story without telling the other. That's how it is with Sarai and Hagar.

It's hard to say how we should classify Sarai and Hagar's relationship. Hagar was Sarai's maidservant. But were they strictly employer-employee? Or were they personally close, like friends? Maybe they were even like sisters, sharing living space the way they did. We only get glimpses of their personal relationship, and it's after trouble strikes. Major friction ensues.

There are so many bits of wisdom to glean from the stories of these two ladies, but it's difficult to avoid feeling sorry about their interpersonal problems. Think of all the wonderful women in your life—your mom, sisters, female friends, mentors, teachers, or neighbors. Thank God for blessing you with the wonderful women whose stories intertwine with yours.

day 22

"[Sarai] said to Abram, 'The Lord has kept me from having children. Go, sleep with my slave; perhaps I can build a family through her.' Abram agreed to what Sarai said."

–GENESIS 16:2

Now, I know what you're thinking. If we judge Sarai by today's standards, she sounds absolutely crazy. Any modern wife would be incredibly upset if her husband had a sexual relationship with another woman—and rightly so! But Sarai was acting in accordance with the custom of her time. A male heir was considered absolutely vital, and Sarai had grown tired of waiting for the heir God had promised to her husband.

Before we judge Sarai too harshly, we should recognize that we don't know how much time passed between Genesis 15 when Abram received the promise of an heir and Genesis 16 when Sarai hands Hagar over to Abram. Perhaps Sarai was well past childbearing years already and thought she *must* fall in line with this ancient custom to make God's words come true. Whatever her motivation, her actions had pretty serious consequences for all involved.

Taking matters into our own hands to this degree rarely produces good results. It's good to be proactive, but we need to balance our initiative with the trust that when God says he'll do something—he will accomplish those things.

day 23

"And [Hagar] conceived. When she knew she was pregnant, she began to despise her mistress. Then Sarai said to Abram, 'You are responsible for the wrong I am suffering. I put my slave in your arms, and now that she knows she is pregnant, she despises me. May the LORD judge between you and me.'"

–GENESIS 16:4–5

Hagar fell into a trap we all do sometimes. When she saw that she was able to do something her mistress wasn't able to do—in this case, give Abram a child—she became haughty. Arrogant. Conceited. She was so puffed up about it, she despised her mistress, the woman whom she had lived with for some time.

Overinflated egos can be big relationship-killers. No one wants to be close with the girl who thinks she's better than everyone else. It's important that we speak positively about ourselves and recognize that we are loved and beautiful, strong and capable in Christ. When we begin to feel superior, we've crossed a line that could spell doom for our most treasured friendships.

It's sad when relationships fall apart, especially when they fall apart because of our wrong attitudes. Is there someone you were once close with, but now you've drifted apart? Pray about what you can do to help set things right, especially if the distance was caused by a mistake you made. Relationships can be healed when we're willing to humble ourselves!

day 24

"And [the angel of the Lᴏʀᴅ] said, 'Hagar, slave of Sarai, where have you come from, and where are you going?' 'I'm running away from my mistress Sarai,' she answered."

–GENESIS 16:8

Everyone messes up. We make bad choices, adopt wrong attitudes, hurt other people. We wish we didn't do these things most of the time, especially when the heat of the moment has passed and we're confronted with the fallout of our actions. Repercussions—bleh. Consequences—ick.

No matter how hard it is to face the music, running away from our consequences is never the best choice. It's the easiest choice, certainly. And sometimes it feels like our only option. When we've tripped up big-time and it feels like there's no way back, running away seems like the logical thing to do.

But God doesn't work this way. The Bible says that when we plant bad choices, we will harvest consequences (it's the "reaping and sowing" principle). This feels like a hard truth. And it is. But through these hard experiences where we must swallow our pride and put aside our fears, we grow. This spiritual growth may not undo whatever mistake we made. But through that growth, we move one step closer to maturity, toward a spirit that looks more and more like Jesus's. It's hard and it hurts. But it's always worth it.

day 25

"Then the angel of the Lord told her, 'Go back to your mistress and submit to her.' The angel added, 'I will increase your descendants so much that they will be too numerous to count.'"

—GENESIS 16:9–10

When you hear the word "submission," what's the first thing that comes to mind? Someone tapping out of an ankle lock in a cage fight? Ahem. Obviously that's not what's meant by biblical submission. And yet the word might strike fear into the heart of a modern woman. Submit? Do I have to? And what does that even mean?

When the Bible tells us to submit, whether to a parent, employer, or the government, it doesn't mean we lose our ability to have opinions, think for ourselves, or demonstrate strength. It *does* mean we humble ourselves and accept the leadership of another person. That in itself requires great strength.

There are times when we shouldn't submit. When those in authority ask you to disobey Jesus's teachings, you must follow Christ's will first. And you never, ever need to submit yourself to abuse. That seems contrary to Hagar's story here, as she was running away from Sarai's mistreatment. But Hagar had a direct command from the Lord, and he protected her. It's a special case. If you find yourself in a position where you're being abused by someone in authority, it's *always* okay to get away and get help.

day 26

"[Hagar] gave this name to the Lord who spoke to her: 'You are the God who sees me,' for she said, 'I have now seen the One who sees me.'"

–GENESIS 16:13

Have you ever felt misunderstood, like no one gets you? Or maybe like no matter how hard you try to relate to others, you're just on a different wavelength than everyone else? It would probably be too ironic if I told you, "You're not alone." But it's true. Many people feel that same sting of loneliness. Some feel it more often than others, but everyone has probably experienced it at one point or another.

Did you know that we have a God who sees us? And not just in the sense that we see an object or person in front of us and can discern its appearance. Our God *sees* us—our whole selves, from our outer appearance, to our inner organs, to our minds and hearts. Our very souls are not only seen but *understood* by God.

If you ever feel alone and lost like Hagar was, remember that there is a God who sees you and everything you're going through. He is there to talk to, to comfort you, and to lead you toward your next step. You never need to feel like no one gets you. God does.

day 27

"God also said to Abraham, 'As for Sarai your wife, you are no longer to call her Sarai; her name will be Sarah. I will bless her and will surely give you a son by her. I will bless her so that she will be the mother of nations; kings of peoples will come from her.'"

–GENESIS 17:15–16

Sarai had her name for many decades. She was probably pretty comfortable with it. And then God decreed that her name would be Sarah instead of Sarai. Why? Sarai means "my princess" in Hebrew. Sarah is a similar name with the same root, but it has grander connotations—almost like "Queen Mother" or "mother of nations." A fitting change for the role God was asking Sarai to assume.

We don't usually change our actual names, but our relationship with God does change our labels, and that's really what God was doing here for Sarai. Can you think of a few labels you ascribed to yourself before God began to change you into Christ's image?

Maybe you used to feel like a screw-up—like nothing you did was right—but now God has removed that label and shown you how loved you are. Or maybe you felt like everything you did was perfect, but now God has removed that label and replaced it with humility to show you places you need to grow. What other labels might God want to replace for you so you can better fulfill his purpose in your life?

day 28

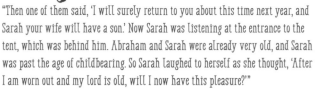

"Then one of them said, 'I will surely return to you about this time next year, and Sarah your wife will have a son.' Now Sarah was listening at the entrance to the tent, which was behind him. Abraham and Sarah were already very old, and Sarah was past the age of childbearing. So Sarah laughed to herself as she thought, 'After I am worn out and my lord is old, will I now have this pleasure?'"

–GENESIS 18:10–12

Sarah received the mother of all promises (bad pun intended). God promised Sarah a pregnancy when she was old enough to be a great-grandmother. I'm sure she would have loved to hear these words decades earlier. But now? When she's very old and has given up on the idea of producing Abraham's heir? That must have been a pretty difficult promise to believe. And indeed, Sarah laughed when she heard it. Who can blame her?

Sometimes we're asked to believe in the impossible. Really, the foundation of our faith can seem "impossible"—the God of the universe born as a man and dying on a cross for our sins. Impossible, yet true. It's important that we build up our belief muscle—the one that flexes and says, "God can do all things, even if we don't understand how." That's faith.

God certainly followed through for Sarah. In Genesis 21, we read that she became pregnant and gave birth to a son, just at the time God promised she would. When God promises us something, he won't go back on it. He always follows through, no matter how impossible his promises may seem.

----

day 29

"Sarah said, 'God has brought me laughter, and everyone who hears about this will laugh with me.' And she added, 'Who would have said to Abraham that Sarah would nurse children? Yet I have borne him a son in his old age.'"

–GENESIS 21:6–7

God has not promised to give us everything we want in life. Sarah had given up on the idea of having biological children, but God blessed her with one anyway. It was a miracle, and God still performs such miracles. Sometimes our answer from God is "no," but sometimes it's "be patient." Oh, it's so hard to be patient, especially when the thing you want is beginning to look physically impossible (perhaps like having a baby when you're ninety . . .).

We can draw strength from examples like Sarah's story. She wasn't perfect in her patience or her belief that God would follow through for her, but we don't tend to be perfect in those areas, either. We have the benefit of being able to see Sarah's whole story, many millennia later, and so we can easily understand that God works out his will in *his* timing. It takes strength to be patient, but letting God's plan unfold is always worth the wait.

day 30

"But Sarah saw that the son whom Hagar the Egyptian had borne to Abraham was mocking, and she said to Abraham, 'Get rid of that slave woman and her son, for that woman's son will never share in the inheritance with my son Isaac.'"

–GENESIS 21:9-10

It's amazing how quickly the tables can turn. Though years had passed since Hagar had borne Ishmael to Abram, it's just a few short chapters for us as we read through Genesis. Maybe that's why it's easier for us to recognize that Sarah is adopting the same arrogance that had so upset her when Hagar displayed it.

In some ways, Sarah is right. Isaac *was* the son of promise, not Ishmael, though God did still have blessings in mind for Ishmael. And Ishmael was wrong to mock. But it seems Sarah was acting out of arrogance, anger, or perhaps fear for her son's position, even though it had been securely promised by God.

Whatever Sarah's motivation, it wasn't love. And it's important that we interact with others in love, especially when we're dealing with someone in a "lower" position than ourselves. Hagar was a servant and her legal position in the household was nowhere near as secure as Sarah's, despite having borne Abraham a child. It's important that we don't abuse positions of power or standing when given the opportunity. Acting with gentleness, even when we're right and someone else is wrong, better reflects Jesus.

day 31

"Early the next morning Abraham took some food and a skin of water and gave them to Hagar. He set them on her shoulders and then sent her off with the boy. She went on her way and wandered in the Desert of Beersheba."

–GENESIS 21:14

Ishmael's mockery and Sarah's anger had some pretty serious consequences for both Ishmael and Hagar. Abraham didn't want to send them away. It says so in Genesis 21:11. In fact, he was "distressed" and only sent them away because God told him to listen to Sarah.

We might wonder what Hagar was thinking as she walked into the desert. Did she trust that God was still looking out for her and her son? Did she wonder if God no longer cared?

Rejection hurts. There's no way around it. But God often uses our most painful experiences to help us rely on him more and to push us to grow to be more like Jesus. God was not finished with Hagar, and he's not finished with us.

day 32

"Then she went off and sat down about a bowshot away, for she thought, 'I cannot watch the boy die.' And as she sat there, she began to sob. God heard the boy crying, and the angel of God called to Hagar from heaven and said to her, 'What is the matter, Hagar? Do not be afraid; God has heard the boy crying as he lies there. Lift the boy up and take him by the hand, for I will make him into a great nation.'"

–GENESIS 21:16–18

Have you ever felt true, deep grief? Maybe you've experienced the loss of a loved one. Maybe you've watched as your family broke apart, or you witnessed a tragic accident. If you have, you can probably relate to Hagar here. She was getting ready to experience one of the greatest tragedies a mother can endure—losing her child.

God is close to us in our grief. Hagar was spared from the tragedy of losing her son to dehydration in the desert. But it doesn't always work out that way. Sometimes, tragedy happens. And when it does, we have to walk through our grief—live it, experience it, deal with it.

But like Hagar in the desert, we're not alone. *El Roi* was the name Hagar gave to God when she first met him—*the God who sees me.* God is not blind to our grief. He is close to our hearts when we suffer, comforting us and easing our burdens.

day 33

"Then God opened [Hagar's] eyes and she saw a well of water. So she went and filled the skin with water and gave the boy a drink."

–GENESIS 21:19

This verse is easy to breeze right past when we read it. Mostly we're just happy that Hagar didn't have to watch her son die of dehydration. So we read this verse and think, "Yay, water!" But if we take a moment to think about this drink of water, it's pretty incredible. The way this is phrased suggests the well was there the whole time. The Bible doesn't say God created a new well. It says he opened Hagar's eyes to see something that was *already there*.

So while Hagar and her son were literally dying of thirst, a well was nearby. Right there. Big drink of water. So why didn't Hagar see it? The Bible doesn't tell us. It only says that God opened her eyes and she saw it. She was able to save her life and her son's life because of it.

We're often in need of a perspective shift. We get in our own way, miss the obvious, and are so focused on our problems that the clear solution escapes us. But, like he did with Hagar, God wants to direct us toward his solutions—his will for our lives.

day 34

"With the coming of dawn, the angels urged Lot, saying, 'Hurry! Take your wife and your two daughters who are here, or you will be swept away when the city is punished.'"

–GENESIS 19:15

We get a few biblical glimpses into Abraham's extended family, first through Abraham's nephew, Lot. Lot's story doesn't have many happy pieces to it—at least, not that we get to read about. Lot settled near the legendarily wicked city, Sodom, to raise his family (yikes). The Lord agreed to rescue Lot's family from Sodom's impending destruction, and that's where Lot's wife is first mentioned—as the angels implore Lot to grab his family and run.

And this wasn't a slight nudge: "Hey, maybe now would be a good time to leave, if you're ready." This was a serious shove: "Go *now*, or your whole family will die!"

Has God ever asked you to flee from something? The moments when we've been asked to run for our lives may not be as dramatic as what Lot and his wife experienced. But we are constantly asked to flee from certain things—bad choices, hurting others, and rejecting God, to name three. What if we brought some of the angels' urgency to fleeing those things? Let's take a moment to reflect on how we can be faithful "fleers" when God wants us to.

----

day 35

"When he hesitated, the men grasped his hand and the hands of his wife and of his two daughters and led them safely out of the city, for the LORD was merciful to them. As soon as they had brought them out, one of them said, 'Flee for your lives! Don't look back, and don't stop anywhere in the plain! Flee to the mountains or you will be swept away!'"

–GENESIS 19:16–17

To fully understand Lot's wife's sad end, we must first understand this piece of the story. God was very merciful to Lot's family for Abraham's sake. They were hand-plucked from the middle of a doomed city and given a chance to escape. Abraham had begged for the city to be spared, if only ten righteous people could be found in it. God agreed, but ten righteous people couldn't be found. Still, even if God was to destroy the city, he sent angels to make sure Abraham's family made it out safely.

How often do we fail to appreciate God's mercies to us? How often do we fail to even notice them? Our day-to-day lives certainly have their share of hardship. But if we're living in relative peace, God has been merciful. If we're able to eat three meals a day, that's a mercy. If we have access to clean water, we've been blessed.

Take a moment to think of the mercies, large and small, that God has granted us today. The biggest mercy of all is our salvation through Jesus. Let's pour out our gratitude to God for that amazing gift.

day 36

"Thus [God] overthrew those cities and the entire plain, destroying all those living in the cities—and also the vegetation in the land. But Lot's wife looked back, and she became a pillar of salt."

–GENESIS 19:25–26

Oh, this hurts. Remember the angel's specific instructions not to look back? Why did Lot's wife disobey? Why didn't she just run for her life with her husband and daughters?

It's possible she was merely curious. Curiosity that leads to disobedience *can* get us in trouble. But this seems unlikely in Lot's wife's case because of how Jesus mentions her in Luke. In Luke 17:32–33, he says to the disciples, "Remember Lot's wife! Whoever tries to keep their life will lose it, and whoever loses their life will preserve it." It seems Lot's wife was looking back toward her old city, longing for her life there. And remember the depths of wickedness found in that place. Perhaps the sharpest lesson from Lot's wife's story is to fight our longings for sin.

From time to time, we all feel the urge to lie or cheat or break the rules. Crazy as it seems, we *want* to sin. But we can learn from Lot's wife and keep our eyes facing forward toward God and his holiness.

day 37

"Jesus replied, 'No one who puts a hand to the plow and looks back is fit for service in the kingdom of God.'"

–LUKE 9:62

We never get to hear words directly from Lot's wife in the Bible. She doesn't have one line of dialogue, so it's hard to know who she might have been. But, because of her ultimate end, she has gone down in history as an example of what happens when we look backward instead of forward.

Sometimes our pasts entice us, beckoning us toward a time when we didn't bother so much with God's view of our hearts or our behavior. The deceptive whispers try to convince us life was easier or better then. Other times, our pasts haunt us, trying to persuade us that we will never be free of our old selves, that we will never be worthy of Jesus's great love.

Both these messages are lies. Jesus offers us a future. We are no longer the same people we used to be. We are new creatures, fit to serve God's son and dwell in his kingdom. This is an amazing truth! There's no reason to look back, no reason to fall back into old habits. Look to the future, beloved, and see what God has in store for you.

day 36

"My prayer is not that you take them out of the world but that you protect them from the evil one. They are not of the world, even as I am not of it."

–JOHN 17:15-16

Lot's family illustrates an important reminder for us—one that still applies, many thousands of years later. It's very easy to let the culture around us influence us. It's very easy to become a product of our environment . . . which might not be so bad, if only our culture always sought to honor God.

Sadly, the opposite tends to be true. Just like Lot's family, we're surrounded by negative influences and a culture that often misunderstands and rejects the God we love. But that doesn't mean God wants us to remove ourselves from our culture. Instead, God wants us to influence culture as we seek to protect our hearts while building his kingdom.

It's a delicate balance. We're meant to be *in* the world but not *of* it. Living in the world is the easy part. Not allowing our culture to pull us away from God's path is the tough stuff. Spend some time today in prayer about this topic specifically. Ask God how you can be a light in this world to affect your culture for the good of his kingdom.

day 39

"Before he had finished praying, Rebekah came out with her jar on her shoulder. She was the daughter of Bethuel son of Milkah, who was the wife of Abraham's brother Nahor."

–GENESIS 24:15

We know Isaac was a special kid—the fulfillment of a promise given to Abraham and Sarah who were far too old to have biological children. And of course, Isaac eventually grew up and got married himself. Rebekah was his wife, and they have a legitimate love story. Arranged marriage was the common custom in those days, and Isaac and Rebekah's marriage *was* arranged—they'd never even met when she agreed to be his wife! But Isaac romantically loved Rebekah, too, which sets them apart.

This doesn't mean their relationship was without bumps. In fact, from Rebekah, we see a spectrum of wonderful and troubling qualities. Like Sarah before her, Rebekah is shown to be a real, flawed, three-dimensional person. Someone we can relate to and learn from, and someone whose story helps us to grow in godliness.

As we read through Rebekah's story, let's pray that God would help us adopt her positive qualities while weeding the negative ones from our hearts.

day 40

"I want you to swear by the LORD, the God of heaven and the God of earth, that you will not get a wife for my son from the daughters of the Canaanites, among whom I am living, but will go to my country and my own relatives and get a wife for my son Isaac."

–GENESIS 24:3–4

The long journey that brought Abraham's servant to Rebekah's front door began here. Abraham's servant was instructed by Abraham to return to Abraham's homeland and find a wife for his son, Isaac. These days, it might sound weird for a dad to request that his son's wife come from his relatives. But in Isaac's time, it was perfectly normal to marry within one's clan—and keep in mind, Abraham's family had grown!

Today, we obviously like a wider gene pool in our marriages, but we can still draw a valuable lesson from Abraham's request. Abraham wanted to find a partner for Isaac who would share his values and understand his faith. The same idea is important for us when we are thinking about dating or even friendships.

This doesn't mean we have to *only* hang out with people who are exactly the same as we are. In fact, we can learn a lot from people with different opinions. And God will often use us as little lights to illuminate an unbeliever's path to Jesus, something that can't ever happen if we only hang out with other Christians. Try to surround yourself with people who are kind and respectful, and look for relationships that will help you grow in your faith.

day 41

"The servant hurried to meet her and said, 'Please give me a little water from your jar.' 'Drink, my lord,' she said, and quickly lowered the jar to her hands and gave him a drink."

–GENESIS 24:17–18

Rebekah is a great example of hospitality, a concept that was extremely important in her culture. We may think of hospitality as entertaining people in our homes, but we can expand the idea well beyond the four walls of a literal house.

Hospitality is welcoming others into our environments. It's about generosity, warmth, and service to others. Hospitality is an attitude we can bring with us wherever we go. If you're at school and you see someone who doesn't seem to have a group to hang out with, you can bring a spirit of hospitality to her by reaching out, inviting her into your circle, or offering a kind word and a friendly face.

These gestures are so simple, and yet they can make a world of difference to someone who feels alone or rejected. Maybe you've been the girl on the outside and so you know exactly how it feels. An attitude of warmth and openness can offer hope to someone who is hurting!

day 42

"Then they said, 'Let's call the young woman and ask her about it.' So they called Rebekah and asked her, 'Will you go with this man?' 'I will go,' she said."

–GENESIS 24:57–58

People generally like to be comfortable. Many of us like routine, familiarity, and safety. Even the free-spirited, spontaneous among us tend to have a comfort zone—somewhere they return to after their exciting adventures in the big, wide world.

But God asks us to step outside of our comfort zones on a daily basis. By loving him and serving him with our lives, we're already in a culturally uncomfortable place. Other people may not understand our faith, and they may dislike or ridicule us because of it. When we're being asked to go to the uncomfortable, unknown places in life, are we willing? Like Rebekah, will we say, "I will go"?

Are there any areas in your life right now where God is asking you to get uncomfortable? Where does God want to grow you or stretch you? Take a few minutes to pray about it. Ask God for the bravery to say, "I will go" when he asks!

---

day 43

"The boys grew up, and Esau became a skillful hunter, a man of the open country, while Jacob was content to stay at home among the tents. Isaac, who had a taste for wild game, loved Esau, but Rebekah loved Jacob."

–GENESIS 25:27-28

Since God was building a nation, it shouldn't surprise us that Isaac and Rebekah had children—twin sons, Esau and Jacob. The boys' relationship started off rocky. As the oldest son, Esau would have inherited twice as much wealth as his brother. It would make sense to assume Esau was the son through whom God would continue to fulfill his promise to Abraham.

But God had other plans. Jacob was chosen as the son of promise. Already there was fertile ground for some serious sibling rivalry. But here we read that, on top of everything else, Isaac and Rebekah played favorites with their boys. Ouch.

Have you ever felt like you're on the wrong side of the favoritism game? Like you've been overlooked or that you don't measure up when compared to someone else? Maybe it's with a parent, but it could also be with a teacher, coach, or even in your group of friends. Favoritism stings, and it never breeds healthy relationships. But we have to remember that we have no control over how others feel about or view us. We can choose to let go of our resentment and be sure we don't fall into the favoritism trap ourselves.

day 44

"When the men of that place asked him about his wife, he said, 'She is my sister,' because he was afraid to say, 'She is my wife.' He thought, 'The men of this place might kill me on account of Rebekah, because she is beautiful.'"

–GENESIS 26:7

Isaac expected some serious consequences if he admitted his beautiful wife Rebekah was, indeed, his wife. It's sad to imagine that simply because Rebekah was physically beautiful, her freedom and Isaac's life were both in danger.

Hopefully we never find ourselves in such an extreme situation. But we do often experience people judging our outward appearances. Perhaps because you're beautiful, people often assume you're not smart. Or maybe because you look athletic, people assume you're not very feminine. Maybe your style is a little offbeat or funky, so people judge you as "other."

It's important that we learn to reject these snap judgments. Other people don't have the power to define us based on the way we look (even if they think they do). *We* get to control our own stories. *We* get to say who we are. Take a moment to reflect on the unique way God created you, and pray for confidence in your beautiful skin.

day 45

"When Isaac had been there a long time, Abimelek king of the Philistines looked down from a window and saw Isaac caressing his wife Rebekah. So Abimelek summoned Isaac and said, 'She is really your wife! Why did you say, "She is my sister"?' Isaac answered him, 'Because I thought I might lose my life on account of her.'"

—GENESIS 26:8–9

Does the whole "she's not my wife; she's my sister" thing sound familiar? We just read an almost identical story about Abraham and Sarah. In both cases, the men lied, either outright or by omission, and nearly caused serious disasters for those who didn't realize they were taking other men's wives as their own. Yikes.

Isn't it odd how Abraham and Isaac both made the same error in judgment when presented with the same situation? We might think that Isaac should have known better, probably growing up hearing about the one time his parents went over to Egypt and almost caused a plague. And it's entirely possible he *did* hear these stories growing up and Abraham *did* try to teach him to do better.

The truth is it's shockingly easy to repeat the mistakes of our parents, even when we don't mean to. Even when we know better, ingrained patterns pop up. Pray about some of the hard-learned lessons your parents have tried to teach you. How can you learn from their mistakes and gain the benefit of their experience and wisdom?

day 46

"Rebekah said to her son Jacob, 'Look, I overheard your father say to your brother Esau, "Bring me some game and prepare me some tasty food to eat, so that I may give you my blessing in the presence of the Lᴏʀᴅ before I die." Now, my son, listen carefully and do what I tell you: Go out to the flock and bring me two choice young goats, so I can prepare some tasty food for your father, just the way he likes it. Then take it to your father to eat, so that he may give you his blessing before he dies.'"

–GENESIS 27:6–10

Oh, Rebekah. She concocted quite the plan here to make sure her favorite son, Jacob, was blessed beyond her husband's favorite, Esau. Esau, as the oldest, was to receive a double inheritance (he ended up selling it to Jacob for a bowl of soup—not a good life choice). Perhaps Rebekah felt like Jacob's position was not secureand her favored boy would get left in the dust.

So, what was so bad about her plan? Aside from the obvious—Rebekah failed to recognize that God had already promised Jacob would be the father of the nation of Israel. It was pronounced long before this trick. Like Sarah, Rebekah seemed to want to take matters into her own hands to force God's promise to come true.

God doesn't need our help to keep his promises. He doesn't need anything from us at all. What he *wants* is our trust and our obedience. When we honor God with our trust in his words, he is glorified all the more when he stays true to his promises.

day 47

"Jacob said to Rebekah his mother, 'But my brother Esau is a hairy man while I have smooth skin. What if my father touches me? I would appear to be tricking him and would bring down a curse on myself rather than a blessing.' His mother said to him, 'My son, let the curse fall on me. Just do what I say; go and get them for me.'"

–GENESIS 27:11-13

Maybe it's no worse than any other kind of deception, but something seems doubly wrong about Rebekah's trickery here. Not only was she not trusting God's promises would come about in their own time and in their own way, she was actively deceiving her husband. Remember, Isaac and Rebekah really loved each other. How sad that, of all people, he was the one she tricked.

We're all vulnerable to the same mistake. Sometimes those we love most—our deepest, most loving relationships—are the ones we take for granted. We may be on our "best behavior" for those who aren't close friends or family. Often, we save the worst of ourselves for those with whom we're most comfortable.

It's good to nurture openness with our inner circles. It's good to have places where we don't have to be "on" all the time, or where we can allow ourselves to feel weak or imperfect. But this shouldn't be an excuse to mistreat those trusted, beloved soul-friends. Rebekah crossed the line here, but we can use her mistake as a reminder to cherish those closest to us.

day 48

"Then Rebekah said to Isaac, 'I'm disgusted with living because of these Hittite women. If Jacob takes a wife from among the women of this land, from Hittite women like these, my life will not be worth living.'"

–GENESIS 27:46

Rebekah may have been acting a little dramatic about her daughters-in-law here. Yes, there were very sharp religious differences between Isaac's family and the surrounding people groups who worshiped idols. Perhaps the difference in values between Rebekah's family and the wives her son Esau had taken really made Rebekah's life miserable.

One thing is certain—we generally don't want a family member to feel upset or uncomfortable because of us in the way Rebekah was upset by Esau's wives. We don't want to be known as a bringer of grief (or drama or bad attitude). This idea can even be applied to our friends and other people close to us, whether by birth, marriage, or choice.

Instead, we want to be known as someone who brings blessing with her presence. What can you do today to bless those around you? How can you bring joy, refreshment, and peace into the lives of others?

day 49

"While he was still talking with them, Rachel came with her father's sheep, for she was a shepherd. When Jacob saw Rachel daughter of his uncle Laban, and Laban's sheep, he went over and rolled the stone away from the mouth of the well and watered his uncle's sheep."

–GENESIS 29:9–10

There aren't many women in the Bible who are given as much room on the stage as Rachel. We get to know a lot about this woman who eventually becomes the beloved wife of Jacob. And that means we get to see the good, the bad, and the ugly. Perhaps this is what makes Rachel (and her sister, whom we'll meet soon) so relatable.

Rachel would eventually become Jacob's wife, but before that, she had a job. We might get the idea that ancient women were chained to their ovens and looms, but they actually shared in a surprising number of duties we tend to associate with men, like tending the flocks and herds. Rachel was a shepherdess. And in biblical days, the animals Rachel tended were highly valuable—a family's wealth could be measured by the quantity and quality of its flocks and herds.

Today, let's thank God that, as modern women, we have choices about how we'd like to spend our lives, both personally and professionally. Not every generation of women before us has enjoyed such freedom. It's a blessing!

day 50

"Then Jacob kissed Rachel and began to weep aloud. He had told Rachel that he was a relative of her father and a son of Rebekah. So she ran and told her father."

–GENESIS 29:11–12

Whoa there, buddy! We just met! Maybe back off on the kissing a little? Truthfully, it's not likely that this was a big Hollywood embrace meant to express romantic love. Jacob was elated to find his mother's relatives, and kissing was used to express many things in ancient Near Eastern cultures.

But in our culture, we wouldn't be likely to kiss a stranger for any reason. In fact, we may struggle to know when it is appropriate to kiss someone we're dating. There isn't one blanket answer for that question. Some Christian couples express their affection for each other in this way during the dating phase of their relationship, and others might choose to wait until their wedding day to kiss!

The main thing is to prioritize the nonphysical aspects of your romantic relationships first. Like building a friendship, nurturing an emotional connection, and establishing mutual respect for each other. These will create firm foundations for strong relationships that will last.

day 51

"Now Laban had two daughters; the name of the older was Leah, and the name of the younger was Rachel."

–GENESIS 29:16

Ah, now we meet Leah, Rachel's big sister. You'd think, as the older sister, Leah would get first mention, or perhaps that she would be the one who caught Jacob's eye. But instead, Leah gets a couple (unflattering) verses sandwiched in the middle of the main story, which is centered on Jacob and Rachel's romantic drama.

And that's pretty much the story of Leah's life, if we only look at the surface. But, like Rachel, Leah gets one of the fullest portraits of all the women in the Bible. We get to know quite a lot about her—what she wanted out of life, what she valued, and what her character was like.

In many ways, Leah's story is sad. But if we dig deeper, we'll find undercurrents of hope, redemption, and embracing God's purpose for our lives, even when we're hurt by those closest to us. Thank God for women like Leah, who show us that, even when it feels like we've been abandoned, God remembers us.

day 52

"Leah had weak eyes, but Rachel had a lovely figure and was beautiful."

—GENESIS 29:17

Weak eyes? It almost seems like we have a strange, biblical comment on Leah's eyesight—that she would be a candidate for LASIK. Or at least glasses (join the club). But the Hebrew phrase for "weak eyes" can mean gentle, kind eyes. Or it can be an insult, suggesting Leah's eyes weren't exactly stunning. And given what follows about Rachel, that may very well be what the original writer meant.

Rachel is "the pretty sister." Ugh. Comparisons like this can be so painful. If you have a sister, cousin, or close female friend to whom you're often compared, you know how this feels. The pretty sister. The smart one. The athletic one. The artsy or musical one. Or how about "the good one"? Ouch.

Whenever we feel like we're compared to someone else and found wanting, it can hurt. But we don't have to own the negative comparisons others foist upon us. We can choose to focus on our strengths, the wonderful things that God and others see when they look at us. We *all* have these qualities, and yet we're so prone to embracing the negative descriptors instead. Think about your positives today. Focus on embracing those great attributes.

day 53

"Jacob was in love with Rachel and said, 'I'll work for you seven years in return for your younger daughter Rachel.'...So Jacob served seven years to get Rachel, but they seemed like only a few days to him because of his love for her."

–GENESIS 29:18, 20

Whoa buddy, again! So quick with the marriage talk! It seems a little abrupt as we read through the story in Genesis. Jacob and Rachel seem to fall in love immediately and jump straight into discussions of marriage arrangements. But when you think about it, marriage *talk* happened quickly. The actual marriage was planned for seven years away. And even by today's standards, that's a very long engagement.

The idea of "true love" can sometimes tie us up in knots. We may watch romantic comedies and think those "love stories" are what true love looks like—the flutteriest butterflies, the most sparks, the biggest romantic gestures. Or we may think it's common (or even possible) to meet a man and know instantly he's our soulmate. (Yikes—let's avoid that territory, ladies.)

But Jacob would probably tell us true love looks a lot like hard work. He labored for *seven years* before he was able to possibly marry Rachel. All relationships that really matter require time and effort. But they're worth it!

day 54

"But when evening came, he took his daughter Leah and brought her to Jacob . . . When morning came, there was Leah! So Jacob said to Laban, 'What is this you have done to me? I served you for Rachel, didn't I? Why have you deceived me?'"

–GENESIS 29:23, 25

The word "leftovers" doesn't bring to mind the prettiest picture. We might think of two-day-old food, stale and soggy, sealed in a plastic container and waiting for some very hungry person with no other options to consider heating it up and braving a bite. Is that what Leah felt like here—the leftover sister?

It's not that Jacob didn't have a right to be angry. He and Laban had an agreement. He was to work for seven long years—which he did—and then receive *Rachel* as his wife. And remember how much he loved Rachel. Instead, Laban tricked him into marrying Leah. Jacob had every right to be upset. But . . . what about Leah?

We don't get a biblical comment on how Leah felt in this moment, but we can imagine she knew exactly how much she was *not* Jacob's first choice. In fact, she would spend much of the rest of her life trying to win his attention. It must have felt like being picked last for a sports team—times a million.

But no matter how others see us, God sees us as his beloved, not his last choice. We're precious, not picked-over.

day 55

"[Laban said], 'Finish this daughter's bridal week; then we will give you the younger one also, in return for another seven years of work.'"

–GENESIS 29:27

The good news for Rachel was, after seven long years, she only had to wait another week before marrying Jacob. The less-good news was that her older sister was now also married to the guy she loved. Awkward.

Even more awkward—do you notice how Laban speaks of Rachel here? "The younger one." He doesn't mention her by name. And he tacks her on to the deal like an afterthought: "Yeah, we'll give her to you too." How did Rachel feel about that? We can guess she was pretty accustomed to being the favored sister, but suddenly, she becomes the unnamed afterthought.

Have you ever been toppled like that? It's amazing how quickly things can flip. Our positions are never secure. One second, we're on the top of the social food chain, and the next, we've plummeted to the bottom. If we look to our social standing to tell us what we're worth, we're putting our trust in a very shaky system! Instead, we can plant our sense of self-worth very securely on God. *He* says we're beloved, and we are—no matter what others think of us.

day 56

"When the Lord saw that Leah was not loved, he enabled her to conceive, but Rachel remained childless. Leah became pregnant and gave birth to a son. She named him Reuben, for she said, 'It is because the Lord has seen my misery. Surely my husband will love me now.'"

–GENESIS 29:31-32

Leah, girl, we hear you. God heard her too. Our Bible says Leah was "not loved," but the Hebrew word (*sane*) literally means "hated." Did Jacob actually hate Leah? Did he despise his own wife? That's a sad thought! It's possible this Hebrew word is simply trying to say Leah was loved much less than Rachel. But even if Jacob didn't have passionate feelings of hatred toward Leah, one thing is sure—Leah was not a favored, treasured wife, and the Lord saw it.

When we're not loved by others—especially those whose love and attention we strongly desire—it cuts. Deeply. But no matter how unloved we are by those who should accept us, it doesn't change God's view of who we are. He isn't swayed by external labels others place on us. God didn't look at Leah and see someone worthless, just because Jacob failed to appreciate her.

Loving someone who doesn't love you back never feels good. But when we're confident that God values and adores us, it becomes easier to shrug off the rejection of others. Let's thank God for his boundless love—that we are seen and known and beloved.

day 57

"When Rachel saw that she was not bearing Jacob any children, she became jealous of her sister. So she said to Jacob, 'Give me children, or I'll die!'"

—GENESIS 30:1

As the favored wife, Rachel didn't have much reason to be jealous of Leah—at first. But by this time, the unloved Leah had been blessed (and blessed Jacob) with four sons. Four of them! The first three times Leah gave birth to a son, she said something to the effect of *"Now* my husband will surely love me!" These sons didn't seem to affect the way Jacob felt about Leah, but they did cause some strong feelings in Rachel.

Learning to manage our jealousy is very important. Envy is the sort of thing that can begin as a tiny seed. If we allow that tiny seed to grow some roots and sprout a few leaves, we'll have a tree of jealousy on our hands before we know it. And those trees are destructive. They cause relationships to crumble, sometimes beyond repair. In Rachel and Leah's case, the jealousy between these two sisters began an escalating race to bear Jacob the most children. The echoes of this rivalry carried into the next generation.

Take a moment to think about any jealousy seeds in your life that are trying to sprout. Dig those things out before they put down roots!

day 58

"Rachel's servant Bilhah conceived again and bore Jacob a second son. Then Rachel said, 'I have had a great struggle with my sister, and I have won.' So she named him Naphtali."

–GENESIS 30:7–8

When Rachel couldn't conceive a child, she began to build a surrogate family through her servant, Bilhah (it's no wonder Jacob ended up with twelve sons . . .). When Bilhah had her first son of Jacob, Rachel felt vindicated, like God had stuck up for her. When Bilhah had her second, Rachel went so far as to say she had won her battle against Leah.

Um, ouch? While we can feel for Rachel's struggle with infertility when she so desperately wanted children, remember that Rachel at least had the love of her husband. These words of triumph over Leah are harsh and unnecessary. But when we feel like we're not getting what we want, or perhaps as though our position is threatened, harsh words can easily slip out. Even when we don't mean them.

It's heartbreaking to think that each of these sisters so badly wanted what the other had. Perhaps they could have been a comfort to one another, but instead, their relationship was full of competition. Have you allowed your desires to fuel harsh words toward someone you care about? Pray about how you can best make amends with that person and avoid unnecessary harshness in the future.

day 59

"Then Leah said, 'What good fortune!' So she named him Gad."

–GENESIS 30:11

Leah had a lot of sons, but still it seemed like Rachel was fast moving in on Leah's territory with the surrogate family built through Bilhah. So Leah started a surrogate family of her own through her maidservant, Zilpah. While this setup sounds increasingly odd to us, the practice was not terribly uncommon. Still, we can probably recognize the strange game of one-upmanship easier than Leah and Rachel could.

When we feel threatened, it's tempting to resort to this sort of thing. Someone moves in on our territory, and we feel the need to push for a position at the top. This can happen in classes at school, on sports teams, in families, and even among groups of friends.

It's important that we remember what Jesus said about wanting to be first in Matthew 20:26: "Whoever wants to become great among you must be your servant." Only those who love sacrificially are "first" in God's eyes. When we bring this attitude of service and humility to our lives, we can better release the idea of one-upping those around us. It's hard to push for position when you're busy loving and serving!

day 60

"During wheat harvest, Reuben went out into the fields and found some mandrake plants, which he brought to his mother Leah. Rachel said to Leah, 'Please give me some of your son's mandrakes.' But she said to her, 'Wasn't it enough that you took away my husband? Will you take my son's mandrakes too?'"

–GENESIS 30:14–15

It's hard to blame Leah for being annoyed. Her favored, beautiful little sister was (politely) demanding a plant that was superstitiously thought to increase fertility. Rachel already had a surrogate family through Bilhah *and* the undying love of Jacob, and now she wanted Leah's vegetables too?!

But if we're being honest with ourselves, we have to admit that we look a lot like Rachel. No matter how many good things we have in our lives, there's just one more thing that will make it better . . . right? It sure feels that way sometimes. Once we get that prized phone or car or dress or boyfriend, will we finally be happy?

Contentment comes with being thankful for our blessings right now, in this moment, however plentiful or sparse they may be. There will *always* be something we don't have that looks attractive, so chasing whatever is on the horizon is a fruitless exercise. Think about the many wonderful blessings God has placed in your life at this moment. Take some time to truly reflect on these things and thank him for his goodness. Satisfaction will follow!

_____

_____

_____

_____

day 61

"Then Leah said, 'God has presented me with a precious gift. This time my husband will treat me with honor, because I have borne him six sons.' So she named him Zebulun."

–GENESIS 30:20

It's almost painful to read Leah's words here. She had given Jacob five sons already (and remember how important sons were in Leah and Jacob's culture). But Leah, naïvely hopeful, says that *this* son—number six—will finally be the one who makes Jacob treat her with the love and respect she should have been getting from day one. We might want to shout at Leah, "Girl! He's not that into you! Let it go!"

But the truth is we're all vulnerable to this. We all have, at one time or another, sought the approval of others. Sometimes, this is healthy—like wanting to please your parents, teachers, or most importantly, God. When it becomes unhealthy is when we allow other humans, even our parents and teachers, to determine what we're worth. If we get our sense of validation from anywhere other than God, we're likely to be disappointed, just like Leah. Know your worth. God treasures you!

day 62

"Some time later she gave birth to a daughter and named her Dinah."

–GENESIS 30:21

After all those sons, Jacob finally has a daughter! Some scholars believe Jacob had multiple daughters because of Genesis 37:35 ("All his sons and daughters came to comfort him . . ."), but others believe the plural refers to all female descendants, including granddaughters. Either way, Dinah is the only daughter who gets a name and a story in the Bible.

Even so, Dinah's brothers were the main attraction here. They were the fathers of the twelve tribes of Israel—kind of a big deal! So . . . does that mean Dinah didn't really matter?

It's easy to feel like we don't matter sometimes. When the attention is focused on others close to us, we can feel overlooked. Maybe your best friend is a hot-shot track star at school. Maybe your cousin got a perfect score on the SATs. Maybe you have a sibling who has special medical needs, so it feels like your parents are always focused on her. The truth is most of us aren't going to have our names go down in the history books. And that's perfectly okay. Each of us matters very much in the lives of those close to us, and God loves and values each of us.

day 63

"[Rachel] became pregnant and gave birth to a son and said, 'God has taken away my disgrace.' She named him Joseph, and said, 'May the LORD add to me another son.'"

–GENESIS 30:23-24

As modern women who aren't judged "worthy" based on the number of sons we have, we may want to tell Rachel she wasn't a disgrace, even without children of her own (and we'd be right!). But it's not really the point here. For Rachel, baby Joseph was a sweet answer to many years of longing for a child. We can only imagine how often Rachel prayed, cried, and hurt over the baby who never seemed to come.

Do you have a close-held dream in your heart? Maybe it has to do with your education or career. Maybe it has to do with being a wife or mother. Maybe it has to do with places you want to see or people you want to meet. Most of us have dreams in at least one of these categories. And the scary truth is we're not promised that all our dreams will come true. What we *are* promised is God knows exactly what we need, when we need it. When we place our dreams and desires in his hands, trusting that he knows what he's doing, we can have peace that our lives are unfolding just the way *he* wants them to.

day 64

"Then Rachel and Leah replied [to Jacob], 'Do we still have any share in the inheritance of our father's estate? Does he not regard us as foreigners? Not only has he sold us, but he has used up what was paid for us. Surely all the wealth that God took away from our father belongs to us and our children. So do whatever God has told you.'"

–GENESIS 31:14–16

It's sad that this is the way Leah and Rachel ended up leaving their father's land. But we can hardly blame them. Their father used them as pawns in his marriage schemes with Jacob. He had used their husband to try to increase his own wealth. Laban did not treat Leah and Rachel as beloved daughters. He treated them like game pieces.

It never feels good when someone uses us for selfish reasons. But it hurts even more when the person using us is someone who is supposed to love and cherish us. How do we respond? How do we deal with that?

The answer varies case by case. Sometimes, gentle confrontation is necessary. Other times, overlooking personal slights will bring us the most peace. And in cases of physical or verbal abuse, it's *always* best to seek help from an adult you trust. It's also important to make sure we do not fall into this trap ourselves. By treating others the way we hope to be treated, we can be sure we're not using the ones we're supposed to love most.

----

day 65

"When Laban had gone to shear his sheep, Rachel stole her father's household gods."
–GENESIS 31:19

Theft is bad enough. We know exactly how God feels about stealing because he covers it in the Ten Commandments. Here Rachel is not only stealing from her father, but she's stealing idols. It's likely Rachel stole the idols to worship them. At the very least, she wanted supernatural protection or blessing.

Rachel's offense is huge and obvious. We may skim past it and think, "Well, I've definitely never stolen or worshiped idols before!" But what about when we expand our definition of theft to include something as small as slacking off at an after-school job or taking an allowance from our parents while doing our chores halfheartedly? What about when we expand our definition of "idol" to include anything that has taken importance over God in our lives, whether that's hobbies, friendships, or boyfriends? It becomes a little easier to see that we're all vulnerable to the same issues that affected Rachel.

Think of the little things in your life that could be described as theft or idolatry. What's one thing you can do today to move away from those things and toward a deeper relationship with God?

day 66

"Jacob answered Laban, 'I was afraid, because I thought you would take your daughters away from me by force. But if you find anyone who has your gods, that person shall not live. In the presence of our relatives, see for yourself whether there is anything of yours here with me; and if so, take it.' Now Jacob did not know that Rachel had stolen the gods."

–GENESIS 31:31–32

What a hasty promise for Jacob to make. For all he knew, one of his small children had stolen Laban's idols. And as it turns out, his beloved wife *was* the guilty party. Rachel hid her theft and didn't end up losing her life, but can you imagine Jacob's regret if she had been caught? God warns not to make hasty oaths in the law (Leviticus 5:4), knowing full well the consequences can be massive.

We need to be careful with our words. Sometimes we think we have all the information—that we have a firm grasp on the situation—when really, we're totally unaware of an important piece of the puzzle. While we're not likely to swear on someone else's life (eep!), we may still give our word, make a promise, or stake our reputation on something. And when we realize we were wrong, it might be too late. The damage is done.

Let's remember to speak with restraint and wait until we have the facts to make strong declarations. Words are powerful. Use them wisely!

----

day 67

"If you mistreat my daughters or if you take any wives besides my daughters, even though no one is with us, remember that God is a witness between you and me."

–GENESIS 31:50

After reading just a few verses back how Leah and Rachel felt about their father's treatment, it's interesting—and surprising—to hear their father Laban warn Jacob about mistreating his daughters. It makes us wonder if Laban didn't realize how selfish he'd been about Leah and Rachel in the past. That he would give this warning to Jacob, in particular, might make us wonder if he didn't realize how badly he'd tried to mistreat Jacob too. Laban sounds a little clueless!

Sometimes the people who hurt us most truly don't realize what they're doing. While it's very important we don't make excuses for other people's bad behavior, it's also important we don't harden our hearts against those who are simply loving us imperfectly. Followers of Jesus are always trying to act more like Jesus, but we fail. Often. We need to make sure we extend the same grace to others that we ourselves need.

Is there someone who hurt you who you've been reluctant to forgive? Pray about it. Does God want you to work out your issues with that person? Or does he want you to overlook an offense and forgive?

day 68

"Now Dinah, the daughter Leah had borne to Jacob, went out to visit the women of the land."

–GENESIS 34:1

We've seen Dinah's first mention in the Bible, and now we come to her story—a horrifying, tragic, and controversial one. We'll look at it closely to uncover nuggets of wisdom while sorting through some of the controversy. And believe it or not, the first controversy is found right here in this phrase: *went out*, or *yasa* in Hebrew

In the past (and even today), people have used Dinah's "going out" to suggest that whatever happened next was Dinah's fault because she went out without her father or brothers by her side. In other words, they say, Dinah was asking for it. This ignores the many other women in the Bible who "went out" with no blame assigned to them or impropriety implied (Jael, Rachel, Rebekah, and Abigail, for example). But it reveals a strange human impulse that is still a problem today: victim-blaming.

When something terrible happens, the first question many ask amounts to "What did you do to cause it?" Not only does this make it very difficult for victims to feel safe coming forward, it heaps undue responsibility on a person already dealing with a trauma. Let's guard carefully against this attitude toward those who are suffering.

day 69

"When Shechem son of Hamor the Hivite, the ruler of that area, saw her, he took her and raped her. His heart was drawn to Dinah daughter of Jacob; he loved the young woman and spoke tenderly to her. And Shechem said to his father Hamor, 'Get me this girl as my wife.'"

–GENESIS 34:2–4

In most of our English translations, this sounds like a straightforward case of sexual assault. The Hebrew is less clear. Some scholars believe Dinah and Shechem had a consensual sexual relationship without being married, which was still a serious violation, though of a different kind that had more to do with social customs.

As modern readers of the Bible, we're left with a troubling question. Was Dinah raped, or did she and Shechem get swept up in a careless, forbidden relationship with catastrophic consequences? It would help us figure out the real story if Dinah's words, thoughts, or feelings were recorded in the Bible. But they're not. The story is told from Shechem's, Dinah's brothers', and Jacob's points of view.

Each of us is writing a story with our life. Everything we do, say, and even think is part of that narrative. And, unlike Dinah, *you* have a voice in your narrative. Thank God for the privilege of having a voice, and then use it well.

day 70

"Meanwhile, Jacob's sons had come in from the fields as soon as they heard what had happened. They were shocked and furious, because Shechem had done an outrageous thing in Israel by sleeping with Jacob's daughter—a thing that should not be done."

–GENESIS 34:7

Whether Shechem's act was forceful or Dinah was a willing participant, Shechem majorly messed up. At this point, he had no idea how badly he'd messed up because he was busy getting ready to marry Dinah. He had fallen head over heels for her and thought this event was the beginning of the rest of his life. He wasn't wrong about the level of impact his choice would have—but the results were clearly far more negative than he anticipated.

Sometimes the pivotal moments of our lives are events outside our control. Sometimes they are the results of someone else's choices. Maybe they are due to events outside everyone's control. But sometimes these milestone moments are a result of our own choices. Those choices may be good ones. Or, like Shechem's, they may be bad ones.

Our actions have consequences. It can be a costly lesson to learn when we learn it the hard way. But we don't have to learn it the hard way. Instead, we can work to recognize how important it is to follow God's path as truly as possible, even in decisions that may seem small at the time.

----

day 71

"The young man, who was the most honored of all his father's family, lost no time in doing what they said, because he was delighted with Jacob's daughter ... Three days later, while all of them were still in pain, two of Jacob's sons, Simeon and Levi, Dinah's brothers, took their swords and attacked the unsuspecting city, killing every male. They put Hamor and his son Shechem to the sword and took Dinah from Shechem's house and left."

–GENESIS 34:19, 25–26

Every single male in an entire city died because of Simeon and Levi's reaction to what happened between Shechem and Dinah. Whatever the nature of Dinah and Shechem's relationship, the end result was the same: Dinah's brothers took some serious revenge on Shechem and his clan.

It's good to stand up for people. Especially people who are being mistreated by others. Seeking justice for those who have been hurt is a good, noble thing to do. But it's definitely possible to take that idea too far. When we cross the line from "justice" into "revenge," we're setting ourselves up to become the one who's doing the mistreating.

Defending others is a good thing, but we have to keep in mind that vengeance belongs to the Lord (Romans 12:19, Deuteronomy 32:35). It's our job to speak up for what's right, but it's God's job to sort out retribution. Let's be careful to leave that to him and his perfect judgment!

day 72

"Rachel began to give birth and had great difficulty. And as she was having great difficulty in childbirth, the midwife said to her, 'Don't despair, for you have another son.' As she breathed her last—for she was dying—she named her son Ben-Oni. But his father named him Benjamin. So Rachel died and was buried on the way to Ephrath (that is, Bethlehem)."

–GENESIS 35:16B-19

It's tragic that Rachel, who wanted children of her own so badly, ultimately died in childbirth. She named her precious new baby "son of my trouble" with her last breaths. Rachel was a complicated woman with flaws and virtues who became a symbol of hope for many people, especially childless women. She is immortalized as a mother of Israel.

All that said, it's probably a good thing Ben-Oni's dad stepped in and renamed him Benjamin, which means "son of my right hand." Names were really important. While the name Ben-Oni wasn't a comment on Benjamin's personality, perhaps it would have felt that way if he'd grown up under that title.

It's tough to avoid living down to the negative labels people slap on us. It's important that, no matter the titles other people want to give us, we take hold of our own identities. You know who you are in Jesus, and "Daughter of God" is the only label that truly matters.

day 73

"There Abraham and his wife Sarah were buried, there Isaac and his wife Rebekah were buried, and there I buried Leah."

–GENESIS 49:31

It's an interesting final twist in Leah's story. She was not the favored wife in life, but in death, she was buried in the family plot while the beloved Rachel was buried by the side of the road. But, while Leah had this final bit of honor in death, her disappointment in life was known by all. Is it any surprise, then, that the rivalry between Leah and Rachel carried on into the next generation? Rachel's oldest son, Joseph, was favored by his father and despised by his half-brothers, Leah's sons.

It's easy to take on the offenses of others, especially when family honor is at stake. But Jesus teaches a very different method of dealing with offenses against us. In Luke 17, he tells us to rebuke brothers and sisters who sin against us, certainly, but then to forgive freely. Paul repeats this teaching in his letters to various churches.

Forgiveness is *hard*. Family feuds are one thing, but even a simple disagreement between two friends can be difficult to reconcile. But when we bring Jesus's spirit of openness (in frankly discussing the offense) and forgiveness (showing the grace to others that's been shown to us), reconciliation *is* possible.

day 74

"The Lord was with Joseph so that he prospered, and he lived in the house of his Egyptian master [Potiphar]."

–GENESIS 39:2

Remember that teensy rivalry between Leah and Rachel? Well, that history, coupled with Jacob's unbalanced favoritism of Rachel's oldest son, Joseph, led to some serious bad blood between Jacob's sons. And that bad blood resulted in Joseph being sold into slavery in Egypt by his brothers. Yikes.

Egypt is where we meet our next biblical woman. She's the wife of Potiphar, the man who owned Joseph—and she's not exactly one we want to emulate. Not everyone in the spotlight is someone we should look up to. You can probably name a bunch of celebrities off the top of your head who would not be good role models to shape your life after.

Like the men profiled in the Bible, we have our fair share of women's stories that should come with warning labels: "Do not try this at home!" And so it is with Potiphar's wife. Let's pray about finding good role models in our lives and following in the footsteps of the right people. Very often they're not those who are in the public spotlight but those God has blessed us with in our personal lives.

day 75

"So Potiphar left everything he had in Joseph's care; with Joseph in charge, he did not concern himself with anything except the food he ate. Now Joseph was well-built and handsome, and after a while his master's wife took notice of Joseph and said, 'Come to bed with me!'"

–GENESIS 39:6-7

Uh-oh. Potiphar's wife's first line of dialogue recorded here pretty much sums it up. She knew exactly what she wanted from Joseph, and she was aggressive about trying to get it. While being driven and determined can be good things, we obviously don't want to be driven and determined to behave badly!

It's interesting to note what Potiphar's wife noticed about Joseph. It wasn't his faithfulness to his God or his work ethic, though Joseph possessed both those virtues. She noticed that he was well-built and handsome. While not many girls would be as brazen as Potiphar's wife (that's a good thing!), *all* of us are vulnerable to being drawn to the wrong things in a guy.

There's nothing wrong with thinking a guy is cute. Of course not! Physical attraction isn't a bad thing. But it becomes a dangerous thing when that's all a potential boyfriend has to offer you. If he's super-hot but he's unkind, insensitive, inconsiderate, or doesn't share your beliefs, he's not going to be someone you should pursue. Pray for discernment in this area—that it would be a guy's heart, not his handsome face, that draws you to him.

_____

_____

_____

_____

day 76

"Now Joseph had been taken down to Egypt. Potiphar, an Egyptian who was one of Pharaoh's officials, the captain of the guard, bought him from the Ishmaelites who had taken him there."

–GENESIS 39:1B

We've backtracked a few verses to remind us of something important. Joseph was a slave. He was a slave who was honored by his master and blessed by God. But he was still a slave. He only had the power granted to him by his master, and that power could be taken away in a heartbeat. Joseph had no true agency.

When we're reading about these ancient people in the Bible, it's easy to think that women never had power. Generally speaking, they had much less freedom and control than men in their society. But here we have an example where our biblical woman has all the power—and she's seeking to abuse it.

As modern women, we're likely to be in a position of power at some point in our lives. It might be in our jobs, our communities, or even our government. And when we do find ourselves in a position of power, it's important that we *don't* do what Potiphar's wife did. Having power is a big responsibility, and we fail in that responsibility when we try to use our power selfishly. Let's pray that when we have power, we'll remain humble and treat everyone with dignity and respect.

day 77

"But he refused. 'With me in charge,' he told her, 'my master does not concern himself with anything in the house; everything he owns he has entrusted to my care. No one is greater in this house than I am. My master has withheld nothing from me except you, because you are his wife. How then could I do such a wicked thing and sin against God?'"

–GENESIS 39:8–9

Hooray, Joseph! Not only does he point out that giving in to Potiphar's wife would be a sin against God, he reminds her that his master (her husband!) has trusted Joseph with his entire household. He would be grossly misusing that trust to commit this sin with his master's wife.

While the exact situation we find here isn't likely to happen in our lives, each of us has been entrusted with something in the past. You are probably entrusted with several things right now, and that list will only grow as you move into adulthood. These may be responsibilities at school, work, or home. You may even have people to take care of, like your siblings or the kids you babysit.

God wants us to remain faithful with these things (and people). Jesus talks about being faithful in Luke 16:10. Those who are faithful with small things will be faithful with large things too. Let's endeavor to always be faithful with the things entrusted to us, both big and small.

day 78

"And though she spoke to Joseph day after day, he refused to go to bed with her or even be with her. One day he went into the house to attend to his duties, and none of the household servants was inside. She caught him by his cloak and said, 'Come to bed with me!' But he left his cloak in her hand and ran out of the house."

–GENESIS 39:10–12

Joseph laid out his logical, virtuous case, but Potiphar's wife wasn't having any of it. She still "spoke to him" every day. Blech. The Bible doesn't tell us how difficult it was or wasn't for Joseph to resist her offers. Maybe he was repulsed. Maybe he had to fight the temptation with everything in him. We don't know.

But we can learn from his example in how to handle sexual temptation. Even though his situation was precarious because Potiphar's wife was the one with the power, Joseph followed the advice Paul writes many years later in 1 Corinthians 6:18 pretty literally: flee from sexual immorality.

Joseph literally ran away from Potiphar's wife. There are some situations where we might literally run away from temptation, too, like a party where no parents or adults are present. But other times, the "running away" will be less literal. Perhaps it means making sure we're not in a situation where we're likely to be tempted. Whatever "fleeing" looks like, it's a good principle to practice when it comes to temptation.

_____

_____

_____

_____

day 79

"She kept his cloak beside her until his master came home. Then she told him this story: 'That Hebrew slave you brought us came to me to make sport of me. But as soon as I screamed for help, he left his cloak beside me and ran out of the house.'"

–GENESIS 39:16–18

The injustice of this part of the story should make us cringe. Not only did Potiphar's wife try to abuse her position of privilege and power, but when Joseph does the right thing and runs away, she accuses him of assaulting her. There's so much wrong with what's going on, it's hard to know where to begin.

While Potiphar's wife's actions are hopefully beyond anything we'll ever personally deal with, there's still a relatable lesson here. When we feel wronged by someone, it's massively tempting to exact revenge. In this case, Potiphar's wife caused Joseph to be thrown in jail. He would have died as a result, if not for God's intervention.

As tempting as it can be to take revenge when given the opportunity, it's important that we resist that impulse. The temporary satisfaction of getting back at someone doesn't compare to the potential damage we cause when we're vindictive. Vengeance can ruin lives, just as it could have done to Joseph. Let's pray for a spirit of patience and forgiveness when others snub us

---

---

day 80

"When his master heard the story his wife told him, saying, 'This is how your slave treated me,' he burned with anger. Joseph's master took him and put him in prison, the place where the king's prisoners were confined."

–GENESIS 39:19–20

Joseph is an excellent example of persevering through hardship and maintaining a good attitude. No matter what happened to him, he seemed to always work hard and excel where he was at. And of course, we know God had his hand on the whole situation and used Joseph to bring about good things for the whole family of Jacob.

But still. Look at what the dishonesty of Potiphar's wife caused. A man was *thrown in prison* because she lied. We don't hear anything else in the Bible from Potiphar or his wife after this. It seems they completely forgot about Joseph. Good thing God didn't . . .

It's impossible to overemphasize the importance of honesty in our lives. It's not only about pleasing God with our actions—though that's a very important part of it. Dishonesty can also have a major effect on those around us. If we don't own up to our wrongdoing, it's very possible someone else will take the fall for our behavior. Take this week to focus on speaking the truth in love.

day 61

"The king of Egypt said to the Hebrew midwives, whose names were Shiphrah and Puah, 'When you are helping the Hebrew women during childbirth on the delivery stool, if you see that the baby is a boy, kill him; but if it is a girl, let her live.'"

–EXODUS 1:15–16

A lot had happened since Joseph went to prison. The story is an epic tale of forgiveness and God's big-picture plan that ends with the sons of Jacob, along with their large families, moving to Egypt. That was the beginning of the nation of Israel—the Hebrew people.

But it didn't take long for Pharaoh, king of Egypt, to become threatened by this new nation-within-a-nation. So, he enslaved the Hebrews, and here we've come to our two midwives, Shiphrah and Puah, who have received the horrifying order to kill any Hebrew boys they deliver. It's interesting to note that the Hebrew text isn't clear whether the midwives themselves were Hebrew, Egyptian, or perhaps a mix of Hebrew and Egyptian lineage.

And in a lot of ways, it's better that we don't know for sure. Ethical issues are bigger than nationality, race, and other such identifiers. It's easy and natural to want to look out for "our own," whoever they may be. But God often asks us to step outside those boxes to discern right from wrong and to *act* in line with what's right. Whether Shiphrah and Puah were Hebrew themselves or not, they were the heroes who saved a nation.

day 82

"If you see that the baby is a boy, kill him; but if it is a girl, let her live."

–EXODUS 1:16

Beloved is a book to celebrate and learn from the beloved girls of the Bible, as we strive to better embrace our own identities as beloved daughters of God. But . . . can we just take a moment to love on the baby boys here?

Why only order the boys to be killed? It's possible Pharaoh expected the Hebrew girls would grow up and intermarry with the Egyptians. If so, killing the boys would provide him the best solution from his viewpoint—eliminate the threat of Hebrew soldiers (the men) while maintaining a large slave population through Hebrew girls. While the worth of women was downplayed in many ancient societies, we see here that being a boy could be every bit as dangerous for different reasons.

Sometimes we get the impression that if we, as women, want to assert ourselves or affirm our strength and independence, we have to do it at the expense of men. But a truly godly perspective affirms the value, dignity, and worth of *every* human being. All people matter to God, and that's why he tells us to love boundlessly without respect to race, religion, nationality, or gender.

day 83

"The midwives, however, feared God and did not do what the king of Egypt had told them to do; they let the boys live."

–EXODUS 1:17

Can you imagine what it would have been like to be in Shiphrah and Puah's position? They were midwives. Their whole job was to bring life into the world—to safely guide babies and mothers through the childbirth process (without the aid of modern medicine   yikes!). But Pharaoh was the king, the highest authority in the land of Egypt. In fact, ancient Egyptians worshiped their kings as gods and viewed their pharaoh as mediator between the common people and the divine. We're supposed to obey our governments . . . right?

Romans 13 does tell us to respect and obey the governments over us. But *not* at the expense of God's commands. Shiphrah and Puah had a choice to make. Which did they care more about, their fear of the king or their respect, love, and fear of God?

Thankfully, they chose their fear of God and did what was right—they let the baby boys live. Shiphrah and Puah are an excellent example of when it's right to disobey the law of the land. They did so peacefully and in a way that preserved life rather than destroyed it.

----

day 84

"Then the king of Egypt summoned the midwives and asked them, 'Why have you done this? Why have you let the boys live?' The midwives answered Pharaoh, 'Hebrew women are not like Egyptian women; they are vigorous and give birth before the midwives arrive.'"

–EXODUS 1:18–19

The midwives eventually have to face the king and answer for the continued survival of the Hebrew baby boys. Gulp. They seem to answer the king without cowering, and we might admire their strength in this frightening situation. But their response isn't exactly true, is it?

The Bible is pretty clear about how important honesty is. Yet the midwives are not condemned for their dishonest answer to Pharaoh. Plus, their sidestepping of the truth allowed them to save many lives. So we might wonder . . . is it ever okay to lie?

Stories like that of Shiphrah and Puah give us room to suppose there are extreme circumstances where lying to save lives might be acceptable. But we had better notice that the *majority* of comments in the Bible regarding lying are not at all favorable. While Shiphrah and Puah did right in this impossible circumstance, our go-to response in almost every situation should be truthfulness.

day 85

"So God was kind to the midwives and the people increased and became even more numerous. And because the midwives feared God, he gave them families of their own."

–EXODUS 1:20–21

There's some perfect circularity happening in this story. Shiphrah and Puah were faithful in saving the Hebrew baby boys, so they were rewarded by God with babies of their own. Makes sense!

God doesn't always work in such neat, straightforward ways, of course. Being faithful with managing your employer's money won't necessarily result in personal riches, for example (if only . . .). But God does reward our faithfulness. Sometimes those rewards are material. Sometimes it comes in the form of a great grade after faithfully studying hard for a test. Other times, the rewards may be spiritual. Faithfully serving at church, for example, helps us grow in maturity by practicing putting others before ourselves. Growing in the image of Jesus becomes its own reward.

While we shouldn't act faithfully simply to receive rewards, it's good to remember that God sees and cares about our faithfulness. Can you think of a time when you were faithful and God rewarded you in some way? Thank him for noticing when we do well!

day 86

"Then Pharaoh gave this order to all his people: 'Every Hebrew boy that is born you must throw into the Nile, but let every girl live.'"

–EXODUS 1:22

It would be so lovely if the story ended with Shiphrah and Puah outfoxing Pharaoh and saving Israel from destruction by rescuing babies. But here we see that Pharaoh wasn't finished. Now, instead of targeting midwives, he has told *all* his people to seek out infant Hebrew boys and toss them into the Nile. Ugh.

The sad truth is those with evil intent will often stop at nothing to carry out their plans. Pharaoh's attempt at genocide failed the first time, so he issued a broader order to meet his ends. But no matter how broad the order, no matter how sweeping the edict, those who love God cannot participate in an injustice like this.

If you keep up on current events, you could probably name a few such injustices in our world that mirror Pharaoh's edict here. As followers of Jesus, it's important that we take no part in these atrocities. Instead, we should be like Shiphrah and Puah—strong forces of good, godly values that stand against such evils.

day 67

"The name of Amram's wife was Jochebed, a descendant of Levi, who was born to the Levites in Egypt. To Amram she bore Aaron, Moses and their sister Miriam."

–NUMBERS 26:59

We've fast-forwarded a bit into the book of Numbers because, while her story is in Exodus, Moses's mother doesn't get named until the genealogies in Numbers. And what a genealogy. Those are some pretty famous kids Jochebed has. You could say Jochebed was a mother of Israel. Her sons would grow up to be the deliverer of the nation (Moses) and the first priest to the nation (Aaron). Miriam was no slouch, herself, remembered as a prophet and songwriter. Miriam also played a vital role in rescuing her brother Moses from Pharaoh's decree.

When we read about the women in this part of biblical history, it's hard not to be struck by their bravery. They weren't passive watchers, meekly following along with whatever was expected of them. They stood up and acted in line with what was right and what they knew God would want them to do. Sometimes they risked their safety—and even their lives—to do so. Thank God we have examples of good, godly women from all eras of history who were willing to be brave.

day 88

"Now a man of the tribe of Levi married a Levite woman, and she became pregnant and gave birth to a son. When she saw that he was a fine child, she hid him for three months. But when she could hide him no longer, she got a papyrus basket for him and coated it with tar and pitch. Then she placed the child in it and put it among the reeds along the bank of the Nile."

–EXODUS 2:1–3

Jochebed's actual story is in Exodus, even though she isn't mentioned by name. We can read, in detail, about the lengths she went to save her child. She stood up to the king's wicked edict twice. First, she hid baby Moses for three months. Then, when he couldn't be hidden any longer, she made a waterproof basket for him to try to keep him safe along the Nile. We can only imagine how she felt when she set him adrift in the water. Were her actions enough to spare his life? Would she ever see him again?

In our digital era, it's easy to feel like we're standing up for something by posting about it on social media. And awareness campaigns that go viral on the internet really can make a difference, so this is no knock on posting about important issues on social media. But are we willing to stand up when it costs us more than the few seconds it takes to hashtag a post?

Jochebed was. She was willing to risk the king's wrath to save her son. We can pray for that kind of bravery and boldness when the Lord calls us to it.

day 89

"His sister stood at a distance to see what would happen to him. Then Pharaoh's daughter went down to the Nile to bathe, and her attendants were walking along the riverbank. She saw the basket among the reeds and sent her female slave to get it. She opened it and saw the baby. He was crying, and she felt sorry for him. 'This is one of the Hebrew babies,' she said."

–EXODUS 2:4-6

The sister mentioned in this passage is, of course, Miriam. And now another woman has entered the picture—Pharaoh's own daughter. Through Jochebed first, then Miriam, and the princess, Moses finds his rescue. A good thing, too, since this baby would grow up to be the vessel of God's rescue for all of Israel.

It's pretty ironic when you think about it. Pharaoh was really concerned about the threat the young men of Israel might pose to his kingdom when they grew up. But ultimately, it was the women who thwarted his plan.

Everyone will be underestimated at some point in her life. It never feels good to be overlooked or thought less of than you deserve. But we can remember the truth that God always sees us for exactly what we are. God knows what we're capable of, what lies in our hearts, and what sort of success we'll go on to achieve for his kingdom. Don't let anyone's small opinion of you make you feel small!

day 90

"Then his sister asked Pharaoh's daughter, 'Shall I go and get one of the Hebrew women to nurse the baby for you?' 'Yes, go,' she answered. So the girl went and got the baby's mother. Pharaoh's daughter said to her, 'Take this baby and nurse him for me, and I will pay you.' So the woman took the baby and nursed him."

–EXODUS 2:7–9

Jochebed's heart must have leapt when Miriam came home with baby Moses. She didn't know if she'd ever see her son again, but now, Pharaoh's daughter wanted Jochebed to nurse her own baby until he was old enough to go live in the palace, where he would receive the finest education available and *not* have to live life as a slave. The deal couldn't have been any sweeter if Jochebed had written it herself.

Jochebed was willing to lay her son on God's mercy. In many ways, it's symbolic of what Jesus asks us to do with our lives. That may sound a little weird at first, but think about what he says in Matthew 16:25: "For whoever wants to save their life will lose it, but whoever loses their life for me will find it."

We have to be willing to lay everything down to follow Jesus. We have to be willing to put all our expectations into a little waterproof boat and set them adrift. God will return the best of them to us—or else show us a new, better plan.

day 91

"When the child grew older, she took him to Pharaoh's daughter and he became her son. She named him Moses, saying, 'I drew him out of the water.'"

–EXODUS 2:10

We might wonder how this part of the story felt for Jochebed. Moses was her baby. She'd had the divinely planned opportunity to nurse her son and care for him in his early years. And then, Jochebed had to give her son to the princess. Since Moses's heritage wasn't a secret, it's very possible he stayed connected to his community and his family throughout his years in the palace. But, even so, Jochebed made a great sacrifice to save her son's life.

It's not easy to let go like Jochebed did. She had some serious motivation—saving her son's actual life—but it was still probably hard to follow through with what she had to do. Most people like to have control, but God often asks us to trust *him*—to release that control over to someone much bigger and greater than ourselves. It's a tall order for us. But when we remember that God has a big-picture plan, letting go of our control becomes a little easier. God sees the whole design and he knows what we need most (even when it's not what we *want* most). Trust in God's good plan for you!

day 92

"By faith Moses' parents hid him for three months after he was born, because they saw he was no ordinary child, and they were not afraid of the king's edict."

–HEBREWS 11:23

Did you notice that we've fast-forwarded all the way through the Bible, deep into the New Testament book of Hebrews? Moses's parents get mentioned in the famous "Heroes of Faith" chapter. And with good reason. They were incredibly gutsy, and they followed God's path without fear.

It's easy to become consumed with fear. There are a lot of scary things out there in this world, and because we have become so technologically advanced, we're able to hear about these scary things from all over the globe on a daily basis.

But did you know the antidote to fear isn't boldness or risk-taking or wildness? No, the true cure for fear is faith— faith like Moses's mother and father showed when they defied the king's edict and did what was right in God's sight. They believed God would care for them and for Moses. And they believed that even if their physical lives weren't saved, they were valuing what God valued (life) and honoring what God honored (faith). When we put our faith in God's promises, he will help us manage our fears. Sometimes he might eliminate those worries altogether, but other times, he helps us act in spite of our fears.

_____

_____

_____

_____

day 93

"His sister stood at a distance to see what would happen to him."

–EXODUS 2:4

We've briefly met Moses's sister, but now we'll give Miriam her own time in the spotlight. When we first meet her, she isn't even named, and she is often remembered, more than anything else, as "sister of Moses." But Miriam's story is rich and full in its own right, and she played an integral role in her famous sibling's story too.

Living in someone else's shadow isn't easy. Most of us don't have famous siblings, but almost everyone has to deal with living in a shadow sometimes. Maybe it's a teammate who is a star on the field, or a fellow singer or actor who *always* seems to be getting the center stage roles. When we work hard and do our best, it can be frustrating to feel stuck in a shadow.

But, like Miriam, our value is not lessened just because someone else gets more airtime. Our supporting roles matter. That sports hotshot needs your assist to score a goal. And that starlet has no show without an excellent chorus to back her up. Miriam's support was key to her brother's story, and your support is key to those around you.

day 94

"Then Miriam the prophet, Aaron's sister, took a timbrel in her hand, and all the women followed her, with timbrels and dancing."

–EXODUS 15:20

Miriam the prophet." It's a brief mention, but it's kind of a big deal. We don't have a huge number of female prophets discussed in the Bible (though there are more than many people realize!). Not only is Miriam called a prophet, she is leading all the women of Israel in a song and dance. Prophet and musician—basically, Miriam was an ancient girl boss.

We're pretty lucky to be born in the era we are. Never before has such a large percentage of the global female population had as much freedom as we enjoy. We have the opportunity to pursue careers, rock out being a stay-at-home wife or mom, stay single and support ourselves, shoot for the very highest levels of education available, compete in professional sports—just about anything we want!

But not all girls around the globe have these opportunities. Women in other cultures often deal with constant threats to their safety, little or no freedom, and barbaric practices left over from centuries past. Remember to pray for these women. There are Christian organizations that specifically offer help to these women and their children. See what you can do to get involved!

day 95

"Miriam sang to them: 'Sing to the LORD, for he is highly exalted. Both horse and driver he has hurled into the sea.'"

–EXODUS 15:21

Miriam is very often depicted in artistic renderings as a musician, leading the women of Israel in victory songs. These battle-victory songs were an important part of Israelite culture. They offered acknowledgment that God was the source of victory and praise for his help, power, and loving care. They were performed by highly skilled artists, like Miriam. This wasn't some random tune she threw together on the spot. This music really mattered.

Music matters in our lives too. Music draws people together under a common culture (think about how you can often tell a big country music fan from a heavy metal fan, just based on the way they're dressed). Music makes us feel good. Listening to it releases the feel-good chemical, dopamine, in our brains. And music is one way God's people have been offering praise to him for millennia.

What are some of your favorite modern songs? Do you have a favorite hymn? A favorite band you'd love to see in concert? Take a moment to thank God for the great gift of music and the many ways it enriches our lives, even if we're not musicians ourselves.

day 96

"Miriam and Aaron began to talk against Moses because of his Cushite wife, for he had married a Cushite."

—NUMBERS 12:1

This is a sad piece of the story. Miriam and Aaron are (wrongly, as we'll see later) speaking out against their own brother. But perhaps even more importantly, they are speaking out against the leader God had anointed. They may have even thought they were doing the right thing, since Moses had married a foreign woman and God generally wanted the Israelites to marry other Israelites so they wouldn't be drawn into the idol-worship of the cultures around them. But they did not seek God on the matter before speaking out against their brother. Instead, they slandered him.

Now, this is very important to understand. Aaron and Miriam were sinning because they were *slandering* Moses—that is, they were accusing this godly man of sinning when he hadn't. This is not the same thing as speaking out against someone in authority who is being abusive.

But we must be very careful when we consider speaking against our Christian leaders—and people, in general. Before saying anything negative or critical, make sure you are speaking the truth from a place of love, and that your motivations are good (and not rooted in jealousy, like Miriam and Aaron's).

day 97

"'Has the LORD spoken only through Moses?' they asked. 'Hasn't he also spoken through us?' And the LORD heard this. (Now Moses was a very humble man, more humble than anyone else on the face of the earth.)"

–NUMBERS 12:2–3

After taking offense at Moses, Miriam and Aaron suggest they are equally qualified to lead Israel. The comment that Moses was the most humble person on earth points out to us, the readers, that Miriam and Aaron's charges against Moses were totally unfair.

Pride and jealousy were likely at the root of their accusations, and pride blinds us all sometimes. When the Bible warns us about pride, it's not talking about being happy for someone, like when you're proud of your best friend for getting accepted to her top choice for college. The Bible is warning us about having a puffed-up ego—becoming so full of ourselves, we leave no room to acknowledge God's hand in our successes. Or becoming so prideful, we hate to see others succeed.

It's difficult but *so* important to sift through our hearts and weed out prideful tendencies. Are our feelings rooted in humility or arrogance? Do we celebrate the successes of others? Do we acknowledge God's blessings in our lives? Take a moment to pray about these heart issues and ask God to show you areas he wants you to work on.

day 98

"At once the Lord said to Moses, Aaron and Miriam, 'Come out to the tent of meeting, all three of you.' So the three of them went out. Then the Lord came down in a pillar of cloud; he stood at the entrance to the tent and summoned Aaron and Miriam."

–NUMBERS 12:4–5

Gulp. This would be like being called to the principal's office times a million. God had some choice words for Aaron and Miriam because they had been unjust in accusing Moses. And God told them that Moses was special, even among his prophets. In other words, "Back off, Miriam and Aaron!"

Part of maturing is learning to accept discipline when we've earned it. And, man, do we earn it sometimes. No matter how hard we try, we all mess up. We all make mistakes. Accepting correction from those in authority over us is an important part of learning from those mistakes. That person in authority may be a teacher or boss, and very often this correction comes from our parents. It may even come from our friends. We are wise to listen to the correction of those who love us—friends, family, and mentors or pastors we're close to. It's not an easy aspect of maturing, but it's an important one!

day 99

"The anger of the LORD burned against them, and he left them. When the cloud lifted from above the tent, Miriam's skin was leprous—it became as white as snow. Aaron turned toward her and saw that she had a defiling skin disease, and he said to Moses, 'Please, my lord, I ask you not to hold against us the sin we have so foolishly committed. Do not let her be like a stillborn infant coming from its mother's womb with its flesh half eaten away.'"

–NUMBERS 12:9–12

Leprosy was no joke in the ancient world. Miriam was experiencing some pretty serious consequences for her accusations against her brother.

Aaron quickly recognizes he and Miriam had acted foolishly and he speaks up on his sister's behalf. And God did actually heal Miriam in this case. But worldly consequences don't often work that way. When we mess up and experience consequences, those consequences tend to stick around. Even if we're sorry.

The best way to avoid worldly consequences is to avoid the mess-ups in the first place. Obviously. Remembering that consequences can be long-lasting can serve as a good motivator for thinking twice about our words and actions. But when we do stumble, we can and should pray to God for mercy. But the correction we experience through consequences will result in growth and—hopefully—wiser choices in the future.

day 100

"So Moses cried out to the Lord, 'Please, God, heal her!'"

–NUMBERS 12:13

This is a short verse, but it contains a very powerful message. Miriam and Aaron have wrongly accused their little brother Moses. Even God took Moses's side and punished Miriam for her arrogance. But instead of leaving Miriam to the consequences she earned, as would be very tempting to do, Moses cries out to God for her. He asks for her healing. He asks God's grace for Miriam, even though she messed up. Even though her mess-up was specifically against Moses.

That's forgiveness. It isn't always easy to read Jesus's teachings about forgiveness in the New Testament. He sets a really high standard for us, and forgiveness can be one of the most difficult things for many people to practice. So it's a good thing we have people—regular human beings, just like us—who displayed this trait well in the Bible.

Have you been wronged before? Most of us have. Have you been able to forgive the friend who wronged you? God can soften our hearts and make it possible if we let him.

day 101

"'Confine [Miriam] outside the camp for seven days; after that she can be brought back.' So Miriam was confined outside the camp for seven days, and the people did not move on till she was brought back."

–NUMBERS 12:14B–15

God answered Moses's plea to forgive Miriam. But on the condition that she was confined outside the camp for a week (there were ceremonial laws surrounding leprosy, after all). The people waited for her and didn't continue their journey until Miriam was allowed to rejoin the community.

Miriam was a leader among the Israelites, but we can imagine she rejoined the group feeling thoroughly humbled. Being an outcast will do that to you. Have you ever been in that position? Cut off from the group, on the outside looking in? It's not a pleasant feeling. And while Miriam's separation from the group was part of a punishment she had earned, the outcasts among us usually didn't do something to "deserve" it.

Jesus made a habit of hanging out with outcasts. In his day, that meant tax collectors and others the people despised. When we're cast out or ostracized, we can remember that Jesus cares for us just like he cared for the outcasts of his day. When we see someone on the outside, we can show them Jesus's love by welcoming them into our groups and letting them know they are not alone.

day 102

"Remember what the LORD your God did to Miriam along the way after you came out of Egypt."

–DEUTERONOMY 24:9

Aw, man. Do you have to bring it up *again*? Miriam may have felt that way when these words were spoken to all of Israel. She had messed up, she knew it, she apologized, and she was restored. Can't we just leave it at that and never speak of it again?

Most of us probably feel that way about our mistakes. Especially those where we experienced some sort of public humbling as a result. When we've realized we made a bad choice and truly turned away from that choice, isn't it only fair to expect that everyone else will move on too?

That's true . . . to a point. But our mistakes can actually help other people, so sometimes our mistakes are worth bringing up again. Miriam's mistake became a lesson for all of Israel—a reminder. We can help other people learn from *our* mistakes so they don't have to learn the hard way. Likewise, we can save ourselves some heartache by being willing to learn from others' errors.

day 103

"I brought you up out of Egypt and redeemed you from the land of slavery. I sent Moses to lead you, also Aaron and Miriam."

–MICAH 6:4

Miriam wasn't as perfect as the rest of us (ahem . . .). She was a woman who had an up-and-down journey. An honored leader and prophet. A woman who let her arrogance cloud her judgment. A woman who was publicly disciplined. An artist immortalized in song. Miriam was all of these things, and more.

But here in the book of Micah, hundreds of years after Miriam lived and God saved his people from Egypt, God once again honors Miriam by referring to her not as a person who made mistakes, but as a woman who he sent, along with her brothers, to save his people from Egypt. It's a powerful redemption for our complex Miriam. Her story didn't end with "she made a huge mistake and God was angry with her."

Our stories are always in progress. Sometimes, when difficult things happen in our lives, it can feel like this is our whole story, now and forevermore. Maybe we worry that our stories are over. But God is always writing a new chapter. When we can't see the whole book, God nudges us to at least flip the page.

day 104

"The daughters of Zelophehad son of Hepher, the son of Gilead, the son of Makir, the son of Manasseh, belonged to the clans of Manasseh son of Joseph. The names of the daughters were Mahlah, Noah, Hoglah, Milkah and Tirzah."

–NUMBERS 27:1

Zelophehad's daughters probably aren't household names for most of us. We don't usually think of the great women of the Old Testament as Sarah, Rebekah, Leah, Rachel . . . and Mahlah, Noah, Hoglah, Milkah, and Tirzah. But even though their names might not be part of our common biblical vocabulary, the story of these five extraordinary ladies is well worth studying.

And that's because their story isn't just a dry history lesson about some people who lived thousands of years ago. In the story of Zelophehad's daughters we see a brilliant resolution of conflict where all sides are heard—and then affirmed by God.

Is that even possible? Can everyone's concerns, questions, and fears on all sides of an issue be addressed in a way where no one feels ignored? The story of Zelophehad's daughters tells us that *yes*, it is possible. And what could be more applicable in our modern age of sharply divided politics and public arguments plastered all over the internet? Win-win outcomes are possible when we're willing to listen to the concerns of others.

day 105

"[They] stood before Moses, Eleazar the priest, the leaders and the whole assembly at the entrance to the tent of meeting."

–NUMBERS 27:2

It's probably fairly easy for us to recognize the gutsiness Zelophehad's daughters show here. They're standing before the whole assembly! That takes some serious boldness, especially in a time when most women didn't have the same level of influence as men. These five women stepped forward to make a request to *change the law*. Whoa.

It's not easy to be bold. It comes more naturally to some of us than others, but we can suppose any of us would have felt nervous in Zelophehad's daughters' shoes. But when we're standing up for what's right, we don't need to be afraid. Countless women have worked very hard over many centuries to give future generations—our generation—a voice. Let's keep using that voice! We can stay strong and speak up for what's right, even when we're not the most powerful person in the room.

day 106

"Our father died in the wilderness. He was not among Korah's followers, who banded together against the LORD, but he died for his own sin and left no sons."

–NUMBERS 27:3

It's easy to read the Old Testament and get frustrated with the ancient Israelites sometimes. It seems like, no matter how present, available, and *real* God shows himself to be, the stubborn Israelites just can't help wandering away. It may be easy to judge, but really, our hearts are a lot like this. We know the realness of Jesus's love, but we're still prone to wander toward bad attitudes and wrong choices. We're more like the Israelites than we might realize.

God used forty years of wandering through a wasteland to teach his community to better trust in him, and now that community was ready to take hold of God's promise. Zelophehad's daughters represent the best of the next generation preparing to inherit God's Promised Land. They point out that their father was not involved in the terrible rebellion of his generation, but that he died for his own sin (possibly the community sin of unbelief in God's promise). They balance their intense boldness with humility and godliness.

That's quite a relevant example for a modern girl! Like Zelophehad's daughters we can be fearless and fierce, godly and good. We don't need to sacrifice one for the others.

day 107

"Why should our father's name disappear from his clan because he had no son? Give us property among our father's relatives."

—NUMBERS 27:4

There is long-standing research showing that women are significantly less likely to ask for raises at work than their male colleagues. Some studies show that men are four times more likely to ask—*four times*! Women tend to make less money than men, on average, and while that is a complex statistic with many contributing factors, one reason for this is that women are more likely to hesitate when it comes to asking for raises.

Zelophehad's daughters understood the power of asking. Even though it was a risk, they stepped forward, made their request, and laid out their reasoning. We can find strength in their example. When we have a solid case and sound reasoning, we don't have to hesitate. And this certainly doesn't just apply to the workplace. It can apply to asking our parents for a new bit of independence we believe we've earned. It can apply to our lives at school and church. Whatever goals we're pursuing in our lives, let's be willing to ask!

day 108

"So Moses brought their case before the Lord, and the Lord said to him, 'What Zelophehad's daughters are saying is right. You must certainly give them property as an inheritance among their father's relatives and give their father's inheritance to them.'"

–NUMBERS 27:5–7

Moses didn't answer the daughters right away. Their request might have flummoxed him. After all, it ran contrary to the law given to them directly from God. Only sons were supposed to inherit land. But, as he usually did, Moses asked God before making any declarations. He was a good leader.

We may get the idea that no women owned land in these days, but that's not the case. Ancient Near East legal codes show us that many cultures of the time allowed daughters to inherit the land of their fathers. But in Israel, the land was a physical representation of God's relationship with his people. This land was about much more than property ownership. Which is why God's response to the daughters' request is so beautiful.

God affirms the rightness of the daughters' request. He acknowledges that this situation is an exception to the original law. He doesn't condemn the daughters for daring to suggest they might have a claim on God's promise. God doesn't condemn us for asking and seeking, either. We have a claim as God's daughters, and it's right for us to embrace it.

day 109

"Say to the Israelites, 'If a man dies and leaves no son, give his inheritance to his daughter. If he has no daughter, give his inheritance to his brothers. If he has no brothers, give his inheritance to his father's brothers.'"

–NUMBERS 27:8–10

Not only did God approve of Zelophehad's daughters and grant their request, he added new language to the law so the Israelites could judge similar matters in the future. He creates a new path to land inheritance—first sons, then daughters, then brothers, then uncles.

Did you notice how daughters came before more distant male relatives? While this still isn't perfectly equal with sons and daughters holding the same position, the way they would today, God again confirms that his beloved daughters matter to him in a real way. Having no land inheritance would have left women vulnerable if their fathers died and they were unmarried. The Israelite women needed this new bit of the law added in to help protect them from this fate, and even in the patriarchal society of ancient Israel, God made sure his daughters would be taken care of.

Did you know you matter to God as much as these ladies? He cared enough to tweak the law to protect them, and he cares about our needs too. Let's take a few moments to thank God for his care of our spiritual, physical, and emotional needs.

day 110

"Every daughter who inherits land in any Israelite tribe must marry someone in her father's tribal clan, so that every Israelite will possess the inheritance of their ancestors."

–NUMBERS 36:8

After Zelophehad's daughters were granted land, the men of the tribe starting worrying about what would happen to their land when women married. Would it go away? Would it be absorbed by another tribe? As we see by God's response, their concerns weren't totally unfounded, and swapping land across tribes would not be an ideal set-up. So . . . now what?

God decreed a compromise—women could inherit the land of their families, as long as they married within their clan to keep their land inheritance within its proper tribe. Like most compromises, it's not exactly perfect. It still restricted the freedom given to Israelite women.

But compromise is a very important part of peaceful problem solving. And complex issues are rarely resolved overnight—especially when they're being addressed for the first time. But when we're dealing with complex problems, mutually beneficial compromises are huge victories. God's solution here was perfect (of course), and it paved the way for women's land rights millennia later.

_____

_____

_____

_____

day 111

"So Zelophehad's daughters did as the LORD commanded Moses."

–NUMBERS 36:10

This verse really sums up Zelophehad's daughters. They did as the Lord commanded Moses. These women were righteous and obedient to God's commands, in addition to being brave. Their story has been used by some women's rights groups from the last two hundred years to lobby for better property ownership opportunities for women. For our generation, it seems odd to imagine gender ever excluded anyone from owning property. Laws have come a long way, and we can thank Zelophehad's daughters (as well as many others) for that.

But it's important to remember that many women around the world don't enjoy this same level of freedom—and that there are many men, women, and children living in the poverty Zelophehad's daughters hoped to avoid. Take a moment to thank God for the roof over your head, whether it's owned, rented, or borrowed. Remember those who are struggling without that basic necessity. Is there a way for you to get involved in helping the homeless in your community or around the world? Helping with this vital need is a wonderful way to show the love of Jesus to others.

day 112

"Then Joshua son of Nun secretly sent two spies from Shittim. 'Go, look over the land,' he said, 'especially Jericho.' So they went and entered the house of a prostitute named Rahab and stayed there."

—JOSHUA 2:1

It's a pretty humble one, as "first mentions" go. She's not Rahab, the business owner or Rahab, the homeowner or even just Rahab. She is Rahab, the Canaanite prostitute. Probably not the title any of us would want to announce our arrival in the Bible.

But, despite this unflattering first mention, Rahab becomes a legitimate hero of the Bible. In fact, she gets three mentions in the New Testament, so long-lasting was her impact. Here in Joshua, Rahab was writing the very beginning of a new story for herself and her family.

Maybe you're in the same position in your family. Maybe you're the first person in your family to believe in God. Or maybe you're simply feeling young and small, unsure how you'll be able to have a positive impact on the kingdom of God. Don't resent starting out from humble beginnings. Rahab rose to be a superstar of faith, and you can too.

day 113

"The king of Jericho was told, 'Look, some of the Israelites have come here tonight to spy out the land.' So the king of Jericho sent this message to Rahab: 'Bring out the men who came to you and entered your house, because they have come to spy out the whole land.'"

JOSHUA 2:2–3

Rahab was risking her safety, and possibly her life, to help the Hebrew strangers. It might make us think of Jesus's words in John 15:13: "Greater love has no one than this: to lay down one's life for one's friends." Those are words of intense bravery.

It runs against our natural instinct (self-preservation) to sacrifice ourselves for others. We may not ever experience a demand for self-sacrifice as dramatic as Rahab did here, although many in the 1940s were faced with a frighteningly similar situation as Jewish refugees fled from Nazis during World War II.

But self-sacrifice happens in quiet ways too. It happens in being an emotional support for a struggling friend, in getting up early on a Saturday to serve your community, in volunteering time, energy, and material resources to help those in need. It happens in putting others first and showing sacrificial love.

day 114

"(But [Rahab] had taken them up to the roof and hidden them under the stalks of flax she had laid out on the roof.) So the men set out in pursuit of the spies on the road that leads to the fords of the Jordan, and as soon as the pursuers had gone out, the gate was shut."

–JOSHUA 2:6–7

Rahab responded to the king's demand with cunning and wisdom. She might have been a person of influence in Jericho because the king seemed to trust her without much question. As we've noted before, it's important to default to honesty in just about all situations. But that doesn't mean we can't use our wits.

God gave us wisdom, common sense, and intelligence for a reason—to be used! It's important that we balance the use of our capable minds with humility and dependence on God's leading. Because even the wisest of the wise, the sharpest of the sharp, makes mistakes.

And what if we feel like we're lacking wisdom? James 1:5 says we can ask for it! Intelligence may be something we're born with, but wisdom is something we can grow in—and it's the more important of the two. Let's pray today for good sense and keen judgment.

day 115

"Before the spies lay down for the night, she went up on the roof and said to them, 'I know that the LORD has given you this land and that a great fear of you has fallen on us, so that all who live in this country are melting in fear because of you.'"

—JOSHUA 2:8-9

This is a fascinating statement from Rahab. Not only does she mention the Lord—not just a god, but the Lord, specifically—she demonstrates faith in this Israelite God by acknowledging that God was powerful enough to bring down the city of Jericho and give it to the Israelites.

Rahab had obviously heard about the Lord at some point, whether via direct revelation from God or because she had studied Moses's teachings. And what she heard was enough to ignite belief in her heart. She went against everything she knew—her culture, her religion, her profession—to act in accordance with that faith.

Sometimes God asks us to interact with our culture—to be willing to meet people where they are without condemnation the way Jesus did with the outcasts of his day. Other times, God will ask us to reject our culture the way Rahab did in this pivotal moment in Israel's history. Discerning when God wants us to do each of these things is difficult but necessary. Pray for God's eyes to see when he wants you to interact with your culture and when he wants you to stand up to it.

day 116

"We have heard how the LORD dried up the water of the Red Sea for you when you came out of Egypt, and what you did to Sihon and Og, the two kings of the Amorites east of the Jordan, whom you completely destroyed. When we heard of it, our hearts melted in fear and everyone's courage failed because of you, for the LORD your God is God in heaven above and on the earth below."

–JOSHUA 2:10–11

Notice what Rahab says here—*we* have heard. The Israelites' reputation preceded them. The whole city of Jericho had heard the news of the Israelites escaping through the Red Sea. All of Jericho was afraid because perhaps they were next on the list to be steamrolled by this wandering people and their powerful God.

But for all their fear, Rahab was the *only* one who actually responded to God in her heart. Response is so important. We can hear the gospel message a million and one times but if we don't respond with faith, it's all for nothing.

This matters in our spiritual lives, and it matters in our daily lives too. Think about some opportunities you might be holding back on. Have you been wanting to try out for a team at school, but you're scared you won't make it? Pray about whether or not God wants you to respond to these opportunities and see where he leads you. He may be nudging you to step out in faith!

day 117

> "Now then, please swear to me by the LORD that you will show kindness to my family, because I have shown kindness to you. Give me a sure sign that you will spare the lives of my father and mother, my brothers and sisters, and all who belong to them—and that you will save us from death."

—JOSHUA 2:12–13

This is the deal that changed Rahab's life. It was more than just a plea to save her life. If the Israelites pulled off the conquering of Jericho, Rahab's family would be the only family spared from the city. They would be joining a new community—the Israelites—and grafting their Canaanite branch into this nomadic nation.

Did Rahab worry about how smoothly the transition would go? Did she wonder if the Israelites would accept her, the Canaanite prostitute, when the law repeatedly warned the Israelites about intermixing with the Canaanite culture? We can imagine she did. And though we'll never deal with this exact situation, perhaps if we've ever been a stranger crossing the threshold of a new church or school for the first time, we can relate a little bit to how she might have felt.

Sometimes when we're a long-term, comfortable member of a group, it's easy to miss it when someone else is experiencing one of these scary moments of being the newbie or outsider. The next time you see someone new, go the extra mile to welcome them to your community.

123

day 118

"But Joshua spared Rahab the prostitute, with her family and all who belonged to her, because she hid the men Joshua had sent as spies to Jericho—and she lives among the Israelites to this day."

–JOSHUA 6:25

When we read through the Old Testament, it's pretty clear to see that God chose Israel as his special people. Though he loves everyone, Israel was his promised people. It's important to understand that in order to realize how cool it is that Rahab, a prostitute who was not a born Israelite, was made a member of God's chosen community.

Even many centuries before Jesus came to Earth, God was already hinting at his master plan—a church made up of people of faith, regardless of their heritage. God looked past Rahab's imperfections and into her heart, which held a spark of faith for the one true God. It didn't matter that she didn't have the "qualifications" to be an Israelite.

Your heart is what matters most to God too. We may get discouraged if we feel like we don't have the right upbringing or the best choices in our past. But none of those things matter to God when we have true faith. God loves you right now, just as you are. While we should always pursue a deeper, better, truer relationship with God, we are beloved even when we are starting out where Rahab did.

day 119

"Salmon the father of Boaz, whose mother was Rahab, Boaz the father of Obed, whose mother was Ruth, Obed the father of Jesse . . ."

—MATTHEW 1:5

We'll read more about Boaz when we get to Ruth's story. But for now, we can simply note that he was a very godly man. And here in the gospel of Matthew, as Matthew is tracing Jesus's lineage, Rahab is noted as Boaz's mother. Because of the way genealogies were written, sometimes skipping generations between important figures, it's possible she was a grandmother or great-grandmother to Boaz. But either way, it's safe to say Rahab continued to make godly values a priority in her family. Her descendant Boaz was the great-grandfather of David, Israel's future king and the man whose line would eventually produce Joseph, Jesus's earthly father.

That's quite a legacy. Rahab, the foreigner and the woman who ran a brothel, was eventually included in Jesus's family line. Her story can encourage us when we feel like there's no way to redeem our stories. Maybe we've made a mistake that feels pretty catastrophic. Maybe we made a choice that resulted in serious spiritual fallout.

Don't despair! God can redeem *any* story, and God can redeem *every* situation. Rahab's full-circle journey proves it.

day 120

"By faith the prostitute Rahab, because she welcomed the spies, was not killed with those who were disobedient."

–HEBREWS 11:31

Not only was Rahab honored as a part of Jesus's lineage, she is mentioned here in Hebrews 11, the "Heroes of Faith" chapter. But . . . do you notice something sad? Even here, where she's being honored for her faith and strength of character, she's still called "the prostitute Rahab."

Some sins are "sticky" like that. Even though Rahab was respected, she never could quite shake the label of her past profession. Sometimes it works that way for us too. Sometimes, when people know about the mistakes we've made or the things we used to struggle with, it's hard for them to view us apart from that.

But do you want some good news? God doesn't have this problem. While he is omniscient and knows everything, Psalm 103:12 tells us that as far as the east is from the west, so far has he removed our sins from us. When we repent and accept forgiveness through Jesus, our sin is wiped away, as far as God is concerned. Humans may not be so perfect in their forgiveness or judgment. But God's truth is the one that really matters. No sin is too sticky for him to remove it from his memory.

day 121

"In the same way, was not even Rahab the prostitute considered righteous for what she did when she gave lodging to the spies and sent them off in a different direction? As the body without the spirit is dead, so faith without deeds is dead."

—JAMES 2:25–26

James is one of the most challenging books in the New Testament. James encourages us to live a life of active faith—faith that is visible to others through our deeds. Basically, James says that what we *do* with our faith matters. And here he uses Rahab as an example of that. Regardless of the sins in her past, she was considered a righteous woman because she acted on her faith. She saved the spies and became a member of the Israelite community.

While it's true that some sins are "sticky," we, like Rahab, have the opportunity to carve out our own futures—our own identities—through our faith-based deeds. She didn't stay stuck in her past. She acted in faith and began a new legacy of righteousness.

What legacy are you weaving today? Are you happy with the way it's turning out so far? If not, you can change it! Pray for bigger faith, deeper conviction, and greater boldness. Because if Rahab is remembered as a righteous woman, we have the ability to mirror her faith and strength as righteous women too.

day 122

"And Caleb said, 'I will give my daughter Aksah in marriage to the man who attacks and captures Kiriath Sepher.'"

–JOSHUA 15:16

Sometimes her name is spelled Achsah or Acsah, but don't be confused. It's all the same girl. Aksah, daughter of Caleb, the man who followed Moses as the leader of Israel. In fact, it was Caleb who brought Israel into the Promised Land because Moses was forbidden to enter. And here we have Aksah, Caleb's only daughter, presented as a prize.

We're modern women, so we probably recoil at the idea of being a spoil of war. And we should. It's a stark reminder that women have, at various points in history, been seen as the property of their fathers—prizes to give away, if and when their fathers saw fit. It's important to note that, while this practice is *in* the Bible, it doesn't mean God approved of it.

It's good to think of ourselves as prizes in one sense— valuable and worthy of being won over. But it's dangerous when we see our worth as dependent on anyone else recognizing that we're valuable. We risk reducing ourselves to objects. Human beings—men *and* women—are worth more than that. God loves and cherishes each of us, and we should never allow others to objectify us as mere prizes.

day 123

"Othniel son of Kenaz, Caleb's brother, [captured Kiriath Sepher]; so Caleb gave his daughter Aksah to him in marriage."

—JOSHUA 15:17

Aksah didn't really have a choice in this matter. If she objected to a marriage with Othniel, we'll never know. Given the cultural norms of Aksah's time, that might not have even occurred to her. Arranged marriages were very common. If you had romantic feelings for your spouse, all the better, but that wasn't necessarily the starting point for most marriages.

While arranged marriage is still common in some parts of the world, it's very unusual in most western cultures. We have the liberty to choose our spouses based on whatever criteria we want—which is a wonderful freedom but can also be an overwhelming responsibility!

It's important we seek relationships built on love, mutual respect, and friendship. A lifelong marriage commitment is no small decision. Let's make sure we're seeking a partner who has the qualities that matter!

day 124

"She replied, 'Do me a special favor. Since you have given me land in the Negev, give me also springs of water.' So Caleb gave her the upper and lower springs. This is the inheritance of the tribe of Judah, according to its clans."

–JOSHUA 15:19–20

Water was vital in the Negev desert. Because Aksah is specifically asking for springs, we might speculate that she didn't have any water sources on the land Caleb had given to her. Whatever the original water situation on the land, notice what her father does—he gives her both the upper and lower springs.

Isn't that exactly like our heavenly father? In spite of all the good things God has already given to us, when we come to him with requests of necessity or deep desire, he hears us and responds. And not only does he respond, he responds with something better than what we originally asked for.

Now, that doesn't mean God gives us whatever we want, whenever we want it. Sometimes his response is a period of silence (ack!). Sometimes his response is a firm no. But God does always give us whatever is *best*, just like a loving father would. When we understand we have a loving father listening to our prayers, we can rest securely and peacefully in what he gives to us. His choices are always wise.

day 125

"But when they cried out to the Lord, he raised up for them a deliverer, Othniel son of Kenaz, Caleb's younger brother, who saved them. The Spirit of the Lord came on him, so that he became Israel's judge and went to war. The Lord gave Cushan-Rishathaim king of Aram into the hands of Othniel, who overpowered him. So the land had peace for forty years, until Othniel son of Kenaz died."

–JUDGES 3:9–11

This judge of Israel was the same Othniel who was Aksah's husband. And she had grown up with Caleb as her father—Caleb, one of the only men of his generation allowed to enter the Promised Land because of his faithfulness. Needless to say, Aksah had some pretty awesome people in her life.

The friends and family we surround ourselves with can have a profound impact on our faith. When we spend time with people who share our faith, who help us grow, and those whom we can trust, we'll see a positive impact on our lives.

So what do you do if you don't feel like you have enough of these influences in your life? Find some! Reach out to a mentor or pastor at church. Ask your friend who is awesome at praying to become your prayer partner. You can even look to your Bible to find role models to emulate. There are many in this book.

day 126

"Now Deborah, a prophet, the wife of Lappidoth, was leading Israel at that time."
—JUDGES 4:4

You'd think that after the Israelites entered the Promised Land, everything would be peachy. But instead (because they were human), they entered into a cycle of falling away from God and his law, being handed over to their enemies, crying out to God, and God sending a deliverer to rescue and lead them. These deliverers were called judges, and Deborah was one of them.

Say what? A female judge of Israel? It's true. Of the fifteen judges mentioned in the Bible, Deborah is the only woman. Was it hard for her to fit in among other Israelite women of her time? Maybe. They were running households and businesses, caring for livestock and fields—no small tasks—but Deborah was leading the nation.

Sometimes being the "only" of something feels like a negative. It can be lonely—the only girl on your debate team, the only girl powerlifting at the gym—or the only Christian girl in the room. But being the "only" one means you're forging a path for others to follow in the future. "Only" means you're brave enough to do something outside the norm. Like Deborah, your "only" can signal your strength.

day 127

"She held court under the Palm of Deborah between Ramah and Bethel in the hill country of Ephraim, and the Israelites went up to her to have their disputes decided."
–JUDGES 4:5

Deborah held court—it may not seem like a terribly significant statement, but it is. It means the people of Israel came to Deborah as their judge. They trusted her wisdom to sort through tough matters. They trusted her discernment to determine what was right. Deborah was treated with respect equal to that of the male judges.

Deborah is one of many historical women who prove that as long as women have been around, they've been capable of leading. One of England's greatest monarchs was Elizabeth I. Or consider her African contemporaries, Amina of Nigeria and Mbande Nzinga of Angola. Or how about military leaders, like Joan of Arc, or leaders of contemporary movements, like Malala Yousafzai, who is the youngest Nobel Prize laureate and advocate for girls' education. Or Hatshepsut, who peacefully ruled Egypt hundreds of years before Deborah lived!

We have a lot of fine examples of female leadership, ladies. Do you feel God prompting you to take a more active leadership role in one or more areas of your life?

day 128

"She sent for Barak son of Abinoam from Kedesh in Naphtali and said to him, 'The Lord, the God of Israel, commands you: "Go, take with you ten thousand men of Naphtali and Zebulun and lead them up to Mount Tabor. I will lead Sisera, the commander of Jabin's army, with his chariots and his troops to the Kishon River and give him into your hands."'"

–JUDGES 4:6–7

Not only was Deborah the legal and military leader of Israel (all the judges were, and she doesn't seem to have been an exception), she was also a spiritual leader. A prophetess. She spoke the very words of God to the people in the same way Moses did. Deborah was a speaker of truth itself.

Let's be real: we're probably not going to be in a position where we'll speak God's words directly to a nation we're leading as Deborah did. But we will have many opportunities to be speakers of truth—every day, in fact, we're given the opportunity to speak truth into the world around us.

Sometimes that truth is the ultimate truth—the gospel message. We are always speaking truth when we tell people about Jesus's work on the cross. But other times, we speak truth by sharing other stories from the Bible. And often, sharing truth looks like spreading God's love to the world around you—a world that desperately needs God's love and the hope that comes with it. Be a speaker of truth today!

day 129

"Barak said to her, 'If you go with me, I will go; but if you don't go with me, I won't go.'"

—JUDGES 4:8

Barak was no weakling. This was a powerful, talented military leader. He's mentioned in the "Heroes of Faith" chapter in Hebrews. And still, he refused to go fight Sisera unless Deborah, God's appointed judge, was with him. That's quite an endorsement for Deborah! She was an incredibly powerful woman, and her reputation preceded her.

Every single person has a reputation, whether we want one or not. Our reputations are almost like clouds of words that surround us—the words other people use to describe us, the stories others have heard about us. These reps go before us and behind us and can influence the way we are treated, talked about, and even *thought* about.

If we *have* to have a reputation, let's do our best to have one like Deborah's. She was known as a woman of power and faith, righteousness and wisdom. It takes a while to build a rep like that. Many wise choices, many good deeds, many acts that displayed the faith in her heart. So let's start building that Deborah-like reputation today!

day 130

"'Certainly I will go with you,' said Deborah. 'But because of the course you are taking, the honor will not be yours, for the LORD will deliver Sisera into the hands of a woman.' So Deborah went with Barak to Kedesh. There Barak summoned Zebulun and Naphtali, and ten thousand men went up under his command. Deborah also went up with him."

–JUDGES 4:9-10

Like several of the biblical women before her, Deborah is the picture of boldness, even when those around her are displaying timidity and hesitation. But what we might notice in particular about Deborah here is the grace with which she addresses Barak. She doesn't shame him, scoff at him, or refuse to help him. She is willing to go, as he asked, and she matter-of-factly states a prophecy that would come to have a double meaning (more on that later).

It's great to be a powerful woman. It's great to be respected and have your awesome reputation go before you. But it's important that we stay balanced—humble, gracious, kind, *and* powerful. Like Deborah.

Remember to respond with grace when you're in a position of power—whether you're the captain of the team, the shift leader at work, president of student council, or in some other leadership role. Those gracious responses are an awesome reflection of God's grace.

day 131

"Then Deborah said to Barak, 'Go! This is the day the LORD has given Sisera into your hands. Has not the LORD gone ahead of you?' So Barak went down Mount Tabor, with ten thousand men following him."

–JUDGES 4:14

Deborah was not a mere bystander in Barak's battle against Sisera. Not only did she give confidence to the commander of Israel's army, but as a prophetess, she represented God's presence to the men. She spoke God's words to them. Deborah played a key part in Israel's victory.

Because Deborah's key role in this battle is recorded in the Bible, it has lived on for thousands of years. While not many people's stories will last for millennia (because, seriously, no matter how cool our deeds are, they're not making it into the Bible), we each have moments in our lives where our participation—our presence—is crucial.

God has placed those key moments on your path. That moment may be a make-or-break decision time for someone else's faith, and you were there with perfect answers to their questions. Or it may be you were in the right place at the right time to perform CPR and save a life. Or a million other things. We can be in those right places at the right times and fulfill our key roles when we follow God's lead in our lives.

day 132

"Sisera, meanwhile, fled on foot to the tent of Jael, the wife of Heber the Kenite, because there was an alliance between Jabin king of Hazor and the family of Heber the Kenite."

–JUDGES 4:17

And here we come to another moment where the stories of two powerful biblical women are intertwined. In the middle of Deborah's narrative, we meet Jael. Jael's background is uncertain, as is this alliance Jael's husband had made with Jabin. The Kenites had been friendly to Israel in the wilderness, so it's possible Heber's treaty with Jabin was a betrayal of Israel—a wrong Jael meant to set right.

Loyalty is important. When we give someone our word, it's honorable to remain true to our promise. But are there times when loyalty becomes a bad thing? Believe it or not, there are. When we place loyalty above doing what's right in God's sight, it can become a very bad thing.

Good loyalty looks like not gossiping about your friends behind their backs. Bad loyalty looks like keeping quiet about a dangerous situation because your friend might feel betrayed if you spoke up. It's important to be honorable and keep our word, but we have to use wisdom and discernment when deciding where our true loyalties lie—with those around us, or with God.

day 133

"Jael went out to meet Sisera and said to him, 'Come, my lord, come right in. Don't be afraid.' So he entered her tent, and she covered him with a blanket."

—JUDGES 4:18

Normally, it wouldn't be acceptable for a man to enter a woman's personal tent like this, unless he was her father or brother, and Sisera was neither to Jael. Perhaps that's why Sisera felt he had found the perfect hiding place. No one would think to look for him in a woman's personal tent, so he'd be safe from all his enemies . . . right? Not exactly, as we'll see.

Sisera could be a poster boy for cowardice. He was the commander of an army, but here he is sneaking off by himself, taking refuge in a woman's tent to try to save his own life. Not exactly heroic, and quite the opposite of the love Jesus showed for us when he laid down his life for us (John 10:11).

Fighting in a war is a pretty extreme situation most of us aren't facing at the moment. But the principles of bravery and self-sacrifice apply in smaller ways too. It can mean protecting someone, saving a life, sticking up for the right thing, or even providing an awesome example for those who look up to you. We are all called to sacrificial bravery. Let's own it!

day 134

"'I'm thirsty,' he said. 'Please give me some water.' She opened a skin of milk, gave him a drink, and covered him up. 'Stand in the doorway of the tent,' he told her. 'If someone comes by and asks you, "Is anyone in there?" say "No."'"

–JUDGES 4:19-20

Jael's behavior is almost . . . motherly. She listens to Sisera's requests and cares for his needs. It wouldn't be so startling, really, except for what happens next. But this nurturing moment from Jael helps complete her portrait—a shocking, but robust, picture of womanhood.

Like Jael, we aren't just one thing. God has created us with many facets—strength, beauty, gentleness, intelligence, goodness, fierceness. We can be—we are—all of these things. These traits are the ways we reflect our Creator God, who is all these things and more.

Jot down a list of some of the wonderful qualities God has given to you. Do you see complementary traits that bring balance to who you are? Take a moment to write down some other areas you'd like to grow in. Let's thank God for the wonderfully robust characters he's given to us all.

day 135

"But Jael, Heber's wife, picked up a tent peg and a hammer and went quietly to him while he lay fast asleep, exhausted. She drove the peg through his temple into the ground, and he died."

—JUDGES 4:21

Okay, so . . . this is the shocking part of Jael's story. There's no getting around it. This was a seriously violent act. And with this single violent act, Jael won Israel's war. While the gruesome nature of the killing might make us cringe, it's impossible to deny that Jael, who was certainly smaller, weaker, and more vulnerable than Sisera, the army commander, stepped up and slayed her giant.

Each of us will face giants in our lives, figuratively speaking. Our giants are problems that seem impossible to solve. Goals that seem far out of reach. Persecution or hurtful behaviors of others. Our giants may even be in our own minds—fear, anxiety, depression, doubt.

Jael's story shows us that God's power is bigger than the biggest giants. Time and time again, the Bible shows us the weaker one overcoming the stronger, the smaller one overcoming the larger. Whatever giant you're facing today, God's got your back and then some.

day 136

"Just then Barak came by in pursuit of Sisera, and Jael went out to meet him. 'Come,' she said, 'I will show you the man you're looking for.' So he went in with her, and there lay Sisera with the tent peg through his temple—dead."

–JUDGES 4:22

When Deborah first prophesied to Barak that the glory of the battle would go to a woman, it would have been fairly safe to assume she was speaking of herself. In one sense, she was, but in the literal sense, Jael was the fulfillment of that prophecy. It was she who took down the mighty leader of the enemy army. In fact, two women claimed victory for Israel that day.

Sometimes God brings about his plans in surprising ways. Planning our futures is a good, necessary exercise. We should be looking toward what's on the horizon—hoping, dreaming, wishing, praying.

But we should also be sure to make room for God's unexpected detours. If we become too attached to the *one* path we have in mind for the future, we might lose out on God's directions. Our plans are good; God's plans are great.

day 137

"On that day Deborah and Barak son of Abinoam sang this song: 'When the princes in Israel take the lead, when the people willingly offer themselves—praise the LORD!'"

–JUDGES 5:1-2

Deborah was one of a kind. She's counted among a handful of female prophets in the Bible. She was the only female judge, and one of a small number of strong, powerful female leaders specifically named in the Bible. But what's one of the coolest things about Deborah? Despite her impressive résumé, this kick-butt woman always points back to God.

Deborah didn't focus on her own power. She highlighted God's power, displayed *through* her. Deborah didn't brag about her many gifts or great capability. She gave glory to the One who bestowed those great gifts upon her.

God has granted us many capabilities too, and each of us is probably gifted a bit differently than the other women around us. But no matter our gifts, no matter our power, we should always acknowledge God as the source of those good things. An attitude like Deborah's keeps us humble.

day 138

"Villagers in Israel would not fight; they held back until I, Deborah, arose, until I arose, a mother in Israel. God chose new leaders when war came to the city gates, but not a shield or spear was seen among forty thousand in Israel."

–JUDGES 5:7–8

We've seen Deborah the prophet, Deborah the musician, Deborah the military strategist, Deborah the judge. But here's a new side of Deborah—a mother in Israel. Whether or not Deborah had biological children isn't the point. She was like a mother to the entire nation. Deborah truly "had it all."

We're lucky to be born in modern times. We get the opportunity to "have it all" too. What does it mean to have it all? It means our lives are wide open to us. If we want to be married, that is something we are free to pursue. If not, women are able to have careers and support themselves. This hasn't always been the case! If we want to have children, we're free to pursue that—biologically, through fostering and adoption, or even through mentoring. If not, we can focus our lives in other directions. We can pursue ministry, higher education, executive careers, the arts, athletics—and about a hundred other things.

Having it all isn't actually about doing *all* these things at once. It's about the freedom to do *any* of these things we choose. Don't waste the freedom of modern womanhood! Grab it and go.

day 139

"Most blessed of women be Jael, the wife of Heber the Kenite, most blessed of tent-dwelling women . . . Her hand reached for the tent peg, her right hand for the workman's hammer. She struck Sisera, she crushed his head, she shattered and pierced his temple."

–JUDGES 5:24, 26

Jael's final mention in the Bible comes within Deborah's victory song. Far from being condemned for her violent act, Jael is praised—most blessed of women.

Normally we wouldn't celebrate such a violent act. And in our modern society such drastic measures seem doubly shocking. But here, Jael used what she had available at the time to bring about God's plan.

There are stories in the Bible that are just flat-out hard to understand sometimes. We don't get a lengthy explanation of every situation, detailing exactly what God thought about each part—which actions he approved of and which he condemned. It's okay to wrestle with that a little. It's okay to research, to pray, to grapple, and especially to seek the counsel and insight of trusted believers. Paying attention to these tough stories and working through them only deepens our understanding and grows our faith.

day 140

"Jephthah the Gileadite was a mighty warrior. His father was Gilead; his mother was a prostitute."

–JUDGES 11:1

From Deborah to Jephthah, about a hundred years and four more judges passed. Obviously, Jephthah is a guy, but we're going to take a look at his life because his story starts here, with his unnamed mother. She gets this very unflattering one-liner as her primary mention in the Bible. We might wonder what single-sentence statement she would have written about herself, if given the opportunity. We might also wonder if she was able to raise her son, given that she was not married to his father. Did Jephthah stay in his father's household instead? We just can't know for sure.

But Jephthah's less-than-ideal circumstances of birth—and the great role he would go on to have in Israel—tell us something important about God. There is no circumstance so shameful that God can't redeem it. There is no one so weak that God can't work through her. There is no situation so hopeless that God can't restore balance.

In fact, God likes to do this. First Corinthians 1:27 says that God chose the weak to shame the strong. In other words, God's power is more clearly on display when he uses unlikely vessels to bring about his plans. Feeling like an unlikely vessel today? Be encouraged! God adores the "unlikely."

day 141

"Gilead's wife also bore him sons, and when they were grown up, they drove Jephthah away. 'You are not going to get any inheritance in our family,' they said, 'because you are the son of another woman.'"

—JUDGES 11:2

If you've spent much time inside a school, a large group of people, or even just on social media, you've probably witnessed your fair share of bullying. Maybe you've even experienced it firsthand. Bullying, especially cyber bullying, has made national headlines for years now, and the stories behind those headlines aren't pretty.

But we see this isn't only a modern problem. While these men should have been people Jephthah could trust, since they were his own half-brothers, he experienced brutal rejection at their hands because of the circumstances of his birth.

Jephthah's story is one that can give great strength to those who have been taunted, rejected, and "driven away," even if not in the literal sense. He didn't let his mistreatment at the hands of his brothers define the rest of his life. He rose above it, and we can too. We should always feel comfortable and empowered to seek help or report it if we're the victims of bullying. But it's also empowering to know there are those who have gone before us who didn't let this sort of rejection crush them long-term.

day 142

"So Jephthah fled from his brothers and settled in the land of Tob, where a gang of scoundrels gathered around him and followed him."

–JUDGES 11:3

Okay, so maybe a "gang of scoundrels" wouldn't be most people's first choice of leaders. But the fact is Jephthah was forced out of his father's home and made do with his circumstances and surroundings. Another fact: God created Jephthah to be a leader—a judge, like Deborah—and no matter where Jephthah went, no matter who he was surrounded by, he was bound to be a leader. That was God's purpose for him.

We can't thwart God's designs or purposes for us, either. When he calls us to something, he's not likely to let it go because our circumstances are tough at the moment, or because we don't feel like working at the thing he's called us to.

The persistent prompting of God may feel like a tiny itch in the backs of our brains, nudging us in a particular direction. Or it could feel like a sledgehammer, shattering our excuses and our fears. Let's be active and prayerful in seeking out God's designs for us.

day 143

"Then the Spirit of the Lord came on Jephthah. He crossed Gilead and Manasseh, passed through Mizpah of Gilead, and from there he advanced against the Ammonites."

–JUDGES 11:29

Jephthah rose to the position and purpose God created him for—judge and leader of Israel. The Spirit of God was on him, and he won great military victories for God's people. This, from the little boy who was born to a prostitute? Yep. He didn't let his humble parentage stop him.

Shame is a very powerful poison. It's different than the guilt or broken-heartedness we feel when we know we've sinned or disappointed God. That type of guilt causes us to turn away from wrongdoing and toward God. It helps us grow in Jesus's image. But shame comes from the enemy, and it seeks to strike at our very hearts. Shame tears us down and makes us feel worthless.

The antidote to the poison of shame is knowing and believing in your true identity, like Jephthah did. Your *true* identity is that you are one of God's beloveds. Don't let shame tell you otherwise!

day 144

"And Jephthah made a vow to the LORD: 'If you give the Ammonites into my hands, whatever comes out of the door of my house to meet me when I return in triumph from the Ammonites will be the LORD's, and I will sacrifice it as a burnt offering.'... When Jephthah returned to his home in Mizpah, who should come out to meet him but his daughter."

–JUDGES 11:30–31, 34

Here we find a profoundly sad mention of another woman in Jephthah's life—his only child, a daughter. Jephthah had made a promise to God he could not break. In return for victory, he would sacrifice the first thing that came out of his door at home. That first thing was his daughter.

There is some debate about whether Jephthah's daughter became a literal sacrifice or if she spent the rest of her life dedicated to the Lord, meaning that she would never marry or have children (which would also be cause for mourning in Israelite culture). Either way, it's clear Jephthah spoke his vow rashly, and he deeply regretted it later.

We have to be so, so careful with our words. Like Jephthah, we can speak words quickly without thinking that later get us in big trouble. Spilling secrets can cost us friendships. Making promises we can't keep can ruin our reputations. And harsh words can wound others. Let's show wisdom by being extra careful with our words.

----

day 145

"And what more shall I say? I do not have time to tell about Gideon, Barak, Samson and Jephthah, about David and Samuel and the prophets."

–HEBREWS 11:32

Jephthah isn't one of our more famous historical figures from the Old Testament. He's not a household name like King David, for example. But he does get a mention in the Hebrews "Heroes of Faith" chapter, right alongside the likes of David and Barak.

While we're focusing mostly on biblical women in this book, it's good for us to look up to men of faith too. And each of these men was pretty special in his own right. But what did they all have in common? Though the Bible details some of their moral failings (ahem, David and Samson), they are also men who stood up for the good of the people instead of seeking their own comfort. They were brave, bold, strong, and good.

We get fascinating glimpses of the women who touched the lives of these men, like Jephthah's mother and daughter. But we can also grow in the godly character traits these men exhibit. What else should God's beloved daughters be but brave, bold, strong, and good?

day 146

"A certain man of Zorah, named Manoah, from the clan of the Danites, had a wife who was childless, unable to give birth. The angel of the Lord appeared to her and said, 'You are barren and childless, but you are going to become pregnant and give birth to a son.'"

–JUDGES 13:2–3

Perhaps the most famous leader from Israel's period of the judges is Samson. He was renowned for his physical strength, notorious for his moral failings, and remembered for his heroic final act. But Samson's life story started here, with his mother. We never get her name. We just know her as Manoah's wife and Samson's mother.

We see that Samson's mom seems like an awesome person. She probably deserves to have her name listed. But even without her actual name, we can appreciate her virtues.

It's easy for our identities to get wrapped up in those around us. So-and-so's daughter. This person's friend. While there's something cool about this—that it speaks to the interconnectedness of all our lives—it's important to remember we are our own people. Our parents, friends, and significant others don't define us.

day 147

> "Now see to it that you drink no wine or other fermented drink and that you do not eat anything unclean. You will become pregnant and have a son whose head is never to be touched by a razor because the boy is to be a Nazirite, dedicated to God from the womb. He will take the lead in delivering Israel from the hands of the Philistines."
>
> –JUDGES 13:4-5

It probably seems weird that before he was even conceived, Samson's mother had specific dietary restrictions and instructions about Samson's hairstyle. But these were important elements of the Nazirite vow. It showed that the one who had taken the Nazirite vow was fully dedicated to God. Consecrated. Sanctified. Set apart.

Did you know you're set apart too? The apostle Paul started out his first letter to the Corinthian church with these words: "To the church of God in Corinth, to those sanctified in Christ Jesus and called to be his holy people" (1 Corinthians 1:2). We are set apart in the name of Jesus, called to be God's holy people in the midst of a world that doesn't always reflect God very well.

That's a mighty calling, beloved. Galatians 5:22–23 says the results of the Holy Spirit in our hearts will be love, joy, peace, patience, kindness, goodness, faithfulness, gentleness, and self-control. Pray about specific ways God might want you to display these virtues that set you apart as a daughter of God.

day 148

"Then the woman went to her husband and told him, 'A man of God came to me . . . he said to me, "You will become pregnant and have a son. Now then, drink no wine or other fermented drink and do not eat anything unclean, because the boy will be a Nazirite of God from the womb until the day of his death."'"

–JUDGES 13:6–7

After the angel visited her, Samson's mother went straight to her husband to fill him in on the situation. She relayed the angel's message, repeating the wild, wonderful prophecy she'd just heard. Both Samson's parents believed the angel's words.

Testimony is vital. "Testimony" is just a fancy, Christian-ese way to say "our stories" or "what we have witnessed." How many of us believe in Jesus Christ because someone else told us about him? Unless we've had an angelic visitation like Samson's mom, all of us probably heard about Jesus from another person. We heard their testimonies—their stories about what they had experienced and knew to be true—and faith was sparked in our hearts. We heard, and we believed.

Like Samson's mom, and like those who first shared their stories of Jesus with us, let's aim to have our powerful words of testimony reach others. Tell about the times God answered prayers for you. Share about how Jesus has changed your heart. You'll be planting faith-seeds in the hearts of your listeners.

day 149

"Then Manoah prayed to the LORD: 'Pardon your servant, LORD. I beg you to let the man of God you sent to us come again to teach us how to bring up the boy who is to be born.'"

–JUDGES 13:8

Manoah's response to his wife's testimony is pretty fantastic. The first thing he does—after believing his wife's words, of course—is to pray for help. In fact, he prayed for specific wisdom in bringing up this boy, who was obviously set apart for a special purpose. Total parenting win, and the baby didn't even exist yet.

It is *always* good to ask for godly advice. When we know we're facing something important, whether big or small, we can pray to God for wisdom, strength, discernment, and help. We can also seek godly advice from those whom we trust and who are mature in their faith.

It makes practical sense to ask for help, but it also displays a humble heart. The person who asks for help is acknowledging that they don't know everything and that they would like to share in the wisdom of others. You can't lose when you approach challenges with that attitude!

day 150

"God heard Manoah, and the angel of God came again to the woman while she was out in the field; but her husband Manoah was not with her. The woman hurried to tell her husband, 'He's here! The man who appeared to me the other day!' . . . The angel of the LORD answered, 'Your wife must do all that I have told her.'"

–JUDGES 13:9–10, 13

The angel appears again and tells Manoah that his wife must be careful to follow his instructions to the letter. Remember, Samson was dedicated to the Lord, so those Nazirite rituals expressed something important. There was no room for little slip-ups or small cheats.

We will also serve a variety of roles in our lives. Maybe right now, your main role in life is that of a student. Our young adult years are set aside as a time to get an education. Sometimes that might feel like a drag, especially when you're spending hours doing endless calculus problems or you're writing your nine millionth essay for the semester. But your education lays a solid foundation for the rest of your life, and it's a privilege many throughout history would've loved to have had.

Our most important roles are funny that way. Sometimes they feel a lot like the monotonous day-in and day-out of life. But God wants us to be faithful in the small, daily tasks, because when you put together the big picture of thousands of small tasks, you'll find that the role you served was crucial after all.

day 151

"The angel of the Lord replied, 'Even though you detain me, I will not eat any of your food. But if you prepare a burnt offering, offer it to the Lord.' (Manoah did not realize that it was the angel of the Lord.)"

–JUDGES 13:16

Manoah did not fully realize who he was talking to here. Yikes! Can you imagine chatting with one of God's messengers and thinking you were talking to a regular person?

Manoah might not have been quick on the uptake, but he treated the angel with respect and kindness and did just what the angel said. There's this great verse in Hebrews that says, "Do not forget to show hospitality to strangers, for by so doing some people have shown hospitality to angels without knowing it" (Hebrews 13:2). That's exactly what Manoah and his wife were doing!

We may traditionally associate showing hospitality with welcoming people into our home, and that's certainly one way to be hospitable. But we can also show hospitality by being welcoming to everyone we meet. We're hospitable when we show genuine interest in other people. Even a simple smile is showing hospitality! Whether we're welcoming people into our homes, sharing a meal with them, or greeting them with warmth, the same message is being conveyed: you matter, and I care about you. You are welcome here.

day 152

"And the Lord did an amazing thing while Manoah and his wife watched: As the flame blazed up from the altar toward heaven, the angel of the Lord ascended in the flame. Seeing this, Manoah and his wife fell with their faces to the ground."

–JUDGES 13:19B–20

It's hard to know how we would react if we saw the angel of the Lord face-to-face like this. But falling to the ground seems like a pretty appropriate response. Those in the Bible who saw angels often responded this way.

While we may not ever have a face-to-face meeting like this in our lifetimes, it's important we respond to God with respect, love, and even awe the way Samson's parents did. The word *awesome* has become a synonym for "great," but God is awesome in the original sense of the word—overwhelming, breathtaking, awe-inspiring. Worthy of worship.

Take a few moments right now to think about the awe-inspiring things God has done in your life. Think of the friends and family he has surrounded you with. Think of the times he has sustained you and answered your prayers. And most awe-inspiring of all, think of this simple truth: God sent his son to the cross *for you*, beloved girl. When we keep these things in mind, we can't help but stand in awe of God's great love for us.

day 153

"Manoah realized that it was the angel of the LORD. 'We are doomed to die!' he said to his wife. 'We have seen God!' But his wife answered, 'If the LORD had meant to kill us, he would not have accepted a burnt offering and grain offering from our hands, nor shown us all these things or now told us this.'"

–JUDGES 13:21B-23

Manoah's wife is so cool. Her response to her husband's (completely understandable) fear is perfect. She doesn't crumble alongside him, melting into a puddle of hysterics. And she doesn't speak harshly to him or tell him he's ridiculous. She simply responds with faith-filled logic. Her faith shines through, as she trusts God to be good and just in his dealings with them. And she applies that faith to their situation in a perfectly logical way. "If God meant to kill us, he wouldn't have shown us the favor he just did." Simple and true. No need to panic.

Keeping your head in a crisis or scary situation can be tough. When emotions well up and adrenaline is pumping, hitting the panic button may be an understandable first response. But, like Manoah's wife, we can instead try to stay calm and respond with both faith and reason. The ability to stay calm in a crisis holds panic at bay and helps us make better decisions. And experts say that those good decision-making skills in the midst of an emergency can save lives.

day 154

"The woman gave birth to a boy and named him Samson. He grew and the Lord blessed him, and the Spirit of the Lord began to stir him while he was in Mahaneh Dan, between Zorah and Eshtaol."

–JUDGES 13:24-25

Samson had such a good start in life. He had strong, godly parents who loved him. The Spirit of God was with him as he grew. He had an important calling that mattered to the wellbeing of his entire nation. We might even say Samson's parents did "everything right," if that's possible. But if you know the story of Samson, you know things didn't turn out well for him. So what happened?

We will look at a couple reasons why Samson's life didn't unfold as perfectly as it started. But no matter what Samson's reasons for straying were, we can learn something important from this family. It doesn't matter what those around us do; *we* are called to be faithful in what God has set before us. Manoah and his wife were faithful. They didn't stray from God and they followed the instructions from the Lord like they were supposed to.

It's hard when the people we love stray. But it's important we guard against wavering because of others' choices. We're each accountable for our own behavior—nothing more and nothing less.

day 155

"[Samson] said to his father and mother, 'I have seen a Philistine woman in Timnah; now get her for me as my wife.' His father and mother replied, 'Isn't there an acceptable woman among your relatives or among all our people? Must you go to the uncircumcised Philistines to get a wife?' But Samson said to his father, 'Get her for me. She's the right one for me.'"

–JUDGES 14:2B–3

Here we see one glimpse of Samson straying from the straight and narrow. When it came time for him to marry, he chose a woman who was not an Israelite. But not only was she not an Israelite, she was a Philistine, and the Philistines were the ones who were oppressing the Israelites. Samson's whole role as judge of Israel was supposed to be to save Israel from these people! We can imagine his parents were deeply disappointed.

It's surprisingly easy to forget our calling as God's beloved daughters—namely to honor him in everything we do. That includes honoring God with who we choose for our friends and our romantic partners. We want to choose people who are good and kind. We want to choose people who are principled and who share our core beliefs. When we choose wisely, keeping these things in mind, we glorify God and save ourselves from the sort of grief Samson experienced because of his poor choices.

day 156

"His parents did not know that this was from the Lord, who was seeking an occasion to confront the Philistines; for at that time they were ruling over Israel."

–JUDGES 14:4

Wait, what? Didn't we just say Samson had strayed and was making a poor choice here? Yeah, we did. And yeah, he was. If it was a bad choice, why did God let him make it?

That's a complicated question. It's a lot like asking why bad things happen—is it because of evil forces, because people are making wrong choices, or is it because God did it? And the answer to all three of those questions is yes. Simultaneously. Evil forces are always conspiring to destroy God's kingdom. People are notoriously making bad, selfish choices that result in suffering (which is why we need a savior in the first place). *And* God is, at least, allowing these things to happen for the time being. Sometimes he's even using bad things for his own good purposes.

We've all made bad decisions that have made us wiser, or had tough situations that have made us stronger. When the bad things happen, we have to remember God is there working things out toward *his* ultimate goal. And we can always trust that his goals are good.

day 157

"Samson went down to Timnah together with his father and mother. As they approached the vineyards of Timnah, suddenly a young lion came roaring toward him. The Spirit of the LORD came powerfully upon him so that he tore the lion apart with his bare hands as he might have torn a young goat. But he told neither his father nor his mother what he had done."

–JUDGES 14:5-6

Stories like this throughout Samson's life illustrate an important truth. God is there, even in the midst of our failures—empowering us, providing for us, strengthening us. As Samson travels with his parents to marry his Philistine fiancée, God empowers him with superhuman strength and he tears a lion to pieces with his bare hands (poor lion).

While we can certainly hope the exact situation will never apply to us, the principle holds true in our lives. God has empowered *you* to do the tasks he's set before you. Even when we mess up, even when we fail, God is always ready to accept us back, restore us, and empower us again.

Be encouraged. God does, of course, care about our choices and how we live our lives. We should always strive for holiness. But there is no mistake so bad—no choice so poor—that God will wash his hands of us.

day 158

"Some time later, he fell in love with a woman in the Valley of Sorek whose name was Delilah."

—JUDGES 16:4

We've skipped over the Philistine woman Samson was supposed to marry (a lot of drama went down at that wedding) and moved on to the most famous woman in Samson's life—Delilah. Delilah was not a woman of strong, godly character. From both Samson and Delilah, we get a lot of "what not to dos."

And yet Samson's story is almost sadder than Delilah's. Delilah wasn't moral in the least, but she was also surrounded by an immoral culture. She didn't know the Lord. She wasn't raised with God's Spirit resting on her the way Samson was. Considering that, she behaved exactly as we might expect. If only Samson had been a godly influence on her instead of sinking down to her moral level!

We should always strive to do justice to our spiritual blessings. Maybe you were born into a family that taught you the ways of God from day one. Awesome! Make sure you pass on that spiritual knowledge to others. Maybe you were born into the opposite situation but you have an amazing story of how you came to know God. Use it! Share with others in that situation to encourage and inspire them.

----

day 159

"The rulers of the Philistines went to her and said, 'See if you can lure him into showing you the secret of his great strength and how we can overpower him so we may tie him up and subdue him. Each one of us will give you eleven hundred shekels of silver.'"

–JUDGES 16:5

This is a startling amount of money. Based on the rate paid for Joseph centuries earlier, Delilah was being offered the equivalent of 275 slaves. That's a huge sum. While we can understand that no matter what she was being offered, Delilah's betrayal was *not* okay, it's pretty easy to understand why she was tempted.

The temptation to look out only for ourselves can be overwhelming. That desire is deeply embedded in human nature—survive at all costs, look out for number one. That's why the sacrificial love Jesus commands of us is so revolutionary. It goes against our very nature. Our natural instinct would be to grab that financial security and run. Which is exactly what Delilah tried to do.

Jesus did the opposite for us. He gave up everything for our benefit. So as followers of Jesus, that's the type of love we are to show others. It's a tall order. But every small step we take away from selfish attitudes toward loving others is a victory.

day 160

"So Delilah said to Samson, 'Tell me the secret of your great strength and how you can be tied up and subdued.' Samson answered her, 'If anyone ties me with seven fresh bowstrings that have not been dried, I'll become as weak as any other man.'"

–JUDGES 16:6–7

There's a little bit of reading between the lines we have to do, but it's safe to say that a traditional interpretation of these interactions involves Delilah using her, uh, feminine wiles to coax Samson into revealing his secret. Yikes. That's why her name has become almost synonymous with "dangerous seductress."

But it's probably safe to say most women who love Jesus would not be tempted to use our sexuality to get what we want at this level. But are we vulnerable to something similar on a smaller scale? What about flirting? Is it wrong to flirt with a guy so he'll do something you want him to? Or is that harmless?

No matter the circumstance, using your sexuality or beauty to tempt or manipulate is wrong. When we do such things, we're devaluing the person we're manipulating, treating them like a toy or game piece. Not only that, we're turning ourselves into a sexual object, which devalues *us*. We're instigating our own objectification. Ick! Let's treat ourselves and the men around us with more respect than that.

day 161

"Then the rulers of the Philistines brought her seven fresh bowstrings that had not been dried, and she tied him with them. With men hidden in the room, she called to him, 'Samson, the Philistines are upon you!' But he snapped the bowstrings as easily as a piece of string snaps when it comes close to a flame. So the secret of his strength was not discovered."

–JUDGES 16:8–9

Samson told Delilah his supernatural strength would be broken if she tied him up with fresh bowstrings. Which was, of course, a lie. Obviously Samson has his own issues here, but let's take a moment to realize what Delilah has done. Samson is her boyfriend, and she's just revealed the supposed source of his strength to his enemies so they can subdue him. After which they plan to torture and kill him. To say Delilah has committed an act of betrayal is understating matters.

Betrayal hurts. Betrayal implies that someone has broken loyalty.

While it can be painful, betrayal is something that can be overcome in a relationship. But it's important we find the fine line between practicing honest forgiveness and protecting ourselves from people who abuse our trust. Forgiveness requires a release of bitterness and anger, but it doesn't mean we have to let our betrayer as deep into our hearts as they once were.

day 162

"Then Delilah said to Samson, 'You have made a fool of me; you lied to me. Come now, tell me how you can be tied.'"

–JUDGES 16:10

Delilah's response to this situation is so audacious, it's almost funny (except it's not). She has just betrayed her man to his enemies, and when she discovers he lied about the proper way to subdue him, she pouts. Straight-up, unabashed, pouts. Because how dare Samson refuse to tell her the best way to capture and kill him! Wow.

While we might not be as disrespectful as Delilah is here, everyone is vulnerable to a similar temptation—emotional manipulation. Delilah tries to use a guilt trip on Samson. She tries to make him feel bad for making her look foolish. Have you ever tried something similar on your parents? Maybe tried to make them feel bad so they'll agree to give you something you want?

It's important we avoid emotional manipulation in all its forms, whether a small guilt trip or a brazen pout session. When we have ulterior motives lurking beneath our words, we chip away at the trust others have in us. Honest and straightforward is always best!

day 163

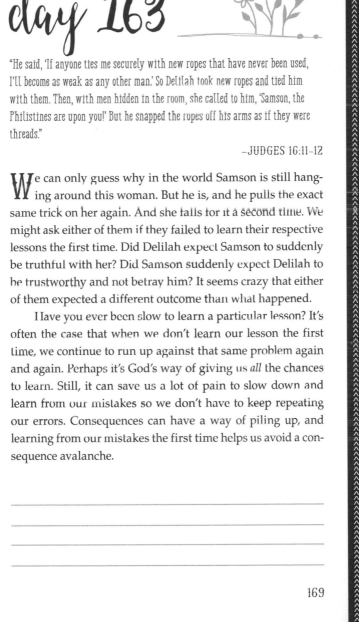

> "He said, 'If anyone ties me securely with new ropes that have never been used, I'll become as weak as any other man.' So Delilah took new ropes and tied him with them. Then, with men hidden in the room, she called to him, 'Samson, the Philistines are upon you!' But he snapped the ropes off his arms as if they were threads."

—JUDGES 16:11–12

We can only guess why in the world Samson is still hanging around this woman. But he is, and he pulls the exact same trick on her again. And she falls for it a second time. We might ask either of them if they failed to learn their respective lessons the first time. Did Delilah expect Samson to suddenly be truthful with her? Did Samson suddenly expect Delilah to be trustworthy and not betray him? It seems crazy that either of them expected a different outcome than what happened.

Have you ever been slow to learn a particular lesson? It's often the case that when we don't learn our lesson the first time, we continue to run up against that same problem again and again. Perhaps it's God's way of giving us *all* the chances to learn. Still, it can save us a lot of pain to slow down and learn from our mistakes so we don't have to keep repeating our errors. Consequences can have a way of piling up, and learning from our mistakes the first time helps us avoid a consequence avalanche.

day 164

"Then she said to him, 'How can you say, "I love you," when you won't confide in me? This is the third time you have made a fool of me and haven't told me the secret of your great strength.'"

–JUDGES 16:15

Delilah takes her emotional manipulation to the next level. She seems to be very aware of Samson's moral weakness—that he doesn't resist beautiful women, even when he should—and she uses it to her greatest advantage, wringing out his attraction to her in order to squeeze what she wants from him.

Why didn't Samson just say no? Why didn't he run away as fast as he could the moment Delilah first betrayed him? Why did he play games with her? By doing so, Samson gave Delilah the leverage to eventually get her way.

Ephesians 4:27 warns us not to "give the devil a foothold." When we act foolishly or give in to temptation in small ways, it opens the door for greater compromise of our principles, more sin, and deeper confusion in our hearts. Let's not give sin that kind of leverage in our lives.

day 165

"With such nagging she prodded him day after day until he was sick to death of it. So he told her everything. 'No razor has ever been used on my head,' he said, 'because I have been a Nazirite dedicated to God from my mother's womb. If my head were shaved, my strength would leave me, and I would become as weak as any other man.'"

–JUDGES 16:16–17

The "nagging wife" is a negative female stereotype that has been perpetuated since . . . well, at least since the time of Delilah. Whether the stereotype is fair or not (most aren't), nagging is something everyone will either do or have done to them at some point in their lives. So what's the big deal about it?

Nagging signifies a lack of confidence in the person being nagged. If your mom is constantly nagging you to do the dishes, it's probably because she doesn't trust you to remember on your own. When we nag people, we're telling them we don't have faith in them. When others nag us, we need to rein in our annoyance and take a moment to ask ourselves *why*. Are they having a hard time trusting us because we've let them down in the past? Can we make an extra effort to follow through this time and begin to rebuild trust?

Nagging is a hard habit to break, just like paying attention to nagging you're used to ignoring can be difficult. But it's worth it! The end result is better, stronger, deeper relationships with those around us.

day 166

"When Delilah saw that he had told her everything, she sent word to the rulers of the Philistines, 'Come back once more; he has told me everything.' So the rulers of the Philistines returned with the silver in their hands ... Then she called, 'Samson, the Philistines are upon you!'"

–JUDGES 16:18, 20A

Oh, this is sad. While Samson made a mistake telling Delilah anything about his strength, it's still sad to see how she betrayed his confidence. Though he shouldn't have, he trusted her, and she repaid him cruelly for it.

When people share sensitive information with us, it's important that we respect their privacy. Proverbs 11:13 tells us, "A gossip betrays a confidence, but a trustworthy person keeps a secret." It's frighteningly easy to slip into gossip, even when we don't mean to. But if you've ever been the subject of other people's gossip, you know just how important it is that we guard our friends' sensitive secrets.

Of course we want to be known as solid, trustworthy people. Let's make an extra effort to squelch the urge to chit-chat about other people's secrets.

day 167

"He awoke from his sleep and thought, 'I'll go out as before and shake myself free.' But he did not know that the Lord had left him. Then the Philistines seized him, gouged out his eyes and took him down to Gaza. Binding him with bronze shackles, they set him to grinding grain in the prison."

–JUDGES 16:20B–21

This is the end of Delilah's story in the Bible, and it's nearly the end of Samson's (though he gets one last moment of strength from God before his ultimate end). Delilah has done a horrible thing to the man she supposedly loved. We don't get to know if she regretted it after she saw what the Philistines did to Samson.

Did you notice Samson's attitude? Though he had broken his Nazirite vow to God, he assumed he'd be able to use his strength to get free. He didn't realize God had left him. Perhaps the biggest mistake of Samson's life was presuming on the grace of God. He had failed to act morally so many times, and God had never taken away his strength before. So what's one more sin, one more failing?

We have to guard against that attitude. God's grace is something to approach with thankfulness and humility. We don't mess up willfully, assuming God will let us skate by. Instead, let's endeavor to honor God with all our decisions from the start.

day 168

"In the days when the judges ruled, there was a famine in the land. So a man from Bethlehem in Judah, together with his wife and two sons, went to live for a while in the country of Moab. The man's name was Elimelek, his wife's name was Naomi, and the names of his two sons were Mahlon and Kilion."

–RUTH 1:1–2A

We've been getting some of the political highlights of this era in Israel's history—stories of the great rulers and deliverers who lived in the time after Israel entered the Promised Land. But our next women aren't military, political, or religious leaders. This is just the story of a family. Although, spoiler alert, this family will become politically powerful later on.

Only two books of the sixty-six in the Bible are named after women, and Naomi, Orpah, and Ruth star in one of them. First, we meet Naomi, the matriarch. These verses appear pretty simple on the surface, but they are oddly silent about the underlying feelings of dislike and suspicion that existed between the Israelites and the Moabites. That key information is important to unlock the full message of the book of Ruth.

Ruth and Naomi's story hints at God's great love for *all* people. He had chosen Israel, but his coming gospel was for everyone, and Ruth shows us that this was God's plan all along. Be encouraged, beloved, that God's heart beats for *you*, no matter who you are or where you come from.

----

day 169

"Now Elimelek, Naomi's husband, died, and she was left with her two sons. They married Moabite women, one named Orpah and the other Ruth."

–RUTH 1:3–4A

Wait, weren't these marriages forbidden? Didn't God tell the Israelites not to marry into the other cultures around them? Yes, but there are several ideas as to why these marriages aren't condemned—that Ruth and Orpah converted before marriage, for example. But another suggestion is that only Moabite *men* were forbidden from entering the assembly of the Lord to their tenth generation. But Moabite women were not.

If that's the case, it's a bit of a reversal from the norm. It would mean Ruth and Orpah actually had an advantage because they were women. Guess what? There are certain advantages we enjoy as modern women too. Like when a gentleman opens a door for you. Some women may feel these gestures are outdated, and hey, if you want to open your own doors, that's totally cool. But you can be a strong, intelligent, godly girl *and* appreciate these gestures offered to us because we're women.

Too often, our world thinks in terms of either/or. Either you're a strong woman *or* you let a man help you. But why not readjust our thinking to both/and?

day 170

"After they had lived there about ten years, both Mahlon and Kilion also died, and Naomi was left without her two sons and her husband."

–RUTH 1:4B–5

That's a very sad verse right there. Naomi was left without her sons and her husband. For many millennia of history and throughout many cultures, a woman had very little means to support herself without male relatives. Childlessness was seen as a curse. Naomi suddenly went from a married mother of two to a childless widow. As we see from her words later, she felt empty.

While our situation may never look exactly like Naomi's, there will be times when we feel emptied out and stripped down. There will be times when we feel broken. To combat feelings of despair, we can remind ourselves of important truths. God loves you. God has a plan for your life, and it isn't for you to remain broken.

The pain is real, and it's okay to acknowledge it. Ignoring it doesn't help you move on. But we can continue to battle our brokenness with truth, and in so doing, reclaim our joy.

----

day 171

"When Naomi heard in Moab that the LORD had come to the aid of his people by providing food for them, she and her daughters-in-law prepared to return home from there. With her two daughters-in-law she left the place where she had been living and set out on the road that would take them back to the land of Judah."

–RUTH 1:6–7

Naomi had left Israel because there'd been a bad famine in the land, and now, after many years in Moab, it was time to return home.

Going home can mean many different things. It can be returning to your physical home after an absence. It can mean reuniting with your family, wherever they may be. It can mean returning to a place where you have bonds, like the church you grew up in or the school you love. Going home can also mean returning to our roots in our relationships with God.

For every person who calls Jesus her savior, there was a time when we were deeply in love with him and when we deeply understood God's love for us. It's easy to get caught up in the busyness of life—even the busyness of church life—and wander away from this "home base" with God. The good news is that we can return whenever we want! We can always pray for God to reignite our sense of home with him, and he will.

day 172

"Then Naomi said to her two daughters-in-law, 'Go back, each of you, to your mother's home. May the LORD show you kindness, as you have shown kindness to your dead husbands and to me.'"

–RUTH 1:8

Naomi is trying to do right by her daughters-in-law here. She's trying to guide them toward what she thinks will be best for them. But she seems to have forgotten what she, a child of Israel, could offer to her pagan daughters-in-law. She could teach them firsthand about the love of the one true God. That's an immense spiritual inheritance she has to share!

It's easy to forget all we have to offer sometimes. When we don't feel particularly blessed with wisdom or gifted with talent, we might decide it's better for those we encounter to spare us a quick nod and go on their merry way. But we shouldn't lose sight of all that God has given us to share with the world.

What are some of the gifts God has given to you? Do you have a heart to serve, the ability to unlock truths in Scripture, the talent for speaking clearly about Jesus and his love? Each of these things—and hundreds more—is so valuable. Remember who you are and what you can share!

day 173

"'May the LORD grant that each of you will find rest in the home of another husband.' Then she kissed them goodbye and they wept aloud and said to her, 'We will go back with you to your people.'"

–RUTH 1:9–10

This is such an awesome display of affection between Naomi and her daughters-in-law. Our culture likes to stereotype a lot of relationships as being difficult or negative—parent/child, teacher/student, boss/employee, and maybe most of all, in-laws. But it doesn't have to be that way!

Some relationships are difficult, and some *people* are difficult, but sometimes we enter into a situation expecting it to be bad before anything bad has actually happened. Naomi and her daughters-in-law, who clearly adore her, defy the stereotype we have of in-law relationships. It's wise for us to enter into new relationships and situations with the belief that this kind of awesomeness is possible. Then, as far as it depends upon us, we can contribute toward making that possibility a reality.

Is there a relationship or situation in your life that you haven't given a fair chance yet? Take a few moments to pray about how you can orchestrate a fresh start.

day 174

"But Naomi said, 'Return home, my daughters. Why would you come with me? Am I going to have any more sons, who could become your husbands? . . . Would you remain unmarried for them? No, my daughters. It is more bitter for me than for you, because the Lord's hand has turned against me!'"

–RUTH 1:11, 13

Naomi is again trying to think of what's best for these young women. She doesn't see the point in all three of them returning to Israel to live as widows. At least in Moab, Ruth and Orpah may have a chance to remarry and have children of their own, right? But this only sounded wise to Naomi because she didn't have access to God's big-picture plan yet.

If only we could see God's roadmap. It would make our life choices quite a lot easier, wouldn't it? We often get the benefit of hindsight. After we've been through something difficult or confusing, we can look back and see exactly what God was doing with all those puzzle pieces that didn't seem to fit together when we were in the middle of them.

But those ah-ha moments tend to come *after* the fact. We remember how our previous situation made sense later, and that can encourage us to keep persevering now. The key is remembering that God does have a plan and then trusting him with the particulars and walking in obedience to what we know he has commanded.

day 175

"At this they wept aloud again. Then Orpah kissed her mother-in-law goodbye, but Ruth clung to her. 'Look,' said Naomi, 'your sister-in-law is going back to her people and her gods. Go back with her.'"

–RUTH 1:14-15

There's nothing particularly wrong with what Orpah did here. She listened to her mother-in-law's urgings and returned home. We might say that Orpah was morally neutral. But she wasn't as strongly committed as Ruth.

Jesus warns us about being lukewarm in Revelation 3:16 when he says, "So, because you are lukewarm—neither hot nor cold—I am about to spit you out of my mouth." Yikes! We don't want Jesus to spit us out, but it's pretty scary how easy it is to be lukewarm. Maybe we don't want to be judged for our faith, so we don't speak out about it. Or perhaps some people we know have a bad impression of Christians, so we stay silent, lest we be lumped in with the others.

While we want to always be gracious and kind to all people of all walks of life, it's important that we're not lukewarm about our faith. We can be vocal, strongly committed, *and* pleasant people all at once!

day 176

"But Ruth replied, 'Don't urge me to leave you or to turn back from you. Where you go I will go, and where you stay I will stay. Your people will be my people and your God my God. Where you die I will die, and there I will be buried. May the Lord deal with me, be it ever so severely, if even death separates you and me.' When Naomi realized that Ruth was determined to go with her, she stopped urging her."

–RUTH 1:16–18

This, perhaps more than any other passage, reveals Ruth's heart. When we contrast her with Orpah, we see how deeply committed Ruth was to Naomi and Naomi's God. She was so committed, she was willing to give up her home and her own people. Ruth knew she had found something better than her birth.

Some people may seem like they have been blessed with absolutely everything. The perfect churchgoing family, parents who completely "get" them, a comfortable financial situation . . . But the truth is, no matter how outwardly perfect anyone's life looks (and we better remind ourselves that everyone has troubles to deal with in their lives), we are all designed for something "better than our birth."

And that's because the world we're all born into is marred by sin. Our world is warped because sin has entered it. It's not as God originally designed it. So, deep down in all our hearts, we're longing for that sinless world, which will return when Jesus does. How cool is that? We were designed for something greater!

day 177

"So the two women went on until they came to Bethlehem. When they arrived in Bethlehem, the whole town was stirred because of them, and the women exclaimed, 'Can this be Naomi?'"

–RUTH 1:19

Ruth and Naomi sure knew how to make an entrance! The whole town was stirred because of their arrival, and the spotlight was on these girls—whether that's what they intended or not!

While we don't want to draw negative attention to ourselves, causing a stir isn't always a bad thing—as long as we're getting attention for the right reasons. Sometimes our accomplishments or talents draw attention to us. We can use that attention as a great platform to give glory to God for those accomplishments. Sometimes people look to us because they consider us a leader. That's a great thing!

So when is attention bad? When we're getting attention for acting out, dressing provocatively, or showing off, that's not really the kind of attention that will glorify God. So if we're going to cause a stir, let's have it be for the right reasons.

day 178

"'Don't call me Naomi,' she told them. 'Call me Mara, because the Almighty has made my life very bitter. I went away full, but the Lord has brought me back empty. Why call me Naomi? The Lord has afflicted me; the Almighty has brought misfortune upon me.'"

–RUTH 1:20–21

Naomi doesn't yet know how the Lord will bring her life full circle. She still feels completely empty. And really, she's justified in feeling that way. She had lost a lot.

The Lord gives and the Lord takes away. That's an easy sentence to write but a terribly difficult truth to grapple with. While we know that God doesn't ever commit evil acts and we should be careful to suggest otherwise, God does sometimes let us experience bitter heartbreak. God does sometimes take away those things he's given to us. In Naomi's case, that meant her husband and two sons. The Lord brought those men into her life, and the Lord took them away.

There will come a time when we don't have to wrestle with this issue. When sin, death, and sickness cease to exist, we will know only the good blessings God wants for us. But now, in this imperfect life, we have to continue growing in trust. We have to trust that God knows what he's doing and that he's holding us close in our darkest, most brokenhearted moments.

_____

_____

_____

_____

day 179

"Now Naomi had a relative on her husband's side, a man of standing from the clan of Elimelek, whose name was Boaz. And Ruth the Moabite said to Naomi, 'Let me go to the fields and pick up the leftover grain behind anyone in whose eyes I find favor.' Naomi said to her, 'Go ahead, my daughter.'"

–RUTH 2:1–2

There were provisions written into the law for the poor in Israel. They were to be allowed to "glean" in the fields behind the field hands while they harvested, which is exactly what Ruth is asking to do.

Ruth is an excellent role model for us in so many ways. We might think that all our awesome biblical women are very powerful (like Deborah), from well-connected families (like Miriam), or that they possessed material wealth (like Sarah). But none of these things is true of Ruth. Yet she is perfectly willing to do whatever honorable activity she must in order to support herself and her mother-in-law. In Ruth, we see that humble means can be noble means.

Caring for those we love and having servants' hearts is never beneath us. Getting our hands dirty (proverbially or literally) through hard work isn't beneath us. Willingness to do these things shows humility that honors God.

day 180

"Boaz asked the overseer of his harvesters, 'Who does that young woman belong to?' The overseer replied, 'She is the Moabite who came back from Moab with Naomi.'"

–RUTH 2:5–6

Now we meet the leading man of Ruth's story, Boaz. He's a great biblical man to study, but we'll get to that later. First, can we take a moment to notice this cool "God moment"? Among all his workers in all his fields, Boaz happens to notice Ruth. And he takes enough notice that he decides to ask about her. If he hadn't noticed her or shown interest in who she was, this entire story might have looked quite different. And Israel's history might have even been different.

Perhaps most of our days are filled with our regular day-to-day activities. But, like Ruth and Boaz have here, some of our days will have God-orchestrated intersections that change our lives. Can you look back on your life up to this point and name a couple of those? Those times when something "happened" to fall into place in just such a way that it helped shape your life from that point forward? These moments don't occur by accident.

Isn't it amazing that the God who created the entire universe cares enough to be so involved in our lives? Let's thank God for his loving oversight over the big things and the details.

day 161

Though we're focusing on Ruth's story, we really can't tell her story without also telling Boaz's part in it. It's really *their* story, and it's one worth telling. In Boaz, we see a godly man who is often held up as the standard of an ideal partner for a godly woman.

Here, Boaz displays his kindness. He made a specific effort to reach out to Ruth. Ruth was a vulnerable member of society. She and Naomi were single women with no means of income and no family to support them. Israelite law provided care for the poor by demanding that land owners let the poor pick up the grain left over after the main harvest work was done. Boaz not only lets Ruth glean in his fields, he urges her not to leave his fields and go elsewhere.

Kindness means showing concern for others and treating them with compassion and gentleness. That's an important trait for a boyfriend or husband, but it's also a wonderful trait to look for in our friends *and* to try to grow in ourselves. What's one way you can demonstrate kindness today?

day 182

"Watch the field where the men are harvesting, and follow along after the women. I have told the men not to lay a hand on you. And whenever you are thirsty, go and get a drink from the water jars the men have filled."

–RUTH 2:9

Boaz made it a priority to protect Ruth. He told his male workers not to touch Ruth. The fact that he felt this necessary highlights once again Ruth's vulnerability in her current situation. Perhaps some men would try to take advantage of the fact that Ruth didn't have a husband, father, or brother to defend her. So Boaz steps in and puts the men on notice that *he* will step in if Ruth is harmed. He's showing her an immense amount of care—and she's practically a stranger!

Even though we enjoy much more social freedom than the women of Ruth's day, we can still be very vulnerable in some ways. Every young woman should learn some self-defense basics, at least, to help her be more empowered and less physically vulnerable. But what about the quality of protectiveness in a partner?

When protectiveness comes from a place of control, it can be a negative. But when it's coming from a place of love and respect—like the kind of care Boaz showed—it's a very good thing. We should be looking for a partner who cares about our physical, emotional, and spiritual wellbeing.

day 163

"At this, she bowed down with her face to the ground. She asked him, 'Why have I found such favor in your eyes that you notice me—a foreigner?' Boaz replied, 'I've been told all about what you have done for your mother-in-law since the death of your husband—how you left your father and mother and your homeland and came to live with a people you did not know before.'"

–RUTH 2:10–11

Ruth asks why in the world Boaz would take such good care of her, a stranger and a foreigner. There are a lot of things Boaz could have noticed about Ruth. Even though the Bible doesn't say so, she is traditionally considered to have been a beautiful young woman. Boaz was a godly man, but he was human. He might have pointed out that he noticed her beautiful face or her lovely figure. But instead, Boaz focuses on Ruth's heart. He focuses on her character. *That* is why she was a standout to him.

Physical attraction is different than lust. Physical attraction is not sinful. God made guys and girls attracted to each other on purpose, and it's a good thing for the human race that he did. But it's still *most* important to find someone who values our inner self above our outer beauty. Outer beauty will fade over time, so a relationship built solely on physical attraction isn't going to last for the long haul. But finding someone who connects with our heart is the start of a solid foundation. And if they also happen to realize we're beautiful? All the better.

_____

_____

_____

_____

day 184

"May the LORD repay you for what you have done. May you be richly rewarded by the LORD, the God of Israel, under whose wings you have come to take refuge."

—RUTH 2:12

After pointing out Ruth's good heart, Boaz turns the focus back to God, calling down blessings on Ruth to repay her for the kindness she showed to her mother-in-law. An ideal partner will be kind, protective in a healthy way, and will focus on our heart even more than our beauty. But he'll also make sure that God is at the center of his life and his thoughts.

Second Corinthians 6:14 contains a warning about being "yoked" to someone who doesn't believe in Jesus (think of two oxen plowing together with one yoke connecting them). While we shouldn't take this as a blanket commandment to stay away from unbelievers, we should consider this warning when choosing the person with whom we'll be spending the rest of our lives. Does he share your values? Does he believe in God? Does he make God a priority in his life? These are important questions to ask ourselves.

It's okay to ask God for discernment in this area. In fact, he wants us to! When only God can see a person's heart, we want to be careful in our judgments.

day 165

"As she got up to glean, Boaz gave orders to his men, 'Let her gather among the sheaves and don't reprimand her.'"

–RUTH 2:15

The law demanded that the poor be allowed to glean the leftovers of the fields. Boaz looked out for Ruth by telling her to stay in his fields where he'd arranged for her protection. And here, he goes even further by making sure she gets far more than the "leftovers." Boaz showed himself to be an ideal partner by going beyond the basics.

We probably don't want a guy to walk up to us and hand us a sheaf of grain (unless you're on a farm . . .). So what might this look like for us? There are probably a thousand different ways someone can go above and beyond. It might be a material gift, like Boaz arranged for Ruth, but it doesn't have to be. Maybe your parents invite your boyfriend over for dinner one night, and he helps your dad clean the kitchen afterward. Maybe he gives you his jacket when it's cold out and you forgot yours.

Those are just some possibilities, but they're all coming from the same place—a heart that loves sacrificially, like Jesus, putting others first. Want to know a secret? That's the way *we* should be loving too, whether for our significant others, family members, or friends.

_____

_____

_____

_____

day 186

"Naomi said to Ruth her daughter-in-law, 'It will be good for you, my daughter, to go with the women who work for him, because in someone else's field you might be harmed.'"

–RUTH 2:22

It's a quick mention—just a single line—but that's a pretty scary reality. Naomi had previously sent Ruth off to glean in the fields she now casually points out are dangerous to Ruth's safety. It's definitely not that Naomi didn't care about Ruth's safety. It's simply that these women didn't have another choice.

While we shouldn't live our lives in fear, it is important to be aware of some ways we might be vulnerable and do what we can to combat that vulnerability. We've already mentioned basic self-defense, but it's worth mentioning again. Many community centers, gyms, and church groups offer self-defense classes. Some martial arts studios specialize in self-defense courses exclusively. If none of these are options, there are many articles and videos on the web to help us learn the basics.

Like Naomi and Ruth, we should be wise about the reality of being a woman and do everything we can to protect ourselves. We might be vulnerable, but that doesn't mean we have to be victims!

day 187

> "Now Boaz, with whose women you have worked, is a relative of ours. Tonight he will be winnowing barley on the threshing floor. Wash, put on perfume, and get dressed in your best clothes. Then go down to the threshing floor, but don't let him know you are there until he has finished eating and drinking. When he lies down, note the place where he is lying. Then go and uncover his feet and lie down. He will tell you what to do."
>
> –RUTH 3:2–4

This is an interesting thing Naomi is asking of her daughter-in-law. She tells Ruth to prepare herself as if for marriage and go meet Boaz in private after he's finished with his evening of harvest celebration. I mean . . . can we all agree this isn't the standard advice most mothers would give to their daughters?

But Naomi's instructions highlight something important. Being bold isn't always an immoral thing. Ruth's act was definitely gutsy, but her behavior is not at all called out as wrong. In fact, Ruth is often pointed to as an example of a very godly biblical woman. She is bold when the situation calls for boldness, gentle when gentleness is best, and is at all times striving to behave honorably. That's quite a role model for us!

If you could, which part of Ruth's character would you inject a little more of into your own life? Do you want to become less timid? Or are you working on upping your gentleness factor when the situation calls for it? Ask God to help you grow in the areas you'd like to most!

day 188

"'I will do whatever you say,' Ruth answered. So she went down to the threshing floor and did everything her mother-in-law told her to do."

–RUTH 3:5–6

Ruth was perfectly willing to do whatever Naomi asked her to do. On many occasions, she shows that she will follow Naomi's specific instructions, especially when they pertain to how to navigate Israelite law and culture.

But the takeaway here isn't that we must always blindly obey whatever anyone tells us to do. The takeaway is that it's good to obey and respect those authority figures in our lives whom we *trust*. Naomi had earned her place in Ruth's heart and Ruth's esteem. We know this because of Ruth's refusal to stay behind in Moab when Naomi returned to Israel. She obeyed Naomi's instructions because she knew Naomi would not steer her wrong.

Who are the respected authority figures in your life you know you can trust? Parents are the most obvious answer, but our respected authority figures may also be teachers, pastors, coaches, or extended family members. When these people give you life advice, remember that they're in your circle of trusted mentors for a reason—and thank God for that! They will always endeavor to steer you right.

_____

_____

_____

_____

day 189

"'I am your servant Ruth,' she said. 'Spread the corner of your garment over me, since you are a guardian-redeemer of our family.'"

–RUTH 3:9B

Ruth is basically proposing marriage to Boaz—or at least asking him to propose. But she does so using language similar to the language Boaz previously used when he told Ruth she had come to take shelter under the wings of the Lord (Ruth 2:12). She now asks Boaz to similarly protect her.

Boaz had proven himself to be a good man who had already been looking out for Ruth's needs and safety. Like Ruth, we should be on the lookout for safe, kind people to let into our inner circles while keeping the toxic folks out.

What makes someone a "safe person"? Safe people are nurturing, trustworthy, and honorable. They show love and respect. They will be concerned about your wellbeing. Not only should we look for friendships or romantic relationships that reflect these qualities, we should do our very best to *be* a safe person for others!

day 190

"'The LORD bless you, my daughter,' [Boaz] replied. 'This kindness is greater than that which you showed earlier: You have not run after the younger men, whether rich or poor. And now, my daughter, don't be afraid. I will do for you all you ask. All the people of my town know that you are a woman of noble character.'"

–RUTH 3:10–11

We focused on several of Boaz's qualities that made him an ideal partner for Ruth. Here, Boaz uses the same word to describe Ruth that the author used to describe him in Ruth 2:1: *noble character*. Boaz was focused on the right things, but so was Ruth! That's one reason she's such a cool role model for us.

It's important for us to look for the right kind of qualities in a romantic partner. "Ideal" personalities will vary, depending on what complements each of us well, but a strong moral character is something everyone should look for in a partner. And not only do we want to look for that in a mate, we want to be women with strong moral character ourselves.

No one will be perfect, of course. But at least caring about our character is a very good start. The more we model our lives after Jesus's, the more we'll grow in all the areas that matter most.

day 191

"So Boaz took Ruth and she became his wife. When he made love to her, the LORD enabled her to conceive, and she gave birth to a son."

—RUTH 4:13

So maybe we wouldn't normally have a devotion that dives right into Boaz and Ruth's bedroom. It feels a little personal, after all. But this son Ruth conceives is important to note. His name was Obed, and he was the father of Jesse, and Jesse was the father of King David. Through David's line, the promised Messiah, Jesus, would be born. So not only had Ruth become an Israelite, but God had grafted her, a Moabite, into Jesus's family tree.

Stories like Ruth's are special. Even though it's found in the Old Testament, Ruth's story hints at God's full plan. He had always planned to redeem, not just the Israelite people, but *all* people through Jesus. No matter someone's nationality, skin color, family history, or previous religious association, Jesus's love is for them. It's for you. It's for all of us.

This idea was revolutionary in the time just after Jesus's life on Earth ended and the apostles began to share the gospel with people who weren't Jewish. And it's pretty revolutionary now. *All people* have the love of Jesus made available to them, and Ruth was a foreshadowing of that fact.

day 192

"The women said to Naomi: 'Praise be to the Lᴏʀᴅ, who this day has not left you without a guardian-redeemer . . . He will renew your life and sustain you in your old age. For your daughter-in-law, who loves you and who is better to you than seven sons, has given him birth.'"

–RUTH 4:14–15

The last chapter of the book of Ruth focuses more on Naomi than it does on Ruth, and it's kind of fitting. The first chapter began with Naomi's brokenness, so the author spends the last chapter focusing on Naomi's redemption.

Naomi led Ruth wisely. She helped the young foreign woman navigate her new life and her new culture. And God brought Naomi full circle through the birth of her grandson. Naomi experienced hope once again.

Naomi's story can give us hope too. No matter how dark a valley we're walking through, we can look at Naomi's life and know that God can bring us through it. Naomi probably never expected her life to take such a dramatic turn—but it did! If you ever find yourself in the sort of broken place Naomi was when we first met her, remember that our God is the God of redemption.

day 193

"[Elkanah] had two wives; one was called Hannah and the other Peninnah. Peninnah had children, but Hannah had none."

–1 SAMUEL 1:2

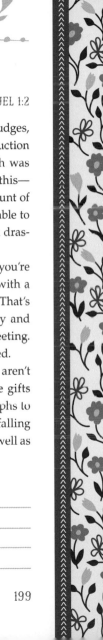

We've come to the very end of the period of Israel's judges, and this short verse gives us a sad, succinct introduction to Hannah. Her husband had two wives, and Hannah was "the one with none." We can guess that a situation like this— one man, two wives—would usually lead to a fair amount of rivalry at the best of times. But when one woman was able to have children and the other wasn't, it had to have been drastically worse.

Dealing with rivalry isn't easy, especially when you're the one with none. Maybe you often feel competition with a sibling, and that sibling excels at something you don't. That's a tough situation. Maybe sometimes we gain a victory and become "the one with some," but those victories are fleeting. If we're chasing those, we'll never be completely satisfied.

The long-term solution is to understand that we aren't created for comparison. You were created with unique gifts to use, particular trials to overcome, and specific triumphs to celebrate. When you embrace your own path and avoid falling into the comparison trap, you can find contentment, as well as the motivation to be the very best *you* possible.

day 194

"Year after year [Elkanah] went up from his town to worship and sacrifice to the LORD Almighty at Shiloh, where Hophni and Phinehas, the two sons of Eli, were priests of the Lord."

–1 SAMUEL 1:3

There were several different types of offerings in Ancient Israel. The ones Elkanah was presenting year after year were fellowship offerings. They were voluntary thanksgiving sacrifices. We'll see a bit later that Elkanah loved Hannah. He saw that she was childless and very unhappy about it. So it's safe to say Elkanah probably did not consider his home life to be perfect. But still he offered thanksgiving to God.

We may experience moments—or even full seasons!—in life where everything feels pretty perfect. Maybe we're happy at home, excelling in school, satisfied in our relationships, hopeful about our careers or other pursuits. But just as often, we might be struggling in one or more of these areas. And let's be real: it's difficult to give thanks when we're struggling.

But examples like Elkanah and Hannah show us that we can still offer heartfelt praise and worship to God, even in our dark times. Praising God when everything isn't perfect reminds us to keep perspective—to keep our hearts humble and tuned to God's voice.

day 195

"Whenever the day came for Elkanah to sacrifice, he would give portions of the meat to his wife Peninnah and to all her sons and daughters. But to Hannah he gave a double portion because he loved her, and the LORD had closed her womb."

–1 SAMUEL 1:4–5

Elkanah fulfilled his role as a husband and father by providing for his wife Peninnah and her children. But he seems to have felt a special tenderness for Hannah. Even if Hannah getting a double portion might be a little unfair, we can appreciate the heart behind Elkanah's actions. He gave her extra because he was showing kindness and favor to a beloved wife who was suffering.

Showing kindness to the brokenhearted is never a wasted effort. If you have ever been the brokenhearted one yourself, you know how much it means when someone cares enough to notice your struggle and directs compassion in your direction.

Do you know anyone who is struggling right now? Is it appropriate to reach out to her? If you're not sure she'd be comfortable talking directly about whatever she's struggling with, maybe there's a simple, kind gesture that would mean a lot right now. A small card or note, an invitation to hang out, or even a funny GIF that made you think of her. These little acts of kindness can mean so much!

day 196

"Because the Lᴏʀᴅ had closed Hannah's womb, her rival kept provoking her in order to irritate her."

–1 SAMUEL 1:6

This is sad. Hannah is suffering here. She desperately wanted children, but God wasn't giving her any yet. Instead of being supportive, Peninnah used Hannah's barrenness to poke at her. Not cool, Peninnah.

But perhaps we should turn the magnifying glass onto ourselves before we judge Peninnah too harshly. The ugly truth is that blessings can make us smug. When the Lord has chosen to bless us with something—material wealth, talent, intelligence, beauty, opportunity—it's very easy to feel superior to those who don't have what we've been given.

Beloved girls, let's guard against this attitude—fiercely. God wants us to use the blessings he's given to us to enrich our lives, yes, but even more importantly, he wants us to use our blessings to bless others. Smug superiority over those who have less than we do in any area is not a blessing to anyone— not to those around us and not to ourselves. Protect your fellow humans and protect your own heart by avoiding this pitfall.

day 197

"This went on year after year. Whenever Hannah went up to the house of the LORD, her rival provoked her till she wept and would not eat."

–1 SAMUEL 1:7

Okay, so we've done a heart-check to make sure we're not being like Peninnah when we deal with those around us. We want to show kindness and compassion, more like Elkanah. But what about when we're the brokenhearted ones? What about when we're Hannah, and someone else is provoking us?

The straight-up truth is that mean girls exist. Bullies exist. Nasty attitudes exist, and sometimes we'll be on the receiving end of them. So how do we deal? What's the correct response?

The answer varies, honestly, though starving or otherwise harming yourself is *never* a healthy response. Sometimes we need to stand up for ourselves. Sometimes it's best to walk away. If someone has passed beyond mean girl and gone into threatening territory, getting help is *always* okay. The main thing is to remember to keep *your* heart right. You can't control a mean girl's heart. But you can make sure you don't become a mean girl in the process of dealing with those who provoke you.

day 198

> "Her husband Elkanah would say to her, 'Hannah, why are you weeping? Why don't you eat? Why are you downhearted? Don't I mean more to you than ten sons?'"
>
> –1 SAMUEL 1:8

Up to this point, Elkanah's been pretty awesome. He's been extraordinarily tender and sensitive toward his struggling wife, Hannah. And while his question here isn't really bad, it's also not particularly sensitive. He's guilt-tripping her a little. Like she doesn't have space to be sad about being childless, as long as she has him. Hrm.

We might have dreams that others don't understand—even those who love us and want good things for us. That's okay. We can always hope people will be sensitive toward our deeply held, most precious desires. But even if the majority of people are delicate with our fragile hopes, we will always run into one or two who just don't get it.

Don't let those few naysayers deter you from your deep dreams—those things you most desire for your life. Often, God has put those deep desires in our hearts, and that's why we burn so passionately about them. Keep chasing your goals! Don't be deterred by those who may not understand.

day 199

> "In her deep anguish Hannah prayed to the LORD, weeping bitterly. And she made a vow, saying, 'LORD Almighty, if you will only look on your servant's misery and remember me, and not forget your servant but give her a son, then I will give him to the Lord for all the days of his life, and no razor will ever be used on his head.'"
>
> –1 SAMUEL 1:10–11

Hannah went to God very openly. She cried. She wept. She may have even wailed. She let him see every bit of her distress. She came to him open-hearted and vulnerable.

Sometimes we get the idea that we need to be proper with God. Perhaps we've learned that showing someone respect means being on our best behavior, so we button our lips, zip up our hearts, and approach God with a detached cool that displays our respect for him.

Hey, it's important to respect God. Absolutely! But perhaps we need to tweak our idea of what "respect" looks like. Reverence, sure. But also openness. Transparency that says, "I trust you. You see me, you love me, and this is the reality of what I'm experiencing right now. It's ugly, and I trust you to love me through the ugliness." To be so open with someone is to respect them deeply. What if we always approached God with all our hearts? What if we always approached God the way Hannah did?

day 200

"As she kept on praying to the LORD, Eli observed her mouth. Hannah was praying in her heart, and her lips were moving but her voice was not heard. Eli thought she was drunk and said to her, 'How long are you going to stay drunk? Put away your wine.'"

–1 SAMUEL 1:12–14

We haven't really talked about Eli, but he was the High Priest over Israel in these days. Not only that, Eli was Israel's judge at the time, like Deborah and Samson before him. Eli was important and well-respected. So this wasn't just some random guy walking up to Hannah and calling her a drunk. This was one of the most important men in Israel!

What's the moral of this story? Everyone makes mistakes. Even those we trust and respect can discern incorrectly or slip up in their judgment. That's why it's so important to be on our guard when looking up to others in our spiritual walks. Having people to look up to is very important. They may be people we know personally, or they may be pastors, preachers, teachers, or writers who speak to many thousands of people. But it's important to remember that, try as our godly leaders might, they mess up sometimes.

When reading or listening to any spiritual teaching, it's important to compare it to what the Word of God says. It's important to listen to your own inner voice and the Holy Spirit's prompting too. Even those who are really trying can make mistakes!

day 201

"'Not so, my lord,' Hannah replied, 'I am a woman who is deeply troubled. I have not been drinking wine or beer; I was pouring out my soul to the Lord. Do not take your servant for a wicked woman; I have been praying here out of my great anguish and grief.'"

–1 SAMUEL 1:15–16

Hannah firmly but respectfully pushes back against Eli's assumption that she's been drinking. She tells him the real reason she appeared out of sorts —that she's distraught and she's bringing her distress before the Lord.

It's okay to do that sometimes. When you've been falsely accused, it's okay to defend our reputations. But there's also a fine line here. Sometimes people are throwing out personal accusations just to get a rise. The internet calls these people trolls, and some of the best internet advice we can possibly observe is *don't feed the trolls*!

Discernment is the key here. We need to look at each situation and decide when it's worth the time and energy to defend ourselves, and when it's best to brush the dust from our shoulders and move on. Don't let your day—or your week—get consumed by trolls who just want to bug you for fun. It's not worth it!

day 202

"Eli answered, 'Go in peace, and may the God of Israel grant you what you have asked of him.' She said, 'May your servant find favor in your eyes.' Then she went her way and ate something, and her face was no longer downcast."

–1 SAMUEL 1:17–18

What was it about Eli's words that finally lifted the cloud of distress that had been following Hannah around for so long? Did Hannah's outlook improve because Eli was a man of God and he had blessed her? Did she sense that perhaps God had heard her prayers and wanted to grant her request now?

It could have been either of these things or several others. But even when it's not a famous person speaking to us, words matter. Words have the ability to crush and the ability to heal. Eli's words were life-giving to Hannah that day. They gave her strength and hope.

How often do we consider the impact of our words? And how often do we just toss out words without thinking about them? Think about your words as you speak this week. Are they crushing words? Healing words? Hurting words? Helping words? Let's try to speak affirming, truthful, enriching words as often as we can!

day 203

"Early the next morning they arose and worshiped before the Lᴏʀᴅ and then went back to their home at Ramah. Elkanah made love to his wife Hannah, and the Lᴏʀᴅ remembered her. So in the course of time Hannah became pregnant and gave birth to a son. She named him Samuel, saying, 'Because I asked the Lᴏʀᴅ for him.'"

–1 SAMUEL 1:19–20

Okay, so we're back in a biblical bedroom. Sorry about that. But since Hannah's whole story centers around her infertility, it's kind of hard to avoid. And this is a happy turn of events, after all. Hannah is finally getting what she so desperately wanted. She gets a baby!

Look, it's important to manage our expectations. It's important to make sure we understand the hard truth that we don't always get what we want. Sometimes God says no. There is no magic formula to ensure God always says yes, and even if there were, we'd probably want to be very wary of such a thing.

But, even after we've triggered all the gloomy truth bombs we can possibly detonate, there's another truth to consider. Sometimes God makes miracles happen. Sometimes God *says yes* and makes the impossible possible. While we don't want to expect that of God every time we ask for something, it's true that sometimes, that's what God does.

day 204

"After he was weaned, she took the boy with her . . . to the house of the LORD at Shiloh . . . [And Hannah said to Eli] 'Pardon me, my lord. As surely as you live, I am the woman who stood here beside you praying to the LORD. I prayed for this child, and the LORD has granted me what I asked of him. So now I give him to the LORD. For his whole life he will be given over to the LORD.' And he worshiped the LORD there."

–1 SAMUEL 1:24, 26-28

How joyous it must have been for Hannah to return to Eli after Samuel was weaned. How wonderful to be able to tell the High Priest, "That thing you prayed for . . . here he is." While we can be sure the occasion was somewhat bittersweet for Hannah, since she was fulfilling her vow to dedicate her son, Samuel, to the Lord's service, what an awesome occasion. It was everything Hannah had asked God for.

Sometimes, after we get that "yes" we've been seeking, it's easy to forget about God. We remember him quickly when we're troubled. It's easy to cry out when we need help. But once we get it, sometimes we forget about our helper.

Let's be like Hannah. Let's keep our promises to God, and remember to give back to him when he gives to us.

day 205

"Then Hannah prayed and said: . . . '[The LORD] raises the poor from the dust and lifts the needy from the ash heap; he seats them with princes and has them inherit a throne of honor. For the foundations of the earth are the LORD's; on them he has set the world.'"

–1 SAMUEL 2:1, 8–9A

This is just a snippet of Hannah's prayer, and the whole thing is really worth reading. The focus of the prayer is God's sovereignty—his freedom, ability, and power to do as he pleases. So her point in these verses isn't that God will take every person who is struggling financially and give him a seat with princes (wouldn't that be nice?). Her point is that God is powerful enough to do these things and many more.

It's hard to accept someone else's rule over our lives sometimes. We want to be independent, so we might cringe at the idea of someone else being in control. But we have to remember that allowing God to rule us isn't the same as allowing another person to control us. God's plans are always good. He wants to bless us, not harm us. He wants good for us, and he is powerful enough to bring about anything he wishes. So giving control to God isn't a bad thing. It's a freeing thing!

day 206

"Then Elkanah went home to Ramah, but the boy ministered before the Lord under Eli the priest."

–1 SAMUEL 2:11

We can't rightly wrap up our look at Hannah without talking about this oldest son of hers (yes, she had more sons and some daughters!). Samuel was a special person in biblical history. He was the final judge of Israel before they asked for a king. If you want to feel comforted during rejection, read Samuel's story (1 Samuel 8)! He felt utterly rejected when Israel asked for a king during his leadership as a judge, but God assured him it was the people who were at fault, not Samuel.

Samuel was a king-maker. He anointed Saul, then David. He was a good, godly leader. A major prophet of Israel. Hannah's boy did well by all standards.

What a cool legacy, both for Samuel and for Hannah. This boy she had prayed for so desperately and promised to the Lord so sincerely left behind a mark of goodness on the world. What kind of mark do you want to leave behind? Do you realize we're working on our "marks" throughout our entire lives? Even now, you're writing your own story, deciding what sort of legacy you'll leave. Let's make it a good one!

day 207

"Now Saul's daughter Michal was in love with David, and when they told Saul about it, he was pleased. 'I will give her to him,' he thought, 'so that she may be a snare to him and so that the hand of the Philistines may be against him.'"

–1 SAMUEL 18:20–21A

We've jumped forward in time a little. Samuel is still alive, but now Saul is King of Israel. And he *hates* David, whom Samuel has anointed to take Saul's place, since Saul turned away from God and didn't rule Israel well. Got all that? It's quite the drama!

Into this drama, we add another element. Saul's daughter Michal was genuinely in love with David, but Saul was so given over to his hatred of David, he tried to use Michal's love for his own evil purposes. He wanted to coax David into an impossible battle with the Philistines by promising Michal's hand in marriage if David could emerge victorious. So he manipulated both Michal and David to try to bring about David's death. Ugh.

Sometimes we can't trust the people we should be able to trust. It would be awesome if every parent always did right. It'd be great if teachers, religious leaders, and law enforcement officers always acted as they should—honorably, as *most* of them do. But that's not the reality. Sometimes, we're dealing with a wolf in sheep's clothing. So we must always be careful about where we place our trust. Trust the true shepherds and avoid the wolves!

day 208

"David [did what Saul asked]. Then Saul gave him his daughter Michal in marriage. When Saul realized that the LORD was with David and that his daughter Michal loved David, Saul became still more afraid of him, and he remained his enemy the rest of his days."

–1 SAMUEL 18:27-29

This is the part where Saul says, "Whoops!" It turned out that David was able to accomplish quite a lot with God on his side. He completed Saul's impossible task and won Michal's hand—much to her joy, we can imagine, since she loved David.

Can you imagine what it was like to be Michal? We don't know for sure when she fell in love with David, but perhaps it was when she was a royal princess and David was still a humble shepherd-musician. She ended up married to a war hero and future king of Israel! These two had a lovely start, and Michal is one of the only women in the Bible whose love is mentioned. Lots of men fall in love with lots of women, but we don't often get a specific comment on how the ladies feel. In Michal's case, we do!

Michal chose well when she fell in love with David, and her example can give us courage to stand by our good choices, even when those around us don't understand.

day 209

"Saul sent men to David's house to watch it and to kill him in the morning. But Michal, David's wife, warned him, 'If you don't run for your life tonight, tomorrow you'll be killed.'"

–1 SAMUEL 19:11

Eek. What a sticky situation for poor Michal. She had every reason to fear for not only David's life but also her own. Though Saul was caught in an intense downward spiral, it wouldn't be unreasonable to suppose Michal still loved him. Perhaps she felt some loyalty toward her father. So that means she's left with a choice between her family and the man she loves.

Hopefully we're never facing a situation this dramatic. But we are likely to find ourselves in a tight spot where our loyalties feel pulled in different directions. Maybe you find yourself trapped in between two feuding friends. Maybe you have divorcing parents fighting over you (ugh . . . so tough). In Michal's case, she had to choose what was right. Her father had murderous intent, and she chose to save David's life. Our situations aren't likely to be this scary, but we can still try to make choices on the side of morality and goodness.

day 210

"As the ark of the Lord was entering the City of David, Michal daughter of Saul watched from a window. And when she saw King David leaping and dancing before the Lord, she despised him in her heart."

–2 SAMUEL 6:16

Unfortunately, this is probably what Michal is most famous for. David wasn't acting kingly enough for her, and she "despised him in her heart." What?! The man she loved? The man she saved from her wicked father? Yep. The same one. How sad!

But it's really easy to trip up the way Michal did. The Bible says "despised him in her heart." We might say Michal was being super judge-y. Now does it hit a little closer to home? There are about a million ways to judge someone. Maybe we raise our eyebrows at someone else's outfit—because it's outdated, odd, doesn't fit well, or is showing too much skin for our tastes. Or maybe we give some side-eye to someone's behavior. Or their taste in music. Or their life choices. Or, or, or. It's definitely far easier to be judge-y than not!

Let's combat this impulse, especially when it's "in our hearts," the way Michal's distaste was. It's easy to imagine that if we don't *say* anything rude to another person, we're in the clear. But the heart matters. And if we're judging or despising in our hearts, we're not practicing kindness as well as we could be.

day 211

"When David returned home to bless his household, Michal daughter of Saul came out to meet him and said, 'How the king of Israel has distinguished himself today, going around half-naked in full view of the slave girls of his servants as any vulgar fellow would!'"

–2 SAMUEL 6:20

Make sure you read Michal's words with a heap of sarcasm, because that's how she meant them. She had taken her judge-y heart and allowed it to spill from her mouth.

Hey, it's possible David was being improper. It's possible those slave girls were seeing a bit more of their king than they needed to (just sayin' . . .). But God accepted David's attitude and rejected Michal's. Why? Because Michal cared more about her husband's outward behavior than his worshipful heart.

It's shockingly easy to care more about the outside than the inside. Maybe you've felt awkward attending a church event because your wardrobe feels inferior to the other girls'. Or maybe you've shied away from serving in the choir or worship team because, even though God's given you the heart for it, you worry about standing in front of all those people. Remember that God cares about your worshipful heart, not your outward appearance. He cares about your love for him, not how polished you are. Let's try to have David's attitude, not Michal's.

day 212

"David said to Michal . . . 'I will celebrate before the Lord. I will become even more undignified than this, and I will be humiliated in my own eyes.'"

–2 SAMUEL 6:21B–22

David had the right focus. Rejoicing, worshiping, praising—all overflowing from a humble heart that loved the Lord. If he had to be undignified in order to let his behavior reflect the joy he felt, he was cool with that.

There's something unsettling to us about a royal figure being human, quirks and all. We want our leaders to be stately, polished, controlled. But David sure broke that mold, and God seemed to be just fine with it. In fact, David's willingness to be imperfect foreshadowed the sacrifice of Jesus on the cross. David's spirit was happy and Jesus's was brokenhearted, but they both set aside their worldly honor to worship God from the depths of their souls.

That's a pretty deep thought. But sometimes it's important for us to think about this stuff. Though Jesus was an even greater king than David—the King of Kings—he allowed himself to be humiliated on the cross for his Father's sake and for our sake. That's an incredible truth! How loved we are.

day 213

"A certain man in Maon, who had property there at Carmel, was very wealthy. He had a thousand goats and three thousand sheep, which he was shearing in Carmel. His name was Nabal and his wife's name was Abigail. She was an intelligent and beautiful woman, but her husband was surly and mean in his dealings—he was a Calebite."

−1 SAMUEL 25:2–3

Abigail's introduction is at once awesome and terrible. She not only gets called out as beautiful, but her intelligence is pointed out. Awesome! But then we get a glimpse into her husband's heart, and he is surly and mean (and his name literally means "fool"). Terrible. They seem quite the mismatched pair.

Abigail probably didn't have a choice of who she would marry. But we do. We have the opportunity to pick someone who will love and appreciate our awesome qualities. Someone whose awesome qualities we get to love and appreciate back. Someone who isn't a mismatch.

It can be hard to wait for someone like that, but perhaps the first lesson we can take from Abigail's story is that we're worth it! And the good men are worth waiting for too.

day 214

"One of the servants told Abigail, Nabal's wife, 'David sent messengers from the wilderness to give our master his greetings, but he hurled insults at them. Yet these men were very good to us. They did not mistreat us . . . Now think it over and see what you can do, because disaster is hanging over our master and his whole household. He is such a wicked man that no one can talk to him.'"

–1 SAMUEL 25:14–15A, 17

David isn't king yet, but he's been anointed as the next in line. He was on the run from Saul and traveling through Nabal's area. He tried to reach out to Nabal and his household, asking for kindness, but Nabal responded in his characteristic mean and surly manner. The servants were understandably concerned. They were part of that household, after all, and who could blame them for wanting to avoid the wrong side of the future king?

So what did they do? Who did they turn to? Abigail, of course! Remember, she was known not only for her beauty but her intelligence. She was wise. She was the perfect person for the servants to go to for advice.

What a cool role model for us. Wouldn't you rather be an Abigail than a Nabal? Let's seek to be the sort of people others come to for advice—those who are wise, measured, judicious, sensible—just like Abigail.

day 215

"Abigail acted quickly."

–1 SAMUEL 25:18A

You go, Abigail! Doesn't she just make you want to cheer? The household servants came to her for help, and she didn't just sit there. She acted quickly. She was decisive and exercised her wisdom in a way that was going to save a lot of people's lives. Abigail is amazing.

Cautiousness and careful planning can be great character traits. We often want to exercise restraint to keep from making hasty decisions. But sometimes, swift action is necessary. So how do we know when to be reserved and when to be bold? Well, we know Abigail acted quickly because her husband's foolish behavior had put the household at risk. David was angry, and he had the power to do something about it. When someone's health, safety, or life is on the line, acting fast is the way to go. We just need to make sure we're tapping into our Abigail-like wisdom, even when we're acting quickly. That will help us make *good* decisions swiftly.

day 216

"She took two hundred loaves of bread, two skins of wine, five dressed sheep, five seahs of roasted grain, a hundred cakes of raisins and two hundred cakes of pressed figs, and loaded them on donkeys. Then she told her servants, 'Go on ahead; I'll follow you.' But she did not tell her husband Nabal."

–1 SAMUEL 25:18B-19

Hmm. That last line might make us wonder if Abigail was being a little deceitful toward her husband, Nabal. After all, we say truthfulness and transparency are supposed to be our default habits. We're supposed to be honest whenever we're able. Was Abigail being truthful and transparent with her husband in this case?

Obviously, she wasn't. At least not right away. But in this case, she was still acting morally because she was prioritizing the lives of the household over volunteering information to Nabal. Sometimes we can't tell people the whole truth, like when we know a secret that isn't ours to share, or when the person we're dealing with isn't trustworthy (like Nabal wasn't). It's important that we discern when to be transparent and when to hold back. You shouldn't tell your friend's crush she likes him, but you *should* tell an adult if a friend needs help. When you're honest with God, he will help you know when secrets should be kept and when they're doing damage.

day 217

"When Abigail saw David, she quickly got off her donkey and bowed down before David with her face to the ground."

–1 SAMUEL 25:23

Abigail's wisdom is on display once again. The first thing she did after dismounting her donkey was to bow down before David. She began her conversation with him from a place of respect. She showed him she was not there to treat him poorly, the way her husband had.

Starting from a place of respect when approaching people goes a very long way. It will almost always help calm an angry person. The same principle applies when opening a conversation with someone who holds different beliefs from you, or someone with whom you've had a disagreement. When we approach these moments with humble, respectful hearts, it makes it easier to listen to others and heal broken or difficult relationships.

Is there someone in your life with whom you tend to have rocky communication? Maybe it's a parent, sibling, or even a friend. Hey, sometimes even the people we choose to have in our lives can rub us the wrong way. Take a moment to think about your interactions. Are you approaching that person with respect or annoyance? Are there any stains of bitterness in your heart you can clean up? It might go a long way in healing that frustration.

day 218

"She fell at his feet and said: 'Pardon your servant, my lord, and let me speak to you; hear what your servant has to say. Please pay no attention, my lord, to that wicked man Nabal. He is just like his name—his name means Fool, and folly goes with him. And as for me, your servant, I did not see the men my lord sent.'"

–1 SAMUEL 25:24-25

There's something really refreshing about Abigail's words here. Her explanation might be considered a little rude (she called her husband a wicked fool, after all), but it still feels right that she said it. Why? Because Abigail was speaking the truth.

While we usually want to consider others' feelings and *not* point out their flaws to others, sometimes we need to call it like we see it. It's okay to call immoral behavior immoral. It's okay to point out that someone who behaves selfishly, foolishly, and harmfully isn't a safe person.

We need to be careful about this, of course. No one is perfect, and we wouldn't want our shortcomings constantly pointed out in public, especially when we're trying to work on them. And there's a fine line between trying to help someone improve a bad habit and just being judgmental or gossiping. But part of the reason Abigail was so effective in convincing David she was sincere was because she was willing to openly acknowledge what was plain to see—that Nabal was not a moral or wise man.

day 219

"And now, my lord, as surely as the LORD your God lives and as you live, since the LORD has kept you from bloodshed and from avenging yourself with your own hands, may your enemies and all who are intent on harming my lord be like Nabal. And let this gift, which your servant has brought to my lord, be given to the men who follow you."

–1 SAMUEL 25:26–27

Abigail says the Lord kept David from bloodshed. God allowed Abigail enough time to approach David and win him over before David acted in anger and killed some of Nabal's household. While David was justified in being offended at Nabal's brush-off, God used Abigail to help control David's temper and keep him from retaliating.

It can be hard to control our tempers when we know someone has wronged us. Why shouldn't we flare up in anger, show our indignation, or exact revenge?

God says that vengeance belongs to him. He's the only one who is perfectly able to judge who is in the right and who is in the wrong. Correctness isn't the fruit of the Spirit, but gentleness is. Let's remember that our role is to turn our anger and offenses over to God. His role is to act as perfect judge.

day 220

"Please forgive your servant's presumption. The Lᴏʀᴅ your God will certainly make a lasting dynasty for my lord, because you fight the Lᴏʀᴅ's battles, and no wrongdoing will be found in you as long as you live."

–1 SAMUEL 25:28

Abigail showed respect to David, but she didn't defer to him because he was rich, impressive in battle, or because he was handsome and charming. No, Abigail pointed to the thing that most set David apart—his relationship with God.

When we're dealing with someone we respect, someone the world holds in high regard, or someone in a position of authority, it can be difficult to stay focused on what matters. Fame, money, good looks, sharp intelligence, smooth words—it can be tempting to become distracted by all of these things. But those who deserve our greatest respect and deepest trusts are the ones who share our love for Jesus and show the evidence of his Spirit in their hearts.

That's not always glamorous. David happened to be a pretty glamorous package—he had a close relationship with God, was future king of Israel, was known for his prowess on the battlefield, and is described in the Bible as handsome. And still, Abigail is most focused on his relationship with God. Like Abigail, let's remember to give respect for the things that matter most in life.

day 221

"Even though someone is pursuing you to take your life, the life of my lord will be bound securely in the bundle of the living by the Lord your God, but the lives of your enemies he will hurl away as from the pocket of a sling. When the Lord has fulfilled for my lord every good thing he promised concerning him and has appointed him ruler over Israel, my lord will not have on his conscience the staggering burden of needless bloodshed or of having avenged himself. And when the Lord your God has brought my lord success, remember your servant."

–1 SAMUEL 25:29–31

We usually think revenge is going to feel great. Even if we're not seeking the sort of revenge someone of David's time might have been—to take the life of the person who offended us—we might get caught up in daydreams about humiliating someone who embarrassed or mocked us, exposing someone who stabbed us in the back, or some other such "smaller" revenge.

We really would do well to follow Abigail's example here. She fought hard for peace. Not only was she protecting the people of her household, she was protecting David's heart. Anger is often fleeting. Something that one minute made us lash out, hurt and furious, may the next minute die down. But when we exact revenge, it can echo on for a lifetime. If David had killed Nabal, he would not have been able to take back that choice once his anger cooled down. Let's remember Abigail's wisdom and actively pursue peace, even with those who have hurt us.

day 222

"David said to Abigail, 'Praise be to the LORD, the God of Israel, who has sent you today to meet me.'"

–1 SAMUEL 25:32

David saw Abigail as a gift from the Lord. He wasn't wrong! Her wisdom saved him and his men from unnecessary bloodshed. She was a wonderful example of a godly woman.

We should seek people who appreciate us for our godly character the way David appreciated Abigail. Whether we're talking about friends, boyfriends, or eventually someone we plan to marry, it's a wonderful blessing to fill our lives with people who understand and appreciate our hearts for God.

Have you ever been in a friendship with someone who just didn't "get" this whole God thing? Those relationships can provide great opportunities to share the love of Jesus with someone who doesn't know him yet. But let's also be sure we fill our lives with those who understand—and better yet, share—our passion for God.

day 223

"Then David accepted from her hand what she had brought him and said, 'Go home in peace. I have heard your words and granted your request.'"

–1 SAMUEL 25:35

Abigail's sigh of relief must have been *huge*. David had accepted her gifts and her words in the way she'd intended them. She'd undone Nabal's foolishness and spared the family from David's wrath. Giant win.

Do you ever have those days that feel like big wins? It's easy to focus on our terrible, horrible, no good, very bad days. Those seem to stick in our minds and hearts, don't they? But it's important for our hearts (and our mental health!) that we're intentional about recognizing the great days. Not only recognizing them, but truly celebrating them.

What's your most recent "win"? Did you ace a big test? Win a big game? Maybe you reconnected with an old friend or became closer with a new friend. All of these things are worth celebrating! Make sure you're taking time to notice the good things and let those moments etch lasting memories in your mind.

day 224

"When Abigail went to Nabal, he was in the house holding a banquet like that of a king. He was in high spirits and very drunk. So she told him nothing at all until daybreak."

–1 SAMUEL 25:36

This is another pretty stark picture of the mismatch between Nabal and Abigail. While she's off smoothing things over with David, Nabal is hosting a giant party and getting drunk. Yikes. But Abigail doesn't disappoint—she handles this situation with wisdom too and decides to hold off speaking to Nabal just yet.

Often, timing is everything. We value honesty, and we value straightforwardness, but sometimes biding our time is the wisest possible choice. If you have a big favor to ask of your mom, it's probably not wise to ask her just as she gets home from work and she's exhausted. If you have bad news to share with your dad, it might not be the best time to spring it on him when he's just had a frustrating conversation with a neighbor.

This really comes down to being aware of and sensitive to other people's situations. Waiting for an opportune moment to make requests or share news not only makes such conversations smoother for you, but you're also showing kindness to the person you're speaking with by considering their feelings.

day 225

"Then in the morning, when Nabal was sober, his wife told him all these things, and his heart failed him and he became like a stone. About ten days later, the LORD struck Nabal and he died."

–1 SAMUEL 25:37–38

Whoa. That's some seriously powerful bad news. It sounds like Nabal probably had a heart attack that eventually led to his death. It's ironic, considering that David was going to retaliate by killing Nabal, and Abigail was able to prevent that from happening. Then the very news of this resulted in Nabal's death, anyway. Sad and ironic.

This is a good lesson in God's sovereignty—which is a fancy word that simply means "control." Sometimes it's really hard for us to accept that God is in control. David probably didn't feel much like turning over control when his anger was burning hot. But by letting go, the end result David was after happened anyway, without David becoming guilty of bloodshed.

Our situations aren't usually so life-and-death dramatic. But the same principle applies. We can accidentally tiptoe into wrongdoing by trying to force our desired result out of a situation. Instead, let's recognize that we have a good, wise, fair God on the throne of our lives and turn over control to *him*. He knows the best outcomes to all our toughest situations.

day 226

"[David said, 'The LORD] has kept his servant from doing wrong and has brought Nabal's wrongdoing down on his own head.' Then David sent word to Abigail, asking her to become his wife. His servants went to Carmel and said to Abigail, 'David has sent us to you to take you to become his wife.'"

–1 SAMUEL 25:39B-40

Wait, what?! Can you imagine how surprised Abigail must have been? When she and David last parted ways, she was returning home to her foolish, wicked husband, whose life she had just spared. We can imagine she had no idea that a few weeks later, Nabal would be dead and David would be asking for her hand.

Sometimes we think we have the "best-case scenario" all figured out. We think we know the most wonderful thing that could possibly happen. Abigail probably thought soothing David's anger and undoing Nabal's mess was the best thing that could happen. And then God surprised her with an unexpected blessing—David as her husband instead.

What's the last "best-case scenario" you asked God for? Imagine for a second that he gave you that, plus something wildly better. It doesn't always work this way, of course. God always gives us what we *need*, and sometimes that's the bare minimum. But sometimes it's a whole lot more!

day 227

"She bowed down with her face to the ground and said, 'I am your servant and am ready to serve you and wash the feet of my lord's servants.' Abigail quickly got on a donkey and, attended by her five female servants, went with David's messengers and became his wife."

–1 SAMUEL 25:41–42

What a turnaround. Poor, mismatched Abigail so impressed King David with her wisdom that he proposed to her as soon as she became a widow. She accepted with grace and poise. Really, we'd expect nothing less of our superwoman, right?

It's not always easy to be as poised as Abigail. Sometimes life's detours throw us for a loop and it's a struggle to get back on our feet. But when we recognize that God never lets us slip through his fingers—that he always has a plan—it becomes easier to manage life's twists and turns with grace, like Abigail.

When was the last time your life took an unexpected turn? Was it a good surprise, like Abigail's, or was it a tough one that left you reeling? Looking back, can you see God's hand in the situation? It can take a long time before we understand *why* certain events happened in our lives. But we know, no matter what we face, that God's plan is being worked for good in our lives. That's a comforting thought!

day 228

"In the spring, at the time when kings go off to war, David sent Joab out with the king's men . . . But David remained in Jerusalem. One evening David got up from his bed and walked around on the roof of the palace. From the roof he saw a woman bathing."

–2 SAMUEL 11:1-2A

Before we move on to our next biblical woman, it's important to get a little context for her arrival—especially since David is about to take a major detour from "man after God's own heart" to "Whoa, dude, you know God can *see* you, right?"

This part of the story is fascinating because it starts with ". . . at the time when kings go off to war." But then it goes on to say what David was doing instead. He sent his generals off to war and he stayed home, idly strolling around the rooftop. And that's when he became distracted by the woman bathing on the roof. Danger!

Distractions have the ability to throw us off-kilter spiritually. We may think of them as harmless at first, but David's story shows us just how much they can knock us off course. Can you think of something that has been drawing your attention away from the important things in life lately? Consider whether it's something that is truly beneficial for you and your growth. If it's not, cut back. And if you think it's harmful, cut it out!

----

day 229

"The woman was very beautiful, and David sent someone to find out about her. The man said, 'She is Bathsheba, the daughter of Eliam and the wife of Uriah the Hittite.'"

—2 SAMUEL 11:2B–3

You may have already noticed that King David was something of a wife-collector. Eight of his wives are named in the Bible, though he probably had more than that, including concubines. We've looked at two so far, and now we've just met the most famous (and probably infamous): Bathsheba.

Poor Bathsheba. She has practically become synonymous with David's sin over the millennia, yet the Bible doesn't tell us her side of the story. We don't know if she loved David, and we don't even know if she was a willing participant in everything that happened. We just know that history remembers her as "the one who David sinned with." The object of his lust.

No matter how history remembers Bathsheba, *we* can choose to remember her as more than an object. The way David looked at her does not define who she was, just as the way others look at us doesn't define our identities.

day 230

"Then David sent messengers to get her. She came to him, and he slept with her. (Now she was purifying herself from her monthly uncleanness.) Then she went back home."

–2 SAMUEL 11:4

This is a disturbing part of the story. Bathsheba was married to someone else, so this was adultery. It's also unclear if Bathsheba was an equal participant or if she was forced or pressured into complying with the desires of her king. Did she feel powerless to resist David's advances? It's a troubling possibility.

It's difficult to know how to respond when someone has done something *to* us, especially when that action was a deep violation in one or more ways. Sometimes people think "turn the other cheek" means "take more abuse without complaint." While it is important to practice forgiveness, mercy, and patience, it's also vital that we feel empowered to maintain boundaries, seek help, or remove ourselves from dangerous or toxic situations. Embracing Christian virtues like forgiveness does *not* mean we must allow abuse to continue.

Are you dealing with a situation where you feel helpless? Do you have a friend currently suffering through abuse? Please, beloved girl, don't feel trapped! There is support out there. Pray about your next step right now, then reach out in faith.

day 231

"The woman conceived and sent word to David, saying, 'I am pregnant.'"

–2 SAMUEL 11:5

Eep. We can suppose this was a moment of pure panic for both Bathsheba and David. Now what were they supposed to do? The sin of adultery is a huge deal, and Bathsheba's pregnancy (while her husband was away fighting wars) certainly threatened to make the king's sin very public, very soon. Commence freak-out.

While being very careful not to excuse David's behavior—because frankly, there's nothing okay about what he did—we can probably all agree that everyone makes mistakes. Not just little mistakes, but huge, massive blunders. We've each probably had a handful of our own, so we can likely relate to the fear and shame David and Bathsheba may have felt.

So what do we do when we realize we've made a big-time stumble? The very thing we fear the most— confess it. That seems like a crazy idea when you're caught in a fear-and-shame tornado. But honestly confessing to someone you trust helps pull you *out* of that downward spiral. It stops the bleeding and helps begin the process of repentance and healing. It's scary, for sure, but it's healthy—and even necessary!

day 232

"Uriah said to David, 'The ark and Israel and Judah are staying in tents, and my commander Joab and my lord's men are camped in the open country. How could I go to my house to eat and drink and make love to my wife? As surely as you live, I will not do such a thing!' . . . In the morning David wrote a letter to Joab and sent it with Uriah."

–2 SAMUEL 11:11, 14

David didn't opt for honest confession. Instead, he tried to cover up his sin. He called Uriah back home, hoping he and Bathsheba would sleep together so her pregnancy wouldn't be questioned. But Uriah refused to stay at home.

But David *still* didn't confess. He sent a letter to his commander, Joab, asking that Uriah would be put on the frontlines in the hopes he would be killed. The real kicker? Uriah was one of David's "Mighty Men"—his closest friends.

There's no one-size-fits-all answer for dealing with betrayal. Sometimes a relationship is so broken, so abused, it's healthiest to cut ties. Oftentimes, forgiveness and reconciliation are possible, but it's a long, slow climb back to trust. The first step in coping is to allow yourself to acknowledge that loss—it hurts, and that's okay! Then move forward in the best, healthiest way possible, keeping in mind Jesus's love for all of us.

day 233

"When Uriah's wife heard that her husband was dead, she mourned for him."
—2 SAMUEL 11:26

David's plan worked. Uriah died in battle, just as the king had hoped. David had now gone from adulterer to murderer in an effort to cover his tracks. Whatever Bathsheba felt about David, this verse implies she loved—or at least cared for—her husband Uriah. She didn't celebrate his death. She mourned for him.

Losing someone close to us is difficult, especially when that person is snatched away unexpectedly. Sometimes we feel like we have to put on a brave face, or else people might think we've lost our faith in God and his plan. But it's important to allow yourself to acknowledge your pain. Talk to others about it, like a godly counselor or mentor. Let others support and comfort you. Give yourself some time and space to heal. Be gentle with your expectations for a while.

And express yourself. Some people do this best in journals. Others like to paint, write music, or build things. Whatever it looks like for you, find a healthy outlet to express your emotions. Healing from grief can be a long, difficult road. But it's fully possible. You don't have to feel stuck!

day 234

"After the time of mourning was over, David had her brought to his house, and she became his wife and bore him a son. But the thing David had done displeased the Lord."

–2 SAMUEL 11:27

David may have thought he was in the clear. He waited until Bathsheba was done mourning, then scuttled her into his household so she could give birth to his baby. No one would count the months *that* closely, right? It seems David, the same man who wrote so many beautiful psalms about God being real and present in his life, had forgotten that nothing is hidden from God. And God was not okay with the terrible things David had done.

In many ways, David's life was not easy. But one constant seemed to be that God's favor almost always rested on him. The Bible says David was a "man after God's own heart" (Acts 13:22). And even so, David was not above the law.

It can be tempting to think that, because we are God's beloved, we have the freedom to do whatever we want while depending on God's grace for our forgiveness. The writers of the New Testament were really careful to explain that this is not what living under grace looks like. God cares about how we act, speak, think, and feel. He cares that we're representing him well to the world. Let's never take advantage of his grace!

day 235

"[Nathan said,] 'Why did you despise the word of the Lord by doing what is evil in his eyes? You struck down Uriah the Hittite with the sword and took his wife to be your own. You killed him with the sword of the Ammonites. Now, therefore, the sword will never depart from your house, because you despised me and took the wife of Uriah the Hittite to be your own.'"

–2 SAMUEL 12:9-10

Oh boy. This is some serious trouble. The prophet Nathan came to the king and let him know about God's displeasure. And, while God didn't stay angry with David forever, Nathan's pronouncement certainly came true. One of his sons openly rebelled against him, and three of his sons died violently. David's legacy was tainted. Most tragically of all, the innocent baby conceived between David and Bathsheba died.

Sometimes our actions are so harmful, the consequences are catastrophic. Those consequences can last a lifetime. Thankfully, forgiveness is always available to us. When we repent and return to God, he will forgive us, just like he forgave David. But forgiveness doesn't usually erase consequences. David's relationship with God was restored. David's heart was restored. But he still had to live with the effects of his choices. Let's be *so* careful to choose wisely the first time. When we listen to the Holy Spirit and the godly counsel in our lives, we can often avoid catastrophe.

day 236

"After Nathan had gone home, the Lᴏʀᴅ struck the child that Uriah's wife had borne to David, and he became ill. David pleaded with God for the child ... On the seventh day the child died."

–2 SAMUEL 12:15, 16A, 18A

Despite all the evil David committed in this situation, our hearts probably still break for him as we read this passage. David knew what the prophet had spoken, but he begged God to spare the baby anyway. It wasn't to be, and God took that baby home.

And that brings us to a hard truth: when we choose selfishly, innocents may suffer. That's uncomfortable. Sometimes it's hard to even acknowledge how many voiceless and vulnerable people are out there. The unborn, the oppressed, the poverty-stricken, the ill, the hurting. It's overwhelming. And it's even harder to acknowledge that we can, by acting selfishly, further add to the pain of these vulnerable groups.

But Jesus-like love allows us to go beyond our selfish actions and do good in the world. Who are the most vulnerable groups in your own community? Can you think of ways to support, help, or encourage that group? If we're intentional about loving the "innocents" of the world, we will be less likely to act selfishly and in ways that harm them—or anyone else.

day 237

> "Then David comforted his wife Bathsheba, and he went to her and made love to her."
> —2 SAMUEL 12:24A

Can we be awkward for a second? Okay, good. Because we're going to talk about sex. Let's put aside the terrible circumstances of how David and Bathsheba got together. However they arrived at this point, they were now husband and wife. Do you notice the language used here to describe their physical union? "He made love to her." Nice, isn't it?

Let's compare that to the way the Bible describes their first union in 2 Samuel 11:4, before David and Bathsheba were married: "He slept with her." Not so nice. There's a difference between marital and extra-marital sex.

The physical union of husband and wife is one of the deepest, most intimate acts imaginable. That's why God has put so many boundaries on sex. That level of intimacy is only to be enjoyed between two married people.

day 238

"[Bathsheba] gave birth to a son, and they named him Solomon. The LORD loved him."
–2 SAMUEL 12:24B

Ah. Redemption! After the horrible rocky start, the rough road to repentance, and the acceptance of their consequences, David and Bathsheba experience redemption. God took their first son home, but he gave them another—the great Solomon, future king of Israel and builder of God's temple, known as the wisest man ever to live.

God loves us too much to leave us stuck. He doesn't want us to wallow in our mistakes or difficult circumstances of the past. He wants us to return to him. Sometimes when we know we've messed up, we try to hide from God. Maybe we pull away from church or our Christian friends. Or perhaps we fall out of the habit of reading our Bibles. But God doesn't want us to run away from him. He wants to restore us.

Do you feel like you've been hiding from God lately? Do you know his love—his acceptance—is always waiting for you?

---

day 239

"[Bathsheba said to David] 'My lord the king, the eyes of all Israel are on you, to learn from you who will sit on the throne of my lord the king after him. Otherwise, as soon as my lord the king is laid to rest with his ancestors, I and my son Solomon will be treated as criminals.'"

–1 KINGS 1:20–21

Obviously some time has passed. Bathsheba is concerned about her son Solomon because David's other sons (by different wives) are already squabbling over the throne. So Bathsheba spoke up. If she hadn't, it's not unreasonable to imagine that David's other sons might have killed or mistreated Solomon.

When you hear the word "assertive," what comes to mind? We don't usually think of it as a biblical virtue. We usually think of someone who is harsh, abrasive, or pushy. But really, it means bold and confident. And we *should* be those things when we understand our identity as beloved daughters of God. Assertiveness doesn't mean arrogance or rudeness.

Without Bathsheba's assertiveness, her son might not have succeeded his father the way he was supposed to. She spoke up, with confidence, for what was right. Let's follow her example!

day 240

"[Bathsheba] came into the king's presence and stood before him. The king then took an oath:... 'I will surely carry out this very day what I swore to you by the LORD, the God of Israel: Solomon your son shall be king after me, and he will sit on my throne in my place.' Then Bathsheba bowed down ... and said, 'May my lord King David live forever!'"

–1 KINGS 1:28B–31

This isn't the very last mention of Bathsheba in the Bible. Solomon goes on to become king, and Bathsheba's transformation is complete. Some people think she began as a complicit adulteress. Others believe she was the victim of David's abuse of power. Either way, she certainly didn't stay stuck in that spot. She rose to the position of powerful Queen Mother, clearly adored and honored by her son, Solomon.

God breathes hope into the most hopeless situations. No matter what your starting point in life, God is able to turn it into something wonderful. He gives us "a crown of beauty instead of ashes" (Isaiah 61:3). Even if we don't get a physical crown, like Bathsheba did (ahem).

Can you think of times in your life when you've seen God replace ashes with beauty? Was there a situation that felt hard, hopeless, or desperate? What did God do to turn it around? Take a moment to thank him for his loving intervention.

day 241

"In the course of time, Amnon son of David fell in love with Tamar, the beautiful sister of Absalom son of David."

–2 SAMUEL 13:1

We're about to begin unraveling one woman's story—Tamar's sad narrative, recorded in painful detail in the Bible. But hers is the story of so many of us. Experts estimate one in seven girls is the victim of sexual abuse before her eighteenth birthday. One out of every seven.

That means if you haven't been the victim of abuse yourself, it's incredibly likely that you know one or more girls who *have* been victimized. Approximately thirty percent of children and teens who are sexually abused are abused by a family member, like Tamar was. Ninety percent of abused children know their abuser. Also? Many victims of childhood sexual abuse never tell anyone about it. The actual statistics are probably worse than these numbers.

So, you see, Tamar's story is our story too. It's the story of at least one in seven girls. Rather than brushing this uncomfortable section of God's Word under the rug, let's thank him for the opportunity to learn about abuse so we can continue to shine a light on it. When we shine a light into the darkest corners of this fallen world, healing can begin.

day 242

"Amnon became so obsessed with his sister Tamar that he made himself ill. She was a virgin, and it seemed impossible for him to do anything to her."

—2 SAMUEL 13:2

Amnon and Tamar were David's children by different mothers, so they were half-siblings. A romantic relationship between them was forbidden by Mosaic Law (Leviticus 18:9), but Amnon was consumed with it anyway. He was obsessed to the point of illness. As a woman, Tamar was automatically vulnerable, and Amnon desperately looked for a way around her defenses.

Manipulators and other unsafe people use similar tactics to control and exploit others. They seek to fulfill unmet emotional and physical needs. They slowly work to isolate their target from others and gradually cross boundaries, becoming increasingly intimate. Then they use threats, blame, and secrecy to maintain their control. None of this is okay.

If you have ever experienced anything like this, know that this is *not your fault*. Abusers want their victims to believe they invited the abuse somehow, but this is a lie. God loves truth, and he does *not* want you to believe these lies about yourself.

day 213

"Now Amnon had an adviser named Jonadab [his cousin]. Jonadab was a very shrewd man . . . 'Go to bed and pretend to be ill,' Jonadab said. 'When your father comes to see you, say to him, "I would like my sister Tamar to come and give me something to eat. Let her prepare the food in my sight so I may watch her and then eat it from her hand."'"

–2 SAMUEL 13:3, 5

How horrifying that Amnon had help from a third party in exploiting his sister Tamar. Jonadab, though he didn't physically assault Tamar, shares blame with his cousin Amnon, as it was his detailed plan that led to Tamar's abuse.

Sometimes we get an incorrect idea of abusers. Like they're all socially inept creepers. But many abusers are charismatic, successful people. They can be charming and helpful, with a large circle of friends and supporters. They are highly manipulative and often use those skills to gain trust and access to their victims. We find abusers in schools, churches, community groups, businesses—everywhere. And even when victims come forward, abusers will always have people who support them.

Seems crazy, doesn't it? It's no wonder so many victims stay silent. But thank God he always knows the truth. He is not fooled by smooth talk or winsome words. And while we can continue to speak up until someone listens to us, we can also turn to God when we feel out-shouted by the supporters of abusers.

day 244

"David sent word to Tamar at the palace: 'Go to the house of your brother Amnon and prepare some food for him.' So Tamar went to the house of her brother Amnon, who was lying down. She took some dough, kneaded it, made the bread in his sight and baked it. Then she took the pan and served him the bread, but he refused to eat. 'Send everyone out of here,' Amnon said. So everyone left him."

–2 SAMUEL 13:7–9

Tamar went to her half-brother Amnon on the orders of her father, King David. How do you suppose David felt when he later discovered what had happened? It's possible he felt some measure of responsibility, even though he couldn't have possibly known what would happen.

Perhaps you've been in this position. Maybe you've discovered after the fact that a terrible situation has been occurring under your nose and you had no idea. If you've been beating yourself up over it, please free yourself from that burden now. *No one*, except the abuser, is responsible for abuse. We have all "missed things" we wish we'd seen sooner. You can be there to support your friend or family member *now* as she finds healing, and we can learn from the past to be prepared to help even more in the future. Let's place responsibility where it belongs—on those who exploit others for their own purposes.

day 245

"Then Amnon said to Tamar, 'Bring the food here into my bedroom so I may eat from your hand.' And Tamar took the bread she had prepared and brought it to her brother Amnon in his bedroom. But when she took it to him to eat, he grabbed her and said, 'Come to bed with me, my sister.'"

–2 SAMUEL 13:10–11

Tamar was trying to obey her father and serve her brother. She was trying to do the right thing. What happened to her was in no way the result of her desires or her choices. How can that be? How can our good intentions go so horribly wrong?

There's no satisfying answer to this, except to understand that we live in a broken world, marred by sin and distorted from what God originally intended. We can do everything "right" and still people may try to hurt us. Not only try, but succeed. Understand, beloved daughter of God, that this is not what God would wish for us. This is a result of mankind's brokenness.

We can take steps to arm ourselves. We can learn self-defense techniques to help us escape if we're physically threatened. We can trust our instincts. When something feels "off," it's okay to get out of that situation, even if you think you might be overreacting. We can look out for warning signs and learn to identify manipulative behavior. We can take precautions to help keep ourselves safe. But please know that the failures of these safety measures *do not* make abuse your fault.

day 246

> "'No, my brother!' she said to him. 'Don't force me! Such a thing should not be done in Israel! Don't do this wicked thing.'"
>
> –2 SAMUEL 13:12

Tamar was very clear. She used the word "no." She appealed to Amnon's morality—to his identity as her brother and child of Israel, a son of God. She even called this act out as wicked. She was crystal clear about her wishes.

Human communication is complex. Tone, nuance, and subtext are all important aspects of communication that exist outside and in between the words actually spoken. So, some ask, does "no" always mean no? Sometimes people who don't intend to become abusers do because they misinterpret some unspoken aspect of communication. They think, in that moment, that no means yes. And that's tragic for everyone involved.

This is why understanding *consent* is so important, even for those of us saving ourselves for marriage. Consent doesn't just apply to sex, but to any level of physical or emotional attention. You should always feel empowered to say no, whether that's to a boyfriend who wants to go further or to someone whose actions make you feel uncomfortable (like when someone you don't know tries to give you a hug).

day 247

"[Tamar said] 'What about me? Where could I get rid of my disgrace? And what about you? You would be like one of the wicked fools in Israel. Please speak to the king; he will not keep me from being married to you.'"

–2 SAMUEL 13:13

Tamar calls on her last resort. She asks Amnon to marry her instead of violating her. If they were married, at least she would not bear the disgrace of having been violated. She would be married to her brother (a forbidden marriage), and we can speculate she would have been miserable because Amnon was a jerk, but this seemed preferable to her.

Tamar didn't have a ton of choices. Even as the daughter of the king, her agency was limited. Agency is an important idea to understand when we're talking about sexual abuse. It's a fancy sociology word that simply means the capacity to act independently and make free choices. Someone's level of agency can be limited due to the circumstances of their birth, as was the case for Tamar. So while we may cringe to imagine offering marriage to a man about to rape us, Tamar was using her limited amount of agency the best way she knew how.

We're blessed to have the amount of agency we do in this modern era. You may not always be the most powerful person in a room, but remember that you have a God-given right to stand up for yourself.

day 248

"But he refused to listen to her, and since he was stronger than she, he raped her."

–2 SAMUEL 13:14

For all of Tamar's good efforts, this was the end result. Amnon took what he wanted. This was an event that would have a catastrophic effect on the rest of Tamar's life, but that didn't matter to Amnon.

Amnon was Tamar's brother. She should have been able to trust him. Instead, he used her in one of the worst ways imaginable. How does someone heal after such a deep violation? Is it even possible? Remember, thirty percent of young people who are abused are abused by a family member—someone they should have been able to trust. How do we heal? How can you help a friend who has been through this heal?

First, we need to understand that it can take years to heal from sexual trauma. Give yourself or your loved one the time needed, however long. Sexual trauma produces shame, and our instinct will be to hide it, deny it, ignore it. Healing begins when we acknowledge what happened, to ourselves and someone who has earned our trust. Allow yourself to grieve, to be angry, to talk to God about it. And *get help*, whether that's from law enforcement, your doctor, a pastor, a qualified counselor, your parents, a trusted friend, or all of the above. There is hope after sexual trauma. There is healing!

---

day 249

"Then Amnon hated her with intense hatred. In fact, he hated her more than he had loved her. Amnon said to her, 'Get up and get out!' 'No!' she said to him. 'Sending me away would be a greater wrong than what you have already done to me.' But he refused to listen to her."

–2 SAMUEL 13:15–16

Tamar's tragedy just gets compounded. Not only has her brother violated her, but now that he has acted on his lust, the obsession he had for Tamar has passed. He doesn't need or want her anymore, so he drives her from the house. She is utterly disgraced.

If you've been abused, maybe you can relate to Tamar's desperation in these verses. She feels like her life is over. She will never be "clean" enough to have a husband, and so if Amnon rejects her, her future is over. We live in quite a different time than Tamar did, but the emotions following sexual trauma haven't changed much.

Listen closely: violations of your body *do not* define your worth and they *do not* define your purity. When your agency is snatched from you and your body is violated, it says nothing about you and everything about your abuser. You are beloved of God, period. The end. Full stop. No one can take that identity from you. Ever. You can find safety, comfort, and empowerment in God's arms.

day 250

"Tamar put ashes on her head and tore the ornate robe she was wearing. She put her hands on her head and went away, weeping aloud as she went. Her brother Absalom said to her, 'Has that Amnon, your brother, been with you? Be quiet for now, my sister; he is your brother. Don't take this thing to heart.' And Tamar lived in her brother Absalom's house, a desolate woman."

–2 SAMUEL 13:19-20

This is the last word we get about Tamar—that she lived in her brother Absalom's house, a desolate woman. That's a very sad ending. This is not a woman who experienced negative consequences because she made bad choices. This is not a woman who experienced God's judgment because she was blasphemous or sinful. This was a woman who was a victim of someone else's sin. And, whether because of the shame she felt or simply as a byproduct of the culture she lived in, the rest of Tamar's life was affected.

You do not have to live that narrative. We have options. We have resources to help us heal following a violation—counseling, prayer support, and abuse victim groups are all examples that can be helpful. We can also seek justice from law enforcement, if we choose. We can live healthy, full lives following sexual trauma. Thank God for the gift of restoration!

_____

_____

_____

_____

day 251

> "When King David heard all this, he was furious. And Absalom never said a word to Amnon, either good or bad; he hated Amnon because he had disgraced his sister Tamar."
> —2 SAMUEL 13:21–22

There is a lot to admire about David. His psalms are beautiful, and they've spoken straight to the emotional heart of mankind for millennia. He often behaved in an exceptionally godly manner (like when he spared Saul's life, even though Saul was out to kill him). But . . . David was not a great parent. He was angry with Amnon, but he never did anything about it. He never defended Tamar or rebuked Amnon. As far as we know, he didn't seek restoration for his daughter. David sat back passively and allowed his family to devour itself.

Sometimes those who should be our advocates don't speak up for us. Worse yet, sometimes they don't believe us. If this has happened to you, you know the pain Tamar must have experienced. You know how it magnifies and compounds your trauma to have your experiences doubted, ignored, or brushed aside.

But take heart. *You* have a voice. And, remember, you have agency. You can be your own advocate and you can speak for yourself. Remember too that God knows and loves truth. He does not doubt or minimize what you've experienced. When imperfect humans behave imperfectly, remember that we have the ultimate advocate on our side.

day 252

"Here is my servant, whom I uphold, my chosen one in whom I delight; I will put my Spirit on him, and he will bring justice to the nations. He will not shout or cry out, or raise his voice in the streets. A bruised reed he will not break, and a smoldering wick he will not snuff out. In faithfulness he will bring forth justice; he will not falter or be discouraged till he establishes justice on earth. In his teaching the islands will put their hope."

–ISAIAH 42:1–4

Sometimes our earthly resources fail. Sometimes the process of healing after trauma like Tamar experienced is slow and painful and lonely. And for many people, though they eventually find healing, they bear the scars of trauma for the rest of their lives.

Read these verses again. They're from the Old Testament, but they're about Jesus. Isaiah was prophesying about the Messiah to come. Jesus is the ultimate bringer of justice. Jesus is the ultimate authority. And he holds us, his bruised reeds and smoldering wicks, close to his heart. When you feel alone, abandoned, or hurt beyond repair, know that Jesus is there, and he is gentle with you.

You're not broken. Bruised, maybe, but not broken. You're a smoldering wick, not an extinguished flame. Don't lose hope.

day 253

"When the queen of Sheba heard about the fame of Solomon and his relationship to the Lord, she came to test Solomon with hard questions. Arriving at Jerusalem with a very great caravan—with camels carrying spices, large quantities of gold, and precious stones—she came to Solomon and talked with him about all that she had on her mind."

–1 KINGS 10:1-2

David's throne eventually passed to his son Solomon. Solomon is remembered as the wisest man who ever lived. His head-knowledge was something to behold. It was so legendary, the queen of Sheba traveled from South Arabia (in present-day Yemen) to pick his brain.

The queen is another fascinating non-Israelite woman who, on some level, recognized God's special relationship with Israel. She came for Solomon's wisdom but also because she'd heard about his relationship with the Lord. Jesus spoke of the queen of Sheba. In Matthew 12:42 he says: "The Queen of the South will rise at the judgment with this generation and condemn it; for she came from the ends of the earth to listen to Solomon's wisdom, and now something greater than Solomon is here." She is an example of someone who doesn't have a relationship with God but who may be seeking him. Amazing!

Do you have any seekers in your life? Those who aren't "church people" but who seem curious about God? Nurture those relationships.

day 254

"Solomon answered all her questions; nothing was too hard for the king to explain to her."

–1 KINGS 10:3

Even today in our modern society, women are sometimes told they shouldn't seek education. Some are even told they shouldn't seek knowledge. But the Bible doesn't condemn the queen of Sheba for her curiosity. It doesn't deride her thirst for knowledge or her quest for wisdom. Nor did Solomon, it seems, because he answered all her questions.

The queen of Sheba sought knowledge like a girl boss. We can feel confident to do the same. What's one area you feel insatiably curious about? Is it math, literature, science, history, religious studies, art, childhood development, technology, music, psychology, economics . . . or something else? All of these areas, and so many more, are open to you.

Imagine there are no limits on the things you can learn about. What would you study? Well, go for it! Seek knowledge like a girl boss.

day 255

"When the queen of Sheba saw all the wisdom of Solomon and the palace he had built, the food on his table, the seating of his officials, the attending servants in their robes, his cupbearers, and the burnt offerings he made at the temple of the Lord, she was overwhelmed."

–1 KINGS 10:4–5

We don't know for sure, but we can imagine that the queen of Sheba felt pretty legit as she cruised into Israel with her caravan of camels. She was a queen, after all, and probably had the best of all that was around her down in Sheba. But when she saw Solomon's court, her perspective shifted a bit. She was overwhelmed by the splendor.

Sometimes we think we're at the top of our game, only to discover we're not. Maybe you were easily the best runner at your school, but when you went to the state championships, you realized you were swimming in a small pond before. Maybe you routinely got the highest grades in your class, so you were shocked when your SAT scores came back as "average."

These aren't pleasant surprises. But we can respond the way the queen did. She didn't throw a tantrum and stomp home, furious that she wasn't as fancy as she'd thought. She stayed and listened to Solomon's wise words. She learned from him. These moments when we realize we're not at the top of our game can be great learning experiences if we approach them with humility.

day 256

"She said to the king, 'The report I heard in my own country about your achievements and your wisdom is true. But I did not believe these things until I came and saw with my own eyes; . . . in wisdom and wealth you have far exceeded the report I heard. How happy your people must be! . . . Praise be to the LORD your God, who has delighted in you and placed you on the throne of Israel. Because of the LORD's eternal love for Israel, he has made you king to maintain justice and righteousness.'"

–1 KINGS 10:6–9

This is a lovely expression from the queen. She gives honor to God here, and by all appearances, it's genuine. But this is a little different from other professions of faith we've seen, like Ruth's. The queen honors God, but not necessarily *only* the Lord. In other words, she acknowledges God, but not to the exclusion of other gods.

It's easy to accidentally follow the queen of Sheba's path here. It's easy to make a surface acknowledgment of God without truly letting him be the number one priority in our lives.

Are you willing to let God have ultimate control of your hopes, dreams, and desires? Are you willing to let him have control of your future? These aren't easy questions! It's okay to wrestle with this. In fact, we need to make this a habit. It's too easy to let our own priorities crowd out God's sovereignty in our lives. Let's practice putting him first, always.

day 257

"And she gave the king 120 talents of gold, large quantities of spices, and precious stones. Never again were so many spices brought in as those the queen of Sheba gave to King Solomon . . . King Solomon gave the queen of Sheba all she desired and asked for, besides what he had given her out of his royal bounty. Then she left and returned with her retinue to her own country."

–1 KINGS 10:10, 13

Solomon and the queen honored each other with their exchange of gifts, just like we would see two ancient kings honor each other. At least in some respect, the queen was treated as an equal. Wealth provided social privilege, just like it does today.

Privilege is a hot-button word these days with lots of social implications. But most people would agree that those born into wealth and power have a social advantage. While we've made great strides in trying to even the playing field (think of how it would have been to be born a serf in the Middle Ages!), we probably still have work to do.

Jesus was concerned with the poor. Jesus was concerned with the vulnerable. It's right for us to be concerned for those who are socially vulnerable too. Think of some socially vulnerable groups in your area. Those who are homeless, chronically ill, disabled, economically disadvantaged, and elderly are some. What can you do to reach out to these groups and show them the love of Jesus?

_____

_____

_____

_____

day 258

"In the thirty-eighth year of Asa king of Judah, Ahab son of Omri became king of Israel, and he reigned in Samaria over Israel twenty-two years. Ahab did more evil in the eyes of the Lord than any of those before him. He not only considered it trivial to commit the sins of Jeroboam, but he also married Jezebel daughter of Ethbaal king of the Sidonians, and began to serve Baal and worship him."

–1 KINGS 16:29–31

It's quite a contrast to go from the queen of Sheba to Jezebel. First, let's fill in a bit of background. David's family was still on the throne—sort of. The kingdom of Israel was now split into two kingdoms, Israel and Judah. David's family ruled Judah and a series of different dynasties ruled Israel. Ahab was part of one of these dynasties, and Jezebel was his wife.

Jezebel is often portrayed as being sexually immoral, but idolatry is truly at the root of her wickedness. You may have seen the Laurel Thatcher Ulrich quote: "Well-behaved women seldom make history." Despite how this quote is often used today, Ulrich was actually lamenting the fact that many women who made a positive impact on society aren't recorded in history the way they ought to be.

Let's seek to make a positive impact, whether we're recorded in history for it or not!

day 259

"While Jezebel was killing off the Lord's prophets, Obadiah had taken a hundred prophets and hidden them in two caves, fifty in each, and had supplied them with food and water."

–1 KINGS 18:4

Yes, you read that right. Jezebel was specifically seeking out God's prophets in order to kill them. She was a murderer—shamelessly so. She persecuted everyone who was actually seeking to follow the Lord. She was the very definition of a wicked queen before fairy tales got ahold of the idea. So Obadiah, a high-ranking servant in Ahab's palace, hid some prophets of God in a cave to save their lives.

Hey, we've spent a lot of time covering some awesomely bold people from the Bible. There is definitely a time for boldness. There's a time to stand up, speak out, and get loud. But it's also okay to hide from evil sometimes. Whether it's our own sin crouching at the door for us or someone else looking to harm us, it's okay not to fight head-on battles with evil every day. Sometimes, we need to flee. The key is to use discernment to figure out when you should fight and when you should run. Let your wisdom, the support of other mature believers, and the leading of the Spirit help you decide which battles to pick!

day 260

"Now Ahab told Jezebel everything Elijah had done and how he had killed all the prophets with the sword. So Jezebel sent a messenger to Elijah to say, 'May the gods deal with me, be it ever so severely, if by this time tomorrow I do not make your life like that of one of them.'"

–1 KINGS 19:1–2

God has a way of bringing some of his brightest lights into the darkest circumstances. During Ahab and Jezebel's reign, Elijah, one of the greatest prophets in history, lived to minister to the kingdom of Israel. And Jezebel *hated* him.

We tend to think in oddly black-and-white terms. Like maybe we think the word "religious" automatically means good or godly. But that's not true. Jezebel was deeply, devoutly religious. She just happened to serve Baal and other false gods. That's why she was so angry with Elijah here. Elijah had won a decisive victory over Jezebel's prophets of Baal, and she was furious about it. He had threatened her religious convictions.

We need to make sure faith, not religiousness, is what's in our hearts. It's perfectly fine to have rituals and liturgical practices as an outflowing of our faith in God. But if we *only* have religious practices and not true faith, we're missing the point.

day 261

"So Ahab went home, sullen and angry because Naboth the Jezreelite had said, 'I will not give you the inheritance of my ancestors.' He lay on his bed sulking and refused to eat. His wife Jezebel came in and asked him, 'Why are you so sullen? Why won't you eat?'"

–1 KINGS 21:4–5

This is the start of one of the very worst stories we have recorded about Ahab and Jezebel. Ahab desperately wanted this particular vineyard that belonged to Naboth. Remember, in Israel land was more than just a plot of dirt. It represented Israel's covenant relationship with God. This land was an ancestral and spiritual inheritance. What Ahab was asking of Naboth was not okay! So Naboth said no, and in so doing, he'd sealed his fate.

At the root of this awful story is covetousness. Ahab wanted something that belonged to someone else, and the lengths he and Jezebel went to in order to obtain what did not belong to them were extraordinary. We need to be very careful to guard our hearts against jealousy and covetousness. We might think it's not such a huge deal because it's a heart-sin—something that happens internally and isn't immediately visible to others. But a lot of nasty things, internal and external, flow from jealousy. That's why it's listed in the Ten Commandments. Let's focus on contentment to combat the seeds of covetousness.

day 262

"Jezebel his wife said, 'Is this how you act as king over Israel? Get up and eat! Cheer up. I'll get you the vineyard of Naboth the Jezreelite.'"

–1 KINGS 21:7

In a different context, Jezebel's words might be positive and encouraging. Get up! Cheer up! You're the king! No pouting. But in this context, her words are actually terrifying. What she's saying is that, as king over Israel, nothing is off-limits for Ahab. He should cheer up, look alive, because no matter what Naboth said about his land, Jezebel was going to get that vineyard for her husband. Yikes.

It's important that we make sure our positions of power or privilege don't go to our heads. It's easy to lose perspective and get full of ourselves when we're given power. But that's such a dangerous place to be! It can lead to bad decisions that hurt other people. Ahab and Jezebel are an extreme example, of course, but it's easy to fall into the same trap in smaller ways if we're not careful.

Let's take a moment to pray for humble hearts and the desire to serve others, especially when we're put in leadership positions. With the right focus, we can be effective, godly leaders.

day 263

"So she wrote letters in Ahab's name, placed his seal on them, and sent them to the elders and nobles who lived in Naboth's city with him. In those letters she wrote: 'Proclaim a day of fasting and seat Naboth in a prominent place among the people. But seat two scoundrels opposite him and have them bring charges that he has cursed both God and the king. Then take him out and stone him to death.'"

–1 KINGS 21:8–10

The depth of Jezebel's dishonesty is astounding. She is willfully, purposely dragging a man's character through the mud. She's openly making sure he has false charges brought against him so he'll be accused of blasphemy and treason, for which the punishment is death. And why would she do this? For his vineyard. Incredible!

The desire for material possessions can blind us. It's easy to get caught up in wanting more, more, more. And when we chase after all that "stuff," sometimes our values begin to slip. Maybe we think it's okay to fudge our timesheets just a little bit if it'll help us get a down payment for our car just a little faster.

Let's keep our focus on the things that truly matter so we don't fall into this trap. What truly matters is our character, our relationship with God, how we treat other people, our inner selves—and none of these have anything to do with material wealth!

day 264

"Then two scoundrels came and sat opposite him and brought charges against Naboth before the people, saying, 'Naboth has cursed both God and the king.' So they took him outside the city and stoned him to death. Then they sent word to Jezebel: 'Naboth has been stoned to death.'"

–1 KINGS 21:13-14

Whatever else we might say about Jezebel, she certainly was crafty. Her plan worked. Naboth was executed for crimes he didn't commit, and then Jezebel was free to fulfill her husband Ahab's desire for . . . a vineyard.

We should be in the habit of doing all we can to preserve human life. Human life matters to God. That's why it's important not to turn a blind eye to the worldwide problems of war, unclean water, starvation, and poverty. We should care about the elderly, the unborn, the sick, and the disabled. We should care about people who are like us and different from us. Why? Because these lives matter to God.

When we look at all the unnecessary loss of life around the world, it can feel overwhelming. So pick *one* thing. Do you have a heart for unwanted babies? For global access to clean water? For medical missions? For elder care? Pick one area where you can help and focus on it. Show the love of God through your care of those who are often overlooked.

day 265

"Then the word of the LORD came to Elijah the Tishbite: 'Go down to meet Ahab king of Israel, who rules in Samaria. He is now in Naboth's vineyard, where he has gone to take possession of it.'"

–1 KINGS 21:17–18

Poor Elijah. Can you imagine what it was like to have his job? It seems like it would be great to hear God's voice directly—and in many ways, it would! But what about when God tells you to go hang out with the wickedest king and queen in Israel's history—two people who just had a man murdered and stole his vineyard? Yeah, that part is less great.

But remember, Elijah was Israel's bright light during this dark time. He was made for this job, made for this time, when Israel needed him. Sometimes God asks a lot of us. But when he does, we can rest easy in the knowledge that we are equipped to complete the tasks he's given to us.

Have you ever been asked to complete some Elijah-like tasks? It's okay to be afraid. It's okay to not love every second of the things God has called us to do. But then, like Elijah, we gather up our strength, let God fill in our weak spots, and rock it out. You got this!

day 266

"'And also concerning Jezebel the Lord says: "Dogs will devour Jezebel by the wall of Jezreel. Dogs will eat those belonging to Ahab who die in the city, and the birds will feed on those who die in the country."' (There was never anyone like Ahab, who sold himself to do evil in the eyes of the Lord, urged on by Jezebel his wife. He behaved in the vilest manner by going after idols, like the Amorites the Lord drove out before Israel.)"

–1 KINGS 21:23–26

Well. To say Ahab and Jezebel deserved this horrible pronouncement over their lives seems harsh . . . but it's probably true. They really were that bad. But you want to know something strange? In verse 27, Ahab hears these words and tears his clothes (usually a sign of mourning and repentance). Check out verse 29, where God speaks to Elijah: "Have you noticed how Ahab has humbled himself before me? Because he has humbled himself, I will not bring this disaster in his day, but I will bring it on his house in the days of his son."

So . . . did Ahab repent? It's not very clear. He is always mentioned as an evil king of Israel. But here we have this weird footnote to his life. Strange, but also hopeful. Because if Ahab can repent, no one is too far gone.

Do you know someone who you've written off as too far gone to come to faith in God? Take a moment to pray for them.

---

day 267

"Then Jehu went to Jezreel. When Jezebel heard about it, she put on eye makeup, arranged her hair and looked out of a window. As Jehu entered the gate, she asked, 'Have you come in peace, you Zimri, you murderer of your master?'"

–2 KINGS 9:30–31

Jezebel's sons were ruling Israel now—or they had been, until Jehu killed them in battle. Now Jehu was coming to Jezreel to take care of the princes' mother, and this is the start of their confrontation that would bring about the fulfillment of the prophecy God had made against Ahab's family. Jezebel has some nasty, barbed words for Jehu. A bit ironic, since she had primped and painted her outward appearance.

But no amount of makeup can conceal what's in our hearts. And truly, not even a show of outward holiness can cover us if what's inside is rotten. Jesus spoke of this when he addressed the Pharisees of his day. He called them white-washed tombs—painted nice and clean on the outside but rotting within.

Let's do a heart check right now. Have you been putting up a good front but inwardly concealing something dark? Maybe there's a hidden bit of bitterness, jealousy, or pride hanging out in there. If so, let's pray about it right now. Let's ask God to remove those hidden seeds of darkness from our hearts.

day 268

"He looked up at the window and called out, 'Who is on my side? Who?' Two or three eunuchs looked down at him. 'Throw her down!' Jehu said. So they threw her down, and some of her blood spattered the wall and the horses as they trampled her underfoot."

–2 KINGS 9:32-33

Oh, man. What a sad end. Jehu breezed into town and shouted up to the servants attending Jezebel, "Hey, why don't you throw her out the window?" *And they did*. At the mere suggestion from Jehu, Jezebel's own servants tossed her to her death. That's how horrible she was to them.

Again, Jezebel represents an extreme, but we can still learn a lesson from this. While we're never likely to be tempted into a life like Jezebel's, we are vulnerable to all the same heart-sins that caused Jezebel's wicked behavior. In this instance, we can imagine she treated her servants poorly and was inconsiderate of them. If we move through life inconsiderate of others, we will never earn their trust, love, or loyalty.

We don't have to be queens for this lesson to apply. The bottom line is to show other people that they matter to you—and that applies to everyone!

day 269

> "Some time later the brook dried up because there had been no rain in the land. Then the word of the LORD came to [Elijah]: 'Go at once to Zarephath in the region of Sidon and stay there. I have directed a widow there to supply you with food.'"
>
> –1 KINGS 17:7–9

We're sticking in the same time period, which you probably guessed, since the verse mentions Elijah. But we are taking a look at a different woman—one a whole lot nicer than Jezebel. Here, God is asking Elijah to go to a place outside of Israel. In fact, he's asking Elijah to go to the area ruled by a pagan king—Jezebel's father. Yikes!

We never get the widow's name. She's known only as the widow of Zarephath. She was not an Israelite, but she's quite a contrast to the princess of her people, Jezebel. Isn't it amazing how often the story of God's people includes "outsiders"?

That's not an accident, you know. Even though God did choose a specific people to be special to him and through whom he could show his plan for redemption, he has always cared about all his human creations. The widow of Zarephath is another example of that. Have you ever felt like a church "outsider"? Know that God's heart is for *you* too.

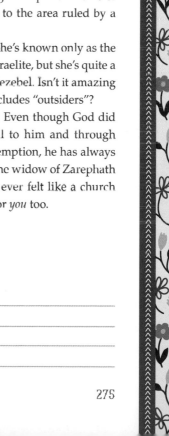

day 270

"So [Elijah] went to Zarephath. When he came to the town gate, a widow was there gathering sticks. He called to her and asked, 'Would you bring me a little water in a jar so I may have a drink?'"

–1 KINGS 17:10

Okay, so maybe we're sneaking in a couple devotions about a biblical man instead of a biblical woman. But Elijah is worth studying!

Elijah shows the kind of reliance on God that should have been characteristic of all Israel. That was the plan, after all—a theocracy where God was their ruler, communicating through his prophets. As long as they followed his law, God would always be on Israel's side. He would give them their land inheritance and protect them. And they would serve and honor him always. But it sure didn't work out that way. The people broke this agreement. They demanded an earthly king (and ended up with those like Ahab . . . ugh). They worshiped other gods. After many centuries of this, we're left with a divided Israel where faithful Elijahs are the exception, not the rule. How sad.

As followers of Jesus, let's do our best to guard against this. If Israel was susceptible to it, so are we! Let's make sure we are constantly checking in with our hearts, confirming we're in line with God's Word, Jesus's example, and the Holy Spirit's leading so we can stay on track.

day 271

> "As she was going to get it, he called, 'And bring me, please, a piece of bread.' 'As surely as the LORD your God lives,' she replied, 'I don't have any bread—only a handful of flour in a jar and a little olive oil in a jug. I am gathering a few sticks to take home and make a meal for myself and my son, that we may eat it—and die.'"
> —1 KINGS 17:11–12

At first it sounds like the widow was being a little dramatic. Almost like she was saying, "Don't mind me. I'm just going to go in this corner and die. Don't trouble yourself." But she wasn't being melodramatic. She and her son really were starving to death.

If you've always had a roof over your head and food on the table, it might be hard to imagine that kind of suffering. But it happens. It happens in developing countries, certainly, but it even happens in our own backyards. Experts estimate that forty-two million Americans struggle with hunger. That's an overwhelming number.

So what can we do to help? First, we can always approach those who are suffering with compassion rather than judgment or coldness. Second, we can demonstrate God's love by meeting physical needs. The two go hand in hand. Telling people God loves them is great. Showing them is often even more powerful!

day 272

"Elijah said to her, 'Don't be afraid. Go home and do as you have said. But first make a small loaf of bread for me from what you have and bring it to me, and then make something for yourself and your son. For this is what the LORD, the God of Israel, says: "The jar of flour will not be used up and the jug of oil will not run dry until the day the LORD sends rain on the land."'"

–1 KINGS 17:13–14

As we read Elijah's request of the widow here, there are two important things to remember. First, remember that Elijah was outside of Israel and Judah. He was in the land where Jezebel's father was king. This was not a people group who had a relationship with God. Second, the widow was literally about to starve. Essentially, Elijah was asking her to give *everything* she had to a God she probably didn't know. Wow.

Take a second to think about what that might mean if God asked you to trust in him so completely, you had to give *all*. Whether that was everything you owned or maybe simply the one thing most important to you. Could you do it? Would you be willing?

Those are tough questions. If you feel like your answer is lacking the zeal you want, you can pray for the Holy Spirit to help you grow in willingness to surrender to God's perfect will.

_____

_____

_____

_____

day 273

"She went away and did as Elijah had told her. So there was food every day for Elijah and for the woman and her family. For the jar of flour was not used up and the jug of oil did not run dry, in keeping with the word of the LORD spoken by Elijah."

–1 KINGS 17:15–16

Despite the obstacles—that this non-Israelite woman and her child were on the brink of death—the widow of Zarephath obeyed Elijah's request. God had softened her heart (see 1 Kings 17:9), and she responded to him with obedience. And do you know what happened? A miracle.

Wouldn't it be awesome if it always worked that way? Miracles do happen even if they're not as spectacular as the miracle of the widow's food. God is still in the business of doing the impossible. But, more often than not, our obedience is answered in much quieter ways. We experience God's blessings, surely, but those aren't usually physics-bending, reality-blasting miracles.

And that's okay. The point of obedience is that we humble ourselves before God and submit to his will, not that we expect a flashy return for our trouble. In fact, Jesus often rebuked the crowds who followed him because they expected flashy miracles but didn't have any real faith behind those expectations. They just wanted a good show. Let's work to submit to God and believe his promises without expecting a "good show" in return.

day 274

"Then the woman said to Elijah, 'Now I know that you are a man of God and that the word of the Lord from your mouth is the truth.'"

–1 KINGS 17:24

The widow's profession is simple but so beautiful. Her culture didn't worship God. But, because of her softened heart, she was able to see that it was through the power of Elijah's God that this miracle had occurred. Not only did she acknowledge it in her mind and heart, she spoke it aloud. So cool!

She's a great example for us. It's easy to forget to point back to God after he has helped us through a tough situation. When we're in crisis, prayer and crying out to God come as naturally as breathing. But when the moment of danger or distress passes, sometimes God slips to the back of our minds.

Let's not forget to acknowledge God when he helps us through tight spots. Our open confession of God's goodness and provision can serve as a strong statement to others who might not know God yet and as a reminder for those who do.

day 275

"The wife of a man from the company of the prophets cried out to Elisha, 'Your servant my husband is dead, and you know that he revered the LORD. But now his creditor is coming to take my two boys as his slaves.'"

–2 KINGS 4:1

Here we have another woman who is unnamed, known simply as "the widow of a prophet" to us. You may have noticed (or not) that we're now dealing with Elisha the prophet instead of Elijah. Elijah mentored young Elisha, and Elisha took over his ministry after Elijah ascended to heaven. Elisha may not be as famous, but he performed twice the number of miracles as his mentor.

Maybe that's why the prophet's widow came to this man of God. She was totally desperate. King Jehoram, Ahab and Jezebel's son, was on the throne. He encouraged Baal worship like his mother had done. The prophet's wife would have been in a precarious situation even with her husband alive, but now that he was dead, she was facing total destitution and the loss of her remaining family. But she was not ashamed to cry out to God and God's representative, the prophet Elisha.

It's okay to ask for help when we feel overwhelmed. It doesn't mean we don't have faith. In fact, it means the opposite. When we're facing an overwhelming situation, crying out for help shows that we believe in God's ability to answer those cries!

day 276

"Elisha replied to her, 'How can I help you? Tell me, what do you have in your house?' 'Your servant has nothing there at all,' she said, 'except a small jar of olive oil.'"

–2 KINGS 4:2

Elisha's response here is perfect. The prophet's widow was in severe distress. Because of her husband's debts, her sons were about to be taken away and turned into slaves. Now, we might ask some hard questions of the husband's debtors. Like, why were they taking away this widow's sons, her only means of support? Why were they enslaving fellow Israelites? But we might also be inclined to ask hard questions of the widow. Why was her husband in debt? Did he not manage his money wisely? Didn't he save up, the way he was supposed to?

But Elisha didn't ask those questions of the widow. He didn't blame her—or her husband, who was a prophet of God—for their tough situation. Instead, he said four of the most important words we can offer to someone in distress: "How can I help?"

Even when we mean well, sometimes an overblown sense of "justice" can prompt us to blame people who find themselves in hard circumstances. And it's true that bad choices *can* lead to hard times. But that's not always the case. And the most compassionate words we can offer are those that seek to help, not place blame.

_____

_____

_____

_____

day 277

"Elisha said, 'Go around and ask all your neighbors for empty jars. Don't ask for just a few . . . Pour oil into all the jars, and as each is filled, put it to one side.' . . . They brought the jars to her and she kept pouring. When all the jars were full . . . the oil stopped flowing. She went and told the man of God, and he said, 'Go, sell the oil and pay your debts. You and your sons can live on what is left.'"

–2 KINGS 4:3–7

Elisha responded to the widow with compassionate, practical help. And God responded with a miracle. She had enough oil to take care of all her husband's debts. Her sons got to stay with her, *and* they had money to live off.

Stories like this remind us of God's power and provision. We need to make sure we're keeping a balanced perspective on such miracles, though. There isn't a magical prayer you can say to ensure God will respond in miraculous ways. There is no formula that guarantees wealth, success, or health.

But, God is an abundant provider. He always gives us what we *need*. In this case, the widow needed a miracle, and God's response was perfect for the situation. Sometimes, what we need, for whatever reason, is the bare minimum. God's response is perfect in that situation too. It's not always easy to surrender to God's plan. But when we realize he is always acting in our best interests, it becomes easier to embrace his plan with joy.

day 278

"One day Elisha went to Shunem. And a well-to-do woman was there, who urged him to stay for a meal. So whenever he came by, he stopped there to eat. She said to her husband, 'I know that this man who often comes our way is a holy man of God. Let's make a small room on the roof and put in it a bed and a table, a chair and a lamp for him. Then he can stay there whenever he comes to us.'"

–2 KINGS 4:8–10

It's interesting that, as Elisha traveled around and ministered, he seemed to interact with women as much or more often than he interacted with men. Here we have a wealthy woman from Shunem, a town in the tribe of Issachar, close to the middle of the kingdom of Israel.

We don't know her name, but she's sometimes called "the Shunamite woman who was hospitable to Elisha." At least she is remembered for one of her virtues! Providing hospitality and contributing to the needs of those in the church, especially those in ministry, is something Paul encouraged the early church to do (Romans 12:13). And we can see that hospitality was vitally important in 2 Kings and throughout the Old Testament (see Job 31:32, Leviticus 19:33–34, for example).

We show hospitality to others because it's an outward expression of God's care and God's grace. Hospitality and caring for the needs of others reflect God's heart of love, compassion, and self-sacrifice.

day 279

> "Elisha said to [Gehazi], 'Tell her, "You have gone to all this trouble for us. Now what can be done for you?"' Gehazi said, 'She has no son, and her husband is old.'... So he called her, and she stood in the doorway. 'About this time next year,' Elisha said, 'you will hold a son in your arms.' 'No, my lord!' she objected. 'Please, man of God, don't mislead your servant!'"
>
> –2 KINGS 4:13A, 14B, 15–16

The Shunamite woman's hospitality would be admirable under any circumstances, but it's especially cool when you consider her whole story. While she was a wealthy woman, she had some unfulfilled desires in her life. She had material wealth, but she'd never had children. Not only was being a mother important in her culture, it seems to have been personally important to her.

But that didn't stop her from blessing other people. That didn't stop her from providing for the prophet. Sometimes it's hard to get into a "giving" state of mind when we don't have everything we want in life. Maybe we fixate on our own desires rather than focusing on the needs of others. Maybe we feel angry, hurt, or bitter that God hasn't responded to our wants the way we'd like.

The Shunamite woman is a great example to help us combat those attitudes! She gave without expectation, without ulterior motive. She gave even though she still had unfulfilled desires of her own. Let's try to approach life with the same generosity she did.

day 280

"'About this time next year,' Elisha said, 'you will hold a son in your arms.' 'No, my lord!' she objected. 'Please, man of God, don't mislead your servant!' But the woman became pregnant, and the next year about that same time she gave birth to a son, just as Elisha had told her."

–2 KINGS 4:16–17

The Shunamite woman was afraid to hope for a child anymore. She had resigned herself to having this dream go unrealized. She didn't dare to believe it might still be possible, and that's why she cried out "No!" when Elisha promised a baby to her. It wasn't that she didn't want a baby. It's that she wanted a baby so badly, she couldn't bear to get her hopes up and have them crushed. Again.

But praise God! The prophet's words were true, and God blessed the Shunamite and her husband with a precious baby boy. She must have been so surprised and delighted. After all these years—after she'd given up on the idea—here was a little son of her own.

God surprises us sometimes, doesn't he? Events we thought were impossible come to pass. Relationships we thought were lost causes are restored. Things we said we'd *never* do become the desires of our heart.

God delights in surprising us. He delights in performing the impossible. Let's believe him when he says he is able to do all things!

day 261

"The child grew, and one day he went out to his father . . . [and] said . . . 'My head! My head!' His father told a servant, 'Carry him to his mother.' After the servant had lifted him up and carried him to his mother, the boy sat on her lap until noon, and then he died."

—2 KINGS 4:18–20

There's no way around it. This part of the story is like a punch in the heart. Our Shunamite woman was doing pretty well before Elisha's prophecy. She didn't have children, true, but it didn't stop her from living joyfully and generously. Then Elisha came into her life, and suddenly, her world turned upside down. She became a mother . . . only to tragically lose her child.

How could this be? How could God give her a child, then allow the boy to be taken away so suddenly? Those are tough questions. In the Shunamite's case, we know God wasn't finished with this family yet. This isn't the end of the story.

What about when we're in the thick of a horrible situation like this ourselves? Sometimes it helps to remember that, in God's perfectly created world, tragedies didn't happen. It's not part of God's original design. And even while we're suffering, our stories aren't over yet, either. God is still moving in our lives. He doesn't always take away the trials, but he does see us through them as we learn to rely on him moment by moment.

day 262

"She called her husband and said, 'Please send me one of the servants and a donkey so I can go to the man of God quickly and return.'"

–2 KINGS 4:22

The Shunamite was a faithful woman of God. She didn't allow her childlessness to cause bitterness in her heart. We can speculate she was pretty good at submitting to God's will for her life, even when it was difficult.

Sometimes, when we think about submitting to God, we might picture a very passive, meek person, allowing her life to happen to her. And maybe there is a time for that—a time when it's right to step back, stand down, and remain still. But submission doesn't always have to look like that. The Shunamite shows us a different kind of godliness—the kind that says, "Yes, Lord, your will be done. But until you tell me otherwise, I'm going to fight for my heart's desire." In this case, the Shunamite's desire was for her precious miracle son. And she had the faith to believe Elisha could help her save the boy. So off she went to see him immediately.

We can be like the Shunamite woman. We can be open to God's will, ready to submit to his clear leading, but still fight for the good and the lovely—those things are worth fighting for.

day 283

> "When she reached the man of God [Elisha] at the mountain, she took hold of his feet. Gehazi came over to push her away, but the man of God said, 'Leave her alone! She is in bitter distress, but the Lord has hidden it from me and has not told me why.' 'Did I ask you for a son, my lord?' she said. 'Didn't I tell you, "Don't raise my hopes"?'"
>
> –2 KINGS 4:27–28

The Shunamite's distress is heartbreaking. She had accepted her life without children, and so she didn't dare to ask Elisha for one—even when he asked her how he could bless her! And now she had experienced deep, true love, followed by the deep pain we feel when we lose someone close to us. She doesn't say it exactly, but we might guess she wouldn't agree that it's better to love and have lost than to never have loved at all.

Love is risky. When we open our hearts to someone, we risk the pain of losing them. We risk the pain of the relationship falling apart or that person abandoning us in some way. And we risk losing them from this earth.

But God says do it anyway. God says to love deeply—not just those who we have chosen to be close to but *everyone*. Our family and friends. Our neighbors. Even our enemies. It's a tall order for some very small humans, but we shoot for that ideal because God has shown us how through Jesus. God was willing to love big, risk big, and lose big, all for our sakes.

day 284

"When Elisha reached the house, there was the boy lying dead on his couch. He went in, shut the door on the two of them and prayed to the Lord ... As he stretched himself out on him, the boy's body grew warm ... [The boy's mother] came in, fell at his feet and bowed to the ground. Then she took her son and went out."

–2 KINGS 4:32–33, 34B, 37

Ah, here's the happy end of the story. Thank goodness! Through the power of Elisha's prayer to God, God's big-picture plan for the boy came full circle. Though the circumstances were distressing for a time, God brought himself glory by allowing the boy to die, then raising him back to life in response to the prophet's prayer. What a display of God's power and ability to heal.

It's not always easy to accept that we go through trials for God's glory. It seems unfair, from our human perspective, especially when our suffering doesn't have the kind of happy, miraculous end the Shunamite got. But suffering can serve as such an important catalyst in our spiritual growth. It stretches our dependence on God, our trust in him, and our belief in his goodness. These things aren't *fun*, surely, but they are *good*.

What's the toughest situation you've been through in the last year? Have you been able to get enough distance from it to see the good God brought about through that tough situation? If you're not there yet, that's okay. You can continue to seek perspective and ask God to heal the wounds you've experienced.

----

day 285

"Ahaziah was twenty-two years old when he became king, and he reigned in Jerusalem one year. His mother's name was Athaliah, a granddaughter of Omri king of Israel. He followed the ways of the house of Ahab and did evil in the eyes of the LORD, as the house of Ahab had done, for he was related by marriage to Ahab's family."

–2 KINGS 8:26–27

We've spent most of our time focused on godly women of the Bible. But every once in a while, we get a Jezebel, whose only purpose in the Word is to show us what *not* to do. Athaliah, like her relative Jezebel, is another one of those women. She was part of Ahab's legacy of evil.

That's a horrible phrase, when you think about it. A legacy of evil. A wickedness and godlessness passed down from generation to generation until the only thing that can be said about your family's mark on history is that it was evil. Yikes.

We can be almost certain that's *not* the legacy we're living right now. But if we're not living a legacy of evil, what kind of legacy are we living? Is it one of godliness, or is it . . . neutral? Think about the mark you're leaving on the world. What good things can you do to make that mark a godly one?

day 286

"When Athaliah the mother of Ahaziah saw that her son was dead, she proceeded to destroy the whole royal family."

–2 KINGS 11:1

At the root of Jezebel's wickedness was her deeply religious idolatry. At the root of Athaliah's wickedness was her thirst for power. Her son had been king, but when he died, she decided she ought to become queen regnant. In order for that to happen, all the heirs to the throne had to be destroyed. So she killed the remnant of her own dynasty, including her grandsons, making sure no one stood ahead of her in line for the throne.

Athaliah was a brutally wicked woman. But the desire for power can even cause otherwise decent people to do some terrible things. Ever watched the way many candidates behave during important elections? Or seen news headlines about businesspeople caught in illegal activity as they sought to build their powerful, successful empires?

Power itself isn't evil. And the drive to be successful isn't bad. But when the thirst for power drowns out all else and makes your moral center wobbly, it's time to reevaluate. Girl boss ambition means behaving ethically while working hard for your dreams. Don't let your drive make you forget who God created you to be!

day 287

> "But Jehosheba, the daughter of King Jehoram and sister of Ahaziah, took Joash son of Ahaziah and stole him away from among the royal princes, who were about to be murdered. She put him and his nurse in a bedroom to hide him from Athaliah; so he was not killed. He remained hidden with his nurse at the temple of the LORD for six years while Athaliah ruled the land."

> –2 KINGS 11:2–3

And speaking of girl bosses, we have a bright light in the midst of Athaliah's dark time. Her name was Jehosheba, and she shows us how compassion and love are strengths. Jehosheba was the daughter of Athaliah's husband, though she may have had a different mother. Joash, Athaliah's grandson, was Jehosheba's nephew. Confused yet? The main thing to understand is that Jehosheba defied a powerful family member to save a very vulnerable one—Joash.

Jehosheba shows us how risky, powerful, and strong love can be. If Athaliah had discovered what Jehosheba had done, Jehosheba would have likely been executed. But Jehosheba was willing to risk it to save a life.

Sometimes, facing the evil of this world can be overwhelming. Where do we even begin to help? We can follow Jehosheba's example and pick *one thing*. One person, one cause, one ministry, and start there. You'd be surprised how great an impact you can have when you focus your efforts!

day 288

"In the seventh year Jehoiada [the priest] sent for the commanders of units of a hundred . . . and had them brought to him at the temple of the Lord. He made a covenant with them and put them under oath at the temple of the Lord. Then he showed them the king's son."

—2 KINGS 11:4

Jehoiada was Jehosheba's husband. Her marriage to this man of God, the priest, may explain why Jehosheba stayed on a good, godly path instead of following in the footsteps of her family members, like Athaliah and Jezebel. Together, she and Jehoiada made a great team.

Jehoiada seemed to have a godly influence on lots of people in his life. When the rescued prince, Joash, became king, he followed the commandments of God as long as Jehoiada was alive. Once the priest died, things went south for Joash, but while his mentor lived, he stayed on the right path.

Jehoiada and Jehosheba show us the importance of godly influences in our lives. We're bombarded with worldly influences all the time through media, politics, and celebrity culture. We need those strong, godly influences in our lives to counteract the negative ones. Who are your godly influences? Parents, pastors, teachers, mentors, leaders, and even your friends can help encourage you in your relationship with God and keep you on the right path. Thank God for these strong voices of truth in our lives!

---

day 289

"Jehoiada brought out the king's son and put the crown on him; he presented him with a copy of the covenant and proclaimed him king. They anointed him, and the people clapped their hands and shouted, 'Long live the king!'"

–2 KINGS 11:12

With Jehoiada's help, little Joash had reclaimed what rightly belonged to him—the throne of Judah, which God had promised to David's line. Athaliah's power-grab lasted for six years, but in the end, God's will would not be thwarted.

Sometimes, we might look around at our world and wonder where God is. We might question whether cultural shifts, certain world leaders, or even natural disasters are part of God's big-picture plan. We can be assured that many, many things happen in this world that God is not okay with. But we can also rest secure in the knowledge that God's plan can't be sidestepped. His ultimate will for the world he created *will* be accomplished, no matter the power-grabs people might make.

It's hard to reconcile those two truths sometimes. We don't always understand why God delays in bringing about justice. In fact, we usually don't understand. But we don't need to understand the details to believe the truth: God always brings about his will in the end, and his will is perfect.

day 290

"When Athaliah heard the noise made by the guards and the people, she went to the people at the temple of the Lᴏʀᴅ. She looked and there was the king, standing by the pillar, as the custom was. The officers and the trumpeters were beside the king, and all the people of the land were rejoicing and blowing trumpets. Then Athaliah tore her robes and called out, 'Treason! Treason!'"

–2 KINGS 11:13–14

This is so ironic, it almost hurts. Athaliah, the woman who had made an unlawful claim to the throne after executing the royal family, was shouting "Treason!" Really, lady? Look in the mirror much?

Even though this example is extreme and easy to scoff at, we're all in danger of the same issue Athaliah was experiencing here. She was so deeply selfish, her view of reality had been distorted. She probably didn't even realize the irony of her claims of treason. She thought she was entitled to the throne, so she grabbed it, and now that a true heir had been discovered, it probably *felt* very much like treason to her.

Our selfishness can blind us sometimes too. When we're focused on only *our* needs, it's easy to become hypocrites without realizing it. It's easy to forget about our own failures while nitpicking others' faults. Let's turn our hearts back toward God and his ideal of sacrificial love to combat our tendency toward selfishness.

day 291

"Jehoiada the priest ordered the commanders of units of a hundred . . . 'Bring her out between the ranks and put to the sword anyone who follows her.' For the priest had said, 'She must not be put to death in the temple of the LORD.' So they seized her as she reached the place where the horses enter the palace grounds, and there she was put to death."

–2 KINGS 11:15–16

Have you ever heard the saying "Live by the sword, die by the sword?" It could almost be misread as a mantra—like an ancient version of "ride or die." It's most definitely not. In fact, it was a warning from Jesus, found in Matthew 26:52, and the NIV translates it like this: "'Put your sword back in its place,' Jesus said to him, 'for all who draw the sword will die by the sword.'"

Athaliah was a perfect example of the consequences of living by the sword. She had committed an unspeakably horrible act against the children of her family. And here, she met her own brutal end. Violence begets violence.

A case can certainly be made for "righteous violence," and theologians have been discussing Just War Theory for centuries. But in the New Testament, it's clear that Jesus set forth an ideal for his followers that values, under most circumstances, peace and gentleness. He commands us not to live by the sword but to show love to others.

day 292

"His daughter was Sheerah, who built Lower and Upper Beth Horon as well as Uzzen Sheerah."

–1 CHRONICLES 7:24

Did you even know there was a person named Sheerah mentioned in the Bible? It wouldn't be surprising if you didn't. She's only mentioned in this one verse! But it's a pretty cool verse, isn't it? She was Sheerah, the city-builder. Cool!

We know female city-builders weren't the norm in Sheerah's day, which is why Sheerah is so notable. But this one verse about her shows us that throughout history, women have been defying expectations. We don't know what else is true of Sheerah, since we only get this one snippet about her. She may have also been a wife, mother, and homemaker, like many of the women of her day. Or she may have only been a builder. But, either way, she was definitely a bit outside the norm!

It's important that we do the work God has equipped us for, not necessarily what our culture expects of us. Culture shifts. Expectations change. But God doesn't. When he gifts you for a certain kind of work or calls you to a certain thing, following through on that gifting or calling is always the right choice. Have you ever defied the norm? You're in good company!

day 293

"Hilkiah and those the king had sent with him went to speak to the prophet Huldah, who was the wife of Shallum son of Tokhath, the son of Hasrah, keeper of the wardrobe. She lived in Jerusalem, in the New Quarter."

–2 CHRONICLES 34:22

We've already seen female prophets Miriam and Deborah, and now we meet Huldah. There are plenty of examples of kick-butt women of God who are explicitly described as being prophets. Some were married, like Huldah and Deborah. Another was a widow (Anna, who we'll get to later). And some, like Phillip's daughters, were young, unmarried women.

Maybe this is a truth so obvious, it doesn't need stating. But maybe not, so let's spell it out anyway. Whatever else God calls you to in your life—marriage, motherhood, career—you are not disqualified from ministry. God can and will use you, if you're willing. We're not all prophets, but we are all useful.

If you could pick one area of ministry for your life, what would it be? There are so many areas of need, so many places to serve, God can use every willing pair of hands to help build his kingdom!

day 294

"She said to them, 'This is what the LORD, the God of Israel, says.'"
–2 CHRONICLES 34:23A

Wait. Huldah spoke words directly from God to the people? Just like a male prophet? Yes! That's what a prophet is, of course. She spoke the very words of God directly to those God wanted to speak to. Just in case you needed more proof that women can be used by God in powerful ways.

Too often, we discount ourselves from powerful ministry. Denominations vary as to what level of leadership women are allowed to hold in their churches. That's the prerogative of each denomination to figure out what they believe the Bible says about this. But even if you are a member of a denomination that doesn't allow women into leadership roles, you can still *minister* in powerful ways.

Too often, we think the word *ministry* means *pastoring*. And that is one way it can be used. But teachers also minister. Mentors minister. Those who serve behind the scenes minister. Those who speak the good news of the gospel wherever they go minister, even though they're not speaking from behind a pulpit. God has prepared ministry opportunities for *you*, using your talents and gifts. Will you take him up on that offer?

day 295

> "On the seventh day, when King Xerxes was in high spirits from wine, he commanded the seven eunuchs who served him . . . to bring before him Queen Vashti, wearing her royal crown, in order to display her beauty to the people and nobles, for she was lovely to look at."
>
> –ESTHER 1:10–11

We've skipped ahead in time, and now the kingdom of Judah is under the rule of the Persians. Xerxes was a Persian king, and Vashti was his wife.

Vashti is often depicted negatively because she wouldn't obey her husband's summons. But let's take a second to consider what was being asked of her here. The king and his friends had been drinking. A lot. Xerxes's sole purpose for calling Vashti into the party was to "display her beauty" to his friends. The cultural context here is important. Women generally lived in seclusion. In his drunken state, Xerxes was breaching cultural protocol to ask Vashti to appear before these men. This was some serious, degrading objectification for the Persian queen.

It's really easy to make snap judgments about others, especially when we don't have the whole story. Let's try reading through Vashti's narrative with a more sympathetic bent to see what we discover about her—and maybe ourselves—in the process.

day 296

"But when the attendants delivered the king's command, Queen Vashti refused to come. Then the king became furious and burned with anger."

–ESTHER 1:12

Here we find Vashti's refusal to comply and Xerxes's rather hysterical response. We'll see his anger snowball out of control to the point that he elevates this incident to a matter of state. Yikes! Governing empires while intoxicated at parties is dangerous business . . .

Vashti is actually a good example for us here. Remember when we talked about the word *agency*—the ability to make free choices? Well, Vashti was exercising her agency. Chances are she knew she'd face harsh consequences. But she freely chose those consequences rather than lowering herself to Xerxes's demeaning command.

Don't ever feel too scared to exercise your agency to remove yourself from (or avoid altogether!) situations that are unsafe or toxic. To put it in more modern terms, Vashti is a great example of standing up to peer pressure.

----

day 297

"'According to law, what must be done to Queen Vashti?' he asked. 'She has not obeyed the command of King Xerxes that the eunuchs have taken to her.'"

–ESTHER 1:15

This might be a little difficult for those of us who live in free societies to wrap our minds around. It didn't matter that Vashti was exercising agency she should have had over her own body. It didn't matter if Xerxes was right to command the queen to go against social custom and appear before the party guests. It only mattered that he *commanded* it, and she was expected to *obey*.

What a terrible thing it is to be caught between obedience and correctness. Vashti was correct not to lower herself. But was she also correct to disobey? Is it ever correct to disobey? Clearly Xerxes and his advisers didn't think so. But what about us?

Obviously, it's never right to disobey God. And we have to use his standard of right and wrong to decide what's correct and what earthly authorities should be obeyed. We should obey our government's laws, unless those laws go against God's laws. We should obey our parents, unless they're asking us to do something unsafe or something God would disapprove of. Those are difficult stands to take. But doing what's right is always better than blind obedience.

day 298

"Then Memukan replied in the presence of the king and the nobles, 'Queen Vashti has done wrong, not only against the king but also against all the nobles and the peoples of all the provinces of King Xerxes. For the queen's conduct will become known to all the women, and so they will despise their husbands ... This very day the Persian and Median women of the nobility who have heard about the queen's conduct will respond to all the king's nobles in the same way. There will be no end of disrespect and discord.'"

–ESTHER 1:16–18

Xerxes and his nobles enlarged this incident until it became cause for national concern. But Vashti had done something that threatened the king's control.

Have you ever felt that kind of heat? We're not likely to cross paths with too many kings, but maybe you've accidentally encroached on the social territory of the most popular person at school. Or maybe you've questioned a teacher in front of the whole class. When those who are in "power" are insecure in some way, it's easy to threaten their sense of control—even when we don't mean to!

Isn't it cool that our ultimate Authority is never threatened by mere words? Isn't it great that we serve a God who isn't insecure and in need of unhealthy control? Let's thank him for being amazing and for giving us wisdom to navigate our earthly authority figures, who are decidedly less perfect.

day 299

"Therefore, if it pleases the king, let him issue a royal decree and let it be written in the laws of Persia and Media, which cannot be repealed, that Vashti is never again to enter the presence of King Xerxes. Also let the king give her royal position to someone else who is better than she."

–ESTHER 1:19

Ouch. Deposed from her position as queen? Banished from the king's presence forever? And the final parting shot—they will start looking for a queen who is "better than she." Double ouch.

If anyone knew what it felt like to be rejected, Vashti sure did. We can hope she had supporters around her who let her know she was loved and valued by them, even if Xerxes had cast her aside. Sadly, as a Persian queen, she probably didn't know the God of the Jewish people. And that's a shame. Because when all our earthly relationships fail, when we feel rejected by everyone on Earth, God is *always* there.

God's presence in our lives doesn't depend on how awesome we feel from one day to the next. His presence is guaranteed, no matter what. He has deemed us "worthy" and "accepted" through the blood of Jesus. There is no surer, stronger foundation upon which to rest when we feel rejected by others.

day 300

"Then when the king's edict is proclaimed throughout all his vast realm, all the women will respect their husbands, from the least to the greatest."

–ESTHER 1:20

Hmm. This is an interesting statement. The nobles thought once they made an example of Vashti, wives all over the empire would "respect" their husbands. But . . . was what Vashti did truly disrespectful? If a woman cowers in fear from her husband, is that truly respect?

This verse seems to show us that the nobles had a bit of a misunderstanding about what respect is. Respect is esteem or honor. We can respect someone, even when we disagree with them. We can honor someone, even if we don't bow to their every request or cave to their every whim. Vashti probably did respect Xerxes, but she did not wish to dishonor and expose herself for the sake of that respect. Xerxes wanted unquestioning obedience.

Have you ever been in a situation where you had to defy someone you respect? It's not an easy position to be in. Remember, you can show honor to someone, even while disagreeing with them. This takes some practice, but it's a very worthy life skill to acquire.

day 301

"Later when King Xerxes' fury had subsided, he remembered Vashti and what she had done and what he had decreed about her. Then the king's personal attendants proposed, 'Let a search be made for beautiful young virgins for the king . . . Then let the young woman who pleases the king be queen instead of Vashti.'"

–ESTHER 2:1–2, 4

So, at some point, Xerxes calmed down, sobered up, and realized he probably needed a new queen. Apparently, the obvious solution was to round up all the beautiful young women nearby and parade them before the king so he could select his favorite and crown her queen.

This is troublesome. While we should avoid judging the hearts of anyone who viewed life through a totally different cultural lens than we do, it's also important to examine incidents like this to figure out what God's view on the matter is.

The way the young women in Xerxes's kingdom were being treated here reflects shallow values—namely that beauty is the first consideration of a woman's worth. There's a lack of agency for these young ladies, too, as you'll see there's no mention of the ladies' wishes or desires, only Xerxes's needs and implied obedience on the part of the women. We're lucky to live in a time when we can reject both these notions. We can value ourselves beyond our physical appearance, as God does, and we are free to embrace our agency.

day 302

> "Now there was in the citadel of Susa a Jew ... named Mordecai ... who had been carried into exile from Jerusalem by Nebuchadnezzar king of Babylon. Mordecai had a cousin named Hadassah, whom he had brought up because she had neither father nor mother. This young woman, who was also known as Esther, had a lovely figure and was beautiful. Mordecai had taken her as his own daughter when her father and mother died."
>
> –ESTHER 2:5–7

It was not uncommon for the Jews taken into exile to adopt Babylonian (the prophet we know as Daniel was also called Belteshazzar, for example) or Persian names. So the woman we know as Esther, was probably called Hadassah by her family, since that was her Jewish name.

Names were significant in the Bible. They often had multiple meanings or were chosen to reflect important events in a person's life or surrounding their birth or conception. So is there any takeaway for us in the fact that God's people often took on names of the culture around them?

While we have to be careful not to become entirely indistinguishable from the culture around us, it seems God's people tended to adopt some of the culture they lived in. Maybe you've heard the old saying "In the world, but not of the world," and that applies here. Being God's people doesn't mean we have to cut ourselves off from the world around us. We don't belong to the world (John 17:16), but we do live in it and we are sent into it to share the light of Jesus.

day 303

"When the king's order and edict had been proclaimed, many young women were brought to the citadel of Susa . . . Esther also was taken to the king's palace and entrusted to Hegai, who had charge of the harem. She pleased him and won his favor. Immediately he provided her with her beauty treatments and special food. He assigned to her seven female attendants selected from the king's palace and moved her and her attendants into the best place in the harem."

–ESTHER 2:8–9

Esther had no choice in whether or not she came before the king. She had no choice as to whether or not she would become queen. And she was living far away from her true home under the rule of an empire not very sympathetic to the Jewish people.

But still she seemed to win people over wherever she went. Was she particularly wise, kind, sweet, funny, passionate, insightful? It could have been any or all of the above. But whatever it was that drew people to Esther, she allowed that to shine through, rather than letting her difficult circumstances overwhelm her.

When was the last time you found yourself in a miserable situation? While we won't find ourselves facing Esther's exact battle, we can follow her example by letting our unique personalities shine, even in our most troublesome times. Not only can we win others over, like Esther did, we can make the situation more bearable for ourselves by maintaining a positive attitude.

day 304

"Esther had not revealed her nationality and family background, because Mordecai had forbidden her to do so."

–ESTHER 2:10

We've seen examples of shockingly, awesomely bold women in the Bible—those ladies who faced immeasurable danger and stood up for what was right, what was godly, and what really mattered. But then we have Esther, who hid the fact that she was Jewish. And yet, she's still a godly role model for us. How is that possible?

There's a time for boldness, surely. But there's also a time for caution. Caution doesn't mean we deny our relationship with God. Esther didn't do that—she just didn't volunteer information that wasn't asked of her. Caution means waiting until the opportune moment to reveal the whole truth, as we'll see Esther do later.

What are some examples of times for caution? Well, maybe you make a new friend who has had bad experiences with Christians in the past. In that situation, it might make the most sense to hold back your relationship with Jesus for a while until this new friend gets to know you and sees you're a genuine person who cares about them and doesn't want to hurt them. It's important to use our discernment and wisdom to decide when to be bold and when to hold back.

day 305

"Before a young woman's turn came to go in to King Xerxes, she had to complete twelve months of beauty treatments . . . Anything she wanted was given her to take with her from the harem to the king's palace. In the evening she would go [to the king] and in the morning return to another part of the harem [with the concubines]. She would not return to the king unless he was pleased with her and summoned her by name."

–ESTHER 2:12-14

The Bible doesn't say it outright, but the obvious implication is that each of the women brought before Xerxes was intimate with him before they were removed to the harem. Esther's "choice" in this situation was likely submit or die.

What a tough position for Esther. And yet God was working through these difficult circumstances. When we read stories like this as modern women, we're understandably troubled. But is it just that millennia have passed and times have changed? Is that why this bothers us?

No, it's because this is opposite of the way God designed marriage and sex. God's original design, far older than Xerxes's empire, was for one man and woman to be joined together in lifelong marriage, *then* for a sexual relationship to take place. Xerxes's model was the exact opposite of this. Culture comes into play, sure, but let's remember to return to God's Word when processing what any culture says about marriage and sex.

day 306

"Now the king was attracted to Esther more than to any of the other women, and she won his favor and approval more than any of the other virgins. So he set a royal crown on her head and made her queen instead of Vashti."

–ESTHER 2:17

We can only guess what it might have been like for the women who waited to be called to Xerxes and those who had been called and were promptly shuttled over to the harem with the other concubines. Did they have much contact with each other? Did they get along? Or was it a den of backstabbing and cattiness, as they each competed for the affection of the same king?

This is an extreme situation, but competition among friends is still a very present reality for us today. If you've ever been up against a friend or acquaintance for the last spot on the team, a part in the school play, a coveted after-school job, a scholarship, or any other prize, you understand what this feels like—and how it can easily destroy friendships.

Competition is a difficult balancing act. We must be careful to value other people's feelings and not sacrifice relationships for our ambitions. At the same time, any friend asking you to display less than the full potential of your awesomeness is only looking out for herself. So let's be careful to compete with kindness in our hearts while being careful not to dull our sparkle.

day 307

"When Mordecai learned of all that had been done, he tore his clothes, put on sackcloth and ashes, and went out into the city, wailing loudly and bitterly. But he went only as far as the king's gate, because no one clothed in sackcloth was allowed to enter it. In every province to which the edict and order of the king came, there was great mourning among the Jews, with fasting, weeping and wailing. Many lay in sackcloth and ashes."

–ESTHER 4:1–3

If you haven't read Esther, do it! It's ten short chapters, and it's quite the rollercoaster. Here, Mordecai was mourning because one of Xerxes's close advisors had hatched a plot to destroy the Jews because of a personal grudge against Mordecai.

This isn't the first and it wouldn't be the last time God's people would have a target on their backs. Even now, Jesus's church often experiences a double standard of judgment and ridicule in the most accepting cultures and horrible persecution and martyrdom in those cultures and political climates where Christianity is not tolerated. The world will always seek to destroy God's followers.

But it's important that we don't become victims. Jesus warned us to expect persecution and opposition (John 15:20–27). Part of following him is accepting this burden with grace—even when it feels impossible!

day 308

"Mordecai told [Hathak] everything that had happened to him, including the exact amount of money Haman had promised to pay into the royal treasury for the destruction of the Jews. He also gave him a copy of the text of the edict for their annihilation . . . to show to Esther and explain it to her, and he told him to instruct her to go into the king's presence to beg for mercy and plead with him for her people."

–ESTHER 4:7–8

The danger to Esther and Mordecai's people was real. Mordecai made sure Ester understood that the Jewish people faced genocide. Not only that, if Esther did what Mordecai asked, her life would be directly threatened. Most of us probably can't begin to understand the terror they must have felt.

And yet, people living in the world today face similar fears. Some people are in danger because their race or culture is in the crosshairs of a different people group. Some people face the threat of violence because of their religious beliefs, and that includes the many Christians around the world who face the possibility of death just for confessing the name of Jesus.

It's easy to forget about these realities today. But it's important to make ourselves remember those who face terror and danger every day. We can pray for their safety and their hearts. This helps us appreciate our own situations and keep our trials in perspective!

day 309

"When Esther's words were reported to Mordecai, he sent back this answer: 'Do not think that because you are in the king's house you alone of all the Jews will escape. For if you remain silent at this time, relief and deliverance for the Jews will arise from another place, but you and your father's family will perish. And who knows but that you have come to your royal position for such a time as this?'"

–ESTHER 4:12–14

These are powerful words from Mordecai, and perhaps the most famous from Esther's story: *for such a time as this.* Mordecai's challenge might be the most famous part of his speech, but did you notice his faithful confession just before his challenge? He feels sure the Jews will be delivered. Why? Because he trusts God will always save a remnant of his people, no matter what they face. But Mordecai was wise enough to recognize that it probably wasn't a coincidence Esther had become queen.

Mordecai's basic point of view still applies to us today. God's purposes will be accomplished no matter what because he's God. But are we willing to say, "Yes, I'm here" and be part of that plan? That was Mordecai's challenge to Esther, and that's a question we can ask ourselves daily.

day 310

"Then Esther sent this reply to Mordecai: 'Go, gather together all the Jews who are in Susa, and fast for me. Do not eat or drink for three days, night or day. I and my attendants will fast as you do. When this is done, I will go to the king, even though it is against the law. And if I perish, I perish.'"

–ESTHER 4:15-16

If Mordecai's challenge was a powerful one, then Esther's faithful response is every bit as powerful. Despite her initial reluctance, Esther straps on her (figurative) sword and gets ready for battle—just another day at the office for our charming, beautiful, girl-boss queen.

Mordecai sensed that Esther had the chance to be part of God's big-picture plan here—and he was right! But Esther had a choice in this moment. She could have backed away and hoped for her own safety and deliverance for her people from some other source. Or she had the opportunity to take a risk, respond in faith, and be part of the plan.

"God moments" happen in our lives too. Those crazy "coincidences" where we're in the perfect place at the perfect time. But, like Esther, we have to respond to those moments. Let's pray God will open our eyes—and our hearts—to better see those times when he wants us to be part of his big-picture plan.

day 311

"On the third day Esther put on her royal robes and stood in the inner court of the palace, in front of the king's hall. The king was sitting on his royal throne in the hall, facing the entrance. When he saw Queen Esther standing in the court, he was pleased with her and held out to her the gold scepter that was in his hand. So Esther approached and touched the tip of the scepter."

–ESTHER 5:1-2

Have you noticed something unusual about the verses from Esther? There are literally no mentions of God.

It's true. Esther is the only book of the Bible that doesn't explicitly mention God. And yet, God is obviously in the story. Esther's big risk was in approaching the king without being summoned. He was within his legal rights to execute her for it. But when she did, he was "coincidentally" in a favorable mood, and he extended mercy to her. In any other book of the Bible, this verse might say, "But God softened Xerxes's heart toward Esther." Here, we don't get that commentary.

And maybe that's why Esther is such a relatable book. God is there, shifting all the pieces into place. But he's also invisible. And that's how God is for us a lot of the time. We know he's there, but we don't often get insight into exactly what he's doing or thinking. Esther's story encourages us that, even though we can't know God's behind-the-scene thoughts all the time, we *can* see him moving clearly, even when he's not mentioned by name.

day 312

"King Xerxes replied to Queen Esther and to Mordecai the Jew, 'Because Haman attacked the Jews, I have given his estate to Esther, and they have impaled him on the pole he set up. Now write another decree in the king's name in behalf of the Jews as seems best to you, and seal it with the king's signet ring—for no document written in the king's name and sealed with his ring can be revoked.'"

–ESTHER 8:7–8

Things worked out very well for Esther, Mordecai, and all the Jewish people. Esther was able to save her people, and the advisor who had it out for Mordecai was punished—harshly. It was the best possible outcome for a vulnerable people who had been facing extinction.

It's true that God's people will often have a target on their backs because the world wants to destroy what God wants to build up. But we must also remember that God is the great deliverer. He doesn't ignore us when we cry for help. Even if the earthly trials we're facing are difficulties we must go through, for whatever reason, God is there with us. He gives us peace in even the most trying circumstances. He reminds us that this world, with all its troubles, is not our permanent home. Sometimes we have worldly deliverance from pain and heartache, but we always have eternal, spiritual deliverance.

day 313

"In the time of Herod king of Judea there was a priest named Zechariah, who belonged to the priestly division of Abijah; his wife Elizabeth was also a descendant of Aaron. Both of them were righteous in the sight of God, observing all the Lord's commands and decrees blamelessly. But they were childless because Elizabeth was not able to conceive, and they were both very old."

–LUKE 1:5-7

We've made it to the New Testament! There are a lot more women in the New Testament than many people realize, and if we're going chronologically, Elizabeth should be the first one we look at.

The beginning of Elizabeth and Zechariah's story is another that falls under the category of "things we might not like to think about." They upheld the Law of Moses as best they could and were faithful followers of God, but they still had not been blessed with a child.

It's not always easy to trust that God knows best in these situations. When we want something badly, that desire can crowd out everything else in our minds. We have to let the truth—that God is always working all things to our good (Romans 8:28)—speak louder than our desires. God has a good plan for each of us. We can trust him and his timing!

day 314

"[The angel said] 'Your wife Elizabeth will bear you a son, and you are to call him John. He will be a joy and delight to you, and many will rejoice because of his birth, for he will be great in the sight of the Lord. He will bring back many of the people of Israel to the Lord their God.'"

–LUKE 1:13B–15A, 16

Elizabeth's story didn't end with an unfulfilled desire. Just like the angel proclaimed, Elizabeth became the mother of John the Baptist, who was an important trailblazer ahead of Jesus's earthly ministry. We have so many miraculous conceptions recorded in the Bible, we might think of them as much more common than they were. But make no mistake—this event was far outside of the "norm." In this case, God's plan was much bigger than the norm.

Sometimes God's plan for our lives turns the norm on its head too. Think about your plans for your future. How many of those plans are based on doing what's expected of you? Sometimes those expectations are great. Other times, we haven't really put in the thought or prayer to discern if we're just plodding in a certain direction because it's our norm or if that's really where God wants us. Take some time to pray about it now, and see what you discover!

day 315

"After this his wife Elizabeth became pregnant and for five months remained in seclusion. 'The Lord has done this for me,' she said. 'In these days he has shown his favor and taken away my disgrace among the people.'"

–LUKE 1:24-25

Can you imagine what it was like to be in Elizabeth's shoes? She went from an elderly, barren woman who considered herself "disgraced" among the people to the mother of a miracle child. Just like that, her entire identity had changed.

God is in the habit of doing that. Our relationship with Jesus brings us from darkness to light. We were blind, now we see. We were dead in our sins, now we live. Believing in Jesus changes our identity in these ways and others.

That's a pretty deep thought! But the apostle Paul wrote about it a lot—becoming a new man (or woman) in Christ. When you're struggling with something—anything from a bad attitude to a serious situation—you can find hope, strength, and encouragement in this fact. You are a new creature in Jesus, with a totally new identity as God's beloved daughter.

day 316

"In the sixth month of Elizabeth's pregnancy, God sent the angel Gabriel to Nazareth, a town in Galilee, to a virgin pledged to be married to a man named Joseph, a descendant of David. The virgin's name was Mary. The angel went to her and said, 'Greetings, you who are highly favored! The Lord is with you.'"

–LUKE 1:26–28

We've reached the most famous woman in the Bible—actually, one of the most famous women in all history! Mary, the mother of Jesus. For two thousand years, people have been reading about, writing about, and painting portraits of Mary. By all accounts, she was a young woman. She wasn't a princess or a prophet or a military leader. She was just a normal girl.

Isn't it cool to think about how much God entrusted to this regular girl? He judged her capable of shouldering this sizable burden—and honor. She wasn't disqualified because she was young or because she was normal. God looked at her heart and said, "Yes. You're the one."

If you're a young woman—and chances are you are, since this book is for you!—be encouraged. God does not disqualify you from big things, either!

day 317

"Mary was greatly troubled at his words and wondered what kind of greeting this might be. But the angel said to her, 'Do not be afraid, Mary; you have found favor with God. You will conceive and give birth to a son, and you are to call him Jesus. He will be great and will be called the Son of the Most High. The Lord God will give him the throne of his father David, and he will reign over Jacob's descendants forever; his kingdom will never end.'"

–LUKE 1:29–33

If most people had sat down to write the plan for mankind's redemption, it probably wouldn't have looked much like what God's plan was. We tend to like superheroes—people who are big, strong, and wear capes and masks. Our culture glorifies those who are talented and beautiful, wealthy and powerful.

But God chose a young woman to give birth to a baby boy, and that boy carried the weight of mankind's redemption on his very human shoulders. Also? Though the boy was human, he was also God himself. So the great big God of the universe took on human frailty in order to make this plan work.

It's a pretty unusual plan! But we serve an extraordinary God. He chooses unlikely vessels and unlikely means. Thank goodness, because that means he chooses us! Let's take a moment to thank God for choosing those who are broken, hurting, timid, or just plain weak. Everyone feels that way sometimes, and we can be thankful that this doesn't disqualify us from serving God.

day 318

"[The angel said] 'Even Elizabeth your relative is going to have a child in her old age, and she who was said to be unable to conceive is in her sixth month. For no word from God will ever fail.' 'I am the Lord's servant,' Mary answered. 'May your word to me be fulfilled.' Then the angel left her."

–LUKE 1:36–38

We've seen a lot of miraculous conceptions in the Bible so far and several declarations from angels beforehand, letting the parent-to-be know it was about to happen. What we don't see as often is a response like Mary's. She responded in faith, not doubt. She said, essentially, "I belong to God—let your words come true." That's a profound demonstration of faith, especially when you consider that Mary was unmarried. The angel's prophecy was even more unbelievable than most. Not only was she to conceive a child, she was to do so while remaining a virgin. What?

Maybe that is what God saw in this regular young woman—the kind of faith that believes in the impossible and the kind of trust that says, "I'm yours, God. Use me as you will." If you're like most people, you could probably use a little more of that kind of faith and trust. Is there an area in your life where you've felt particularly doubtful about trusting God? Spend some time today focused on practicing Mary-like faith in that tough area. God honors those efforts.

day 319

"When Elizabeth heard Mary's greeting, the baby leaped in her womb, and Elizabeth was filled with the Holy Spirit. In a loud voice she exclaimed: 'Blessed are you among women, and blessed is the child you will bear! But why am I so favored, that the mother of my Lord should come to me? As soon as the sound of your greeting reached my ears, the baby in my womb leaped for joy. Blessed is she who has believed that the Lord would fulfill his promises to her!'"

–LUKE 1:41–45

This is such a cool moment. Elizabeth and Mary were related, and after Mary had spoken to the angel, she went to see her relative. This was what happened when they met each other. John the Baptist, in utero, leapt at Mary's presence. Crazy!

There was a lot of direct Holy Spirit intervention happening in this moment. And it's no wonder. It was a pretty special moment, never to be repeated again. The Holy Spirit was talking to tiny John and to Elizabeth. While this definitely isn't the norm, have you thought about the fact that you have the same Holy Spirit living inside of you? The Holy Spirit who is God and knows everything.

We take that for granted sometimes. But it's such an awesome truth! When we're feeling alone, discouraged, weak-willed, or unable, we can remember the power of the One who lives in us. He is there to enable, equip, and encourage us. That's amazing!

day 320

"And Mary said: 'My soul glorifies the Lord and my spirit rejoices in God my Savior, for he has been mindful of the humble state of his servant. From now on all generations will call me blessed, for the Mighty One has done great things for me—holy is his name.'"

–LUKE 1:46–49

This is the beginning of a really lovely song from Mary where she expresses everything that is on her heart just after the amazing moment with her relative Elizabeth. It's reminiscent of one of David's psalms.

The written word is an amazing gift. We write to communicate with others, of course, but we also write to pour ourselves out onto the paper—to express what's deep inside and might be difficult to express verbally. Some people do this better in song. Or art. Or dance. Anything that takes what's in our hearts and allows it to be poured outward is accomplishing the same purpose.

How do you best express those deep emotions? Even if you don't feel particularly gifted in any of these areas, journaling is for everyone! When you're writing in a journal, you can feel free to express yourself without ever worrying about showing it to anyone or having anyone else judge it. You can even use the journaling lines in this book to jot down some of your inmost thoughts as you read.

day 321

"Mary stayed with Elizabeth for about three months and then returned home."
—LUKE 1:56

This may seem like a strange verse to highlight. It's not exactly full of meaty spiritual content to ponder. But that's okay! The Bible is such a cool book in part because the vast majority of its verses contain little nuggets of truth or tiny treasures to discover, even when they're not profound on the surface.

Mary stayed with her relative Elizabeth for an extended period of time. Despite their age difference, they seemed to have gotten along well and enjoyed each other's company. Close relationships with family and friends are such blessings. Siblings, cousins, and friends seem like obvious choices for these close relationships. But, like Mary and Elizabeth, an age difference doesn't have to stand in the way of two people forming a tight, supportive bond. You can have that kind of relationship with a parent or grandparent too.

Do you have a handful of people like that whom you trust on a deep level? If you don't and you'd like some, pray that God would send some people into your life, or that he would help you nurture relationships you have already to get them to that level. The closeness is priceless.

day 322

"When it was time for Elizabeth to have her baby, she gave birth to a son. Her neighbors and relatives heard that the Lord had shown her great mercy, and they shared her joy."

–LUKE 1:57–58

That's a simple little statement, but such a powerful one: Elizabeth's neighbors shared her joy. Elizabeth had long wished for a child. She gave birth to a healthy son, and her neighbors rejoiced with her.

Romans 12:15 says: "Rejoice with those who rejoice; mourn with those who mourn." Also a simple statement, but not always easy to practice. Sometimes we poke at those who mourn by blaming them for their hard circumstances or offering cold "comfort" that has the undertones of judgment. And sometimes it's easier to feel jealousy than joy when something amazing or wonderful happens to someone else.

But when we can offer genuine joy for those who rejoice and genuine sorrow for those who mourn, it has a positive effect on our hearts. We grow in empathy, understanding, and selflessness, which makes us more compassionate, loving people. It's an awesome way to reflect Jesus to others!

day 323

"On the eighth day they came to circumcise the child, and they were going to name him after his father Zechariah, but his mother spoke up and said, 'No! He is to be called John.' They said to her, 'There is no one among your relatives who has that name.' Then they made signs to his father, to find out what he would like to name the child. He asked for a writing tablet, and to everyone's astonishment he wrote, 'His name is John.'"

–LUKE 1:59-63

We've shared some thoughts about defying tradition or turning the norm on its head. Elizabeth does it again here by giving her baby son a name not shared by anyone in her or her husband's families.

But you'll notice she didn't "rebel" for the sake of it. She didn't defy expectations because she was desperate to stand out or because she wanted to disrespect her culture. She did it because she was being obedient to God's instructions, delivered through the angel.

It's okay to defy expectations and go against the grain. In fact, sometimes that's exactly what we *must* do. But it's important we do it for the right reasons. Expectations and norms should take a backseat to God's leading, just like they did for Elizabeth and Zechariah.

day 324

"This is how the birth of Jesus the Messiah came about: His mother Mary was pledged to be married to Joseph, but before they came together, she was found to be pregnant through the Holy Spirit. Because Joseph her husband was faithful to the law, and yet did not want to expose her to public disgrace, he had in mind to divorce her quietly."

–MATTHEW 1:18–19

There's a lot to digest here. Joseph and Mary were engaged, which was as good as married in those days. When Mary became pregnant before she and Joseph had gotten married, of course his obvious assumption would be that she had gotten pregnant by another man. In other words, Mary looked a lot like an adulteress. And he was not okay with adultery. But even before he knew the totally unique circumstances of Mary's pregnancy (and that she was, indeed, not an adulteress), he wanted to protect her. He could have made her disgrace public and had her punished as the law prescribed. Instead, he was going to walk away from the engagement ("divorce," as the verse says) quietly. Wow.

Joseph was a good man. He was upright and godly, but he still remained compassionate. While we may be focusing on biblical role models who are women in this book, Joseph is an excellent role model for us too. It can be really difficult to maintain the balance of righteousness and compassion, but Joseph gives us a great example of how to do just that.

---

day 325

"So [the shepherds] hurried off and found Mary and Joseph, and the baby, who was lying in the manger. When they had seen him, they spread the word concerning what had been told them about this child, and all who heard it were amazed at what the shepherds said to them. But Mary treasured up all these things and pondered them in her heart."

–LUKE 2:16–19

Joseph was visited by an angel and got clued in about the very special family he and Mary were about to begin. They did end up marrying, and Joseph was there for the birth of the Messiah. Which brings us to this very familiar stable.

Mary was in the habit of treasuring and pondering things in her heart. Wise girl. Especially when you consider the extraordinary events of her life, it's no wonder Mary had a particular need to really chew on these wild happenings. Her thoughtful temperament probably equipped her to handle her special role with grace.

We're bombarded with new information all the time. We ask our brains—and our hearts—to process *a lot*. And while all of it may be more mundane than the things Mary needed to process in her life, it's no wonder that we get fatigued.

We would be wise to adopt Mary's practice of quiet reflection. It allows our minds to slow down, process, evaluate, compare, and digest.

day 326

"There was also a prophet, Anna, the daughter of Penuel, of the tribe of Asher. She was very old; she had lived with her husband seven years after her marriage, and then was a widow until she was eighty-four. She never left the temple but worshiped night and day, fasting and praying."

–LUKE 2:36–37

Another female prophet! Anna doesn't have a ton of space devoted to her story, but she was a pretty cool lady. She was married for a relatively short time, then her husband died. She lived the rest of her life as a widow and devoted most—maybe all—of her time to worshiping God. Wow!

Anna is a great encouragement for those who feel called to devote their lives to God's service instead of marriage or family. But even those of us who do want to be married and have children can adopt a little bit of Anna's spirit.

What's one way you can serve the kingdom this week? Maybe it means helping out at your church, or maybe it means ministering to that friend who has been asking about God lately. Or maybe it means simply showing the love of Jesus by helping a friend through a tough time. Wherever the need, you can draw inspiration from Anna by serving with your whole heart and with a constant focus on your love for God.

day 327

"Coming up to them at that very moment, [Anna] gave thanks to God and spoke about the child to all who were looking forward to the redemption of Jerusalem."

–LUKE 2:38

Anna was a legitimate prophet. She knew who this baby boy was the moment his parents brought him into the temple courtyard. And she didn't stay quiet about it. She marched up to Jesus's family, thanked God, and preached about the redemption to come. Not only was she legit, she was bold.

Sometimes we shy away from sharing our faith with others. That may be because a lot of people have had bad experiences with "church people" or because we think we have to preach fire and brimstone and judgment on people. But there's another option. Instead of preaching judgment, we can share our hope, like Anna.

What's the difference? Well, the gospel does require us to turn away from our sins. But the main message of Jesus is that he saved us because he loves us. When we realize what Jesus did for us, turning away from things that displease God comes more naturally—no brimstone required.

day 328

"Near the cross of Jesus stood his mother, his mother's sister, Mary the wife of Clopas, and Mary Magdalene. When Jesus saw his mother there, and the disciple whom he loved standing nearby, he said to her, 'Woman, here is your son,' and to the disciple, 'Here is your mother.' From that time on, this disciple took her into his home."

–JOHN 19:25–27

We've skipped through the rest of Jesus's ministry for a moment to get one final picture of Mary, Jesus's mother. While Jesus died on the cross, Mary was there. Can you imagine her grief? Even if she fully understood who he was and what would happen next, her heart must have been breaking.

In those final moments of Jesus's life, he thought of his mother. John was Jesus's best friend, and before Jesus died, he made it clear he wanted John to become like a son to Mary and take care of her in her old age. Mary had other sons, but Jesus was asking John to take *his* place. And John fulfilled his duty— from that time on, Mary became a part of John's household.

Friends who are like family are a precious gift. Having heart friends like that in no way takes away from your actual family. But if we're lucky enough to have friends who love and support us like family should, we can embrace that blessing. Do you have any friends in your life like that right now? Take a moment to pray for them and to thank God for bringing them into your life.

day 329

"Now he had to go through Samaria. So he came to a town in Samaria called Sychar, near the plot of ground Jacob had given to his son Joseph. Jacob's well was there, and Jesus, tired as he was from the journey, sat down by the well. It was about noon. When a Samaritan woman came to draw water, Jesus said to her, 'Will you give me a drink?'"

–JOHN 4:4-7

To understand the New Testament stories that mention Samaritans, it's important to get a little history lesson. Let's fill in some blanks.

Samaritans and Jews shared Israelite ancestry, but after Israel split into two kingdoms, they started to go their separate ways. By Jesus's time, there was a lot of tension between these two groups. In short, Samaritans were "other," as far as the Jews were concerned. They were an unclean, "impure" people.

Isn't it crazy that these kinds of tensions have existed for so long? We still deal with them today all over the world. But the love of Jesus is a tremendous force of reconciliation. Jesus reached across the divide to the "others" of his day.

A simple act of kindness like Jesus's reaches across the divide. A smile, a kind word, a show of concern—these small acts demonstrate to people that you don't see them as "other." Though you may be up against some strong cultural tensions, you can show that you care by making the first move.

day 330

"The Samaritan woman said to him, 'You are a Jew and I am a Samaritan woman. How can you ask me for a drink?' (For Jews do not associate with Samaritans.) Jesus answered her, 'If you knew the gift of God and who it is that asks you for a drink, you would have asked him and he would have given you living water.'"

–JOHN 4:9–10

There was a lot that could have potentially separated Jesus from the woman at the well. The fact that she was a woman, for one—Jesus and this woman were not considered social equals in biblical times. And there's obviously the fact that she was a Samaritan. Jesus could have turned away, ignored the woman, or even been rude to her—that's what his culture would have expected. But even early in his ministry, Jesus is seen breaking through all those barriers to reach out to this woman drawing water.

There is nothing that disqualifies us from receiving God's grace. There is no sin in your past—no boundaries of culture, ethnicity, or gender—that separates you from redemption. It's hard for us to believe that sometimes, but it's true. It's the foundation of Jesus's work on earth—to bring *all mankind* back to his Father. No one is left out. The offer of salvation is for all. Praise God! Let's take a few minutes to thank God for the amazing gift of grace, open to everyone.

----

day 331

"'Sir,' the woman said, 'you have nothing to draw with and the well is deep. Where can you get this living water? Are you greater than our father Jacob, who gave us the well?' . . . Jesus answered, 'Everyone who drinks this water will be thirsty again, but whoever drinks the water I give them will never thirst. Indeed, the water I give them will become in them a spring of water welling up to eternal life.' The woman said to him, 'Sir, give me this water so that I won't get thirsty and have to keep coming here to draw water.'"

–JOHN 4.11–15

To be fair, Jesus was speaking in riddles a little bit. He told stories in such a way that it was easy to miss the full truth of what he was saying if his listeners weren't carefully weighing his words. Most people at this time didn't know he was the son of God—that his stories were so much more than just interesting tales.

We're in the position of knowing who Jesus is. But even though we understand exactly who he is and we pay careful attention to his words, we *still* miss the spiritual significance of his messages sometimes. Like the woman at the well, we focus on the practical matters and miss the spiritual truth beneath the surface.

Let's be careful not to get swept up in the practical so much that we miss the spiritual. Let's make sure we're listening carefully to Jesus's spiritual truths, even as the busyness of practical matters tries to grab our attention.

day 332

"He told her, 'Go, call your husband and come back.' 'I have no husband,' she replied. Jesus said to her, 'You are right when you say you have no husband. The fact is, you have had five husbands, and the man you now have is not your husband. What you have just said is quite true.'"

–JOHN 4:16–18

Ouch. Jesus didn't tiptoe around the truth. He called out the woman at the well quite plainly. She must have felt like she was standing naked before this Jewish stranger as he pointed out her less-than-stellar behavior when it came to men. Jesus was not harsh with the woman, but we can still understand how embarrassed she must have felt.

There's really no hiding our misdeeds from God. Just as Jesus knew all about this woman's situation, he knows all about ours. There's no faking it when your God is omniscient.

Does that freak you out? It's understandable if it does. No one wants their past—or current!—mistakes pointed out. But that's one thing that's so amazing about God. He sees everything about us so clearly, even the not-so-great stuff, and *still* he offers us grace, love, and reconciliation. Jesus doesn't want us to continue down a bad path, just like he didn't want the woman to continue down her bad path. That's why we're equipped with the Holy Spirit's help and guidance. We just need to follow his leading!

day 333

"'Sir,' the woman said, 'I can see that you are a prophet. Our ancestors worshiped on this mountain, but you Jews claim that the place where we must worship is in Jerusalem.' 'Woman,' Jesus replied, 'believe me, a time is coming when you will worship the Father neither on this mountain nor in Jerusalem . . . Yet a time is coming and has now come when the true worshipers will worship the Father in the Spirit and in truth, for they are the kind of worshipers the Father seeks.'"

–JOHN 4:19–21, 23

Have you ever felt like you have to clean yourself up before approaching Jesus? Have you ever felt like you don't belong in church until you've scrubbed your life of everything God might find displeasing?

If you've ever felt that way, you're not alone. But stories like this one about the Samaritan woman show us that God meets us right where we are. Jesus shared a very deep truth with this woman—even while she was in the midst of some really bad lifestyle choices. Jesus cared about those lifestyle choices, of course, but it didn't stop him from showing compassion to this woman and sharing God's plan with her.

This is important when we feel unworthy. It's also important when we're dealing with others struggling with feelings of unworthiness. Do you know anyone dealing with that right now? You can follow Jesus's example by approaching that person with truth *and* compassion.

day 334

"The woman said, 'I know that Messiah' (called Christ) 'is coming. When he comes, he will explain everything to us.' Then Jesus declared, 'I, the one speaking to you—I am he.'"

—JOHN 4:25-26

This is really amazing. Because we know this truth backward and forward, having read the climax of Jesus's life—his death on the cross and his resurrection—it's easy to skim over this part of the story and not fully grasp its significance.

But look carefully at Jesus's words here. This is his most direct confession of who he is until his trial before Pilate. He is very open with this woman and says plainly to her that he is the Messiah. He hedged with others. He dodged the question sometimes. He didn't even speak this plainly with his own disciples most of the time. But he was open with this Samaritan woman who was living a sinful life. Wow!

She was clearly a seeker of truth. Jesus must have sensed her readiness to hear and digest who he was. Maybe you have a friend who is a "seeker." Have you thought about how you can reach out to that friend? Take a few moments to pray for an organic opportunity to talk about God with your friend. God often uses us to share deep spiritual truths of who Jesus is!

day 335

"Herod had given orders to have John arrested and . . . put in prison . . . because of Herodias, his brother Philip's wife, whom he had married. For John had been saying to Herod, 'It is not lawful for you to have your brother's wife.' So Herodias nursed a grudge against John and wanted to kill him. But she was not able to, because Herod feared John and protected him, knowing him to be a righteous and holy man. When Herod heard John, he was greatly puzzled; yet he liked to listen to him."

—MARK 6:17–20

It would be great if all our New Testament ladies were godly role models or had great stories of redemption. We do have many stories like that. Sadly, we also have a few brutal examples of very bad behavior. Herodias is one of these examples. She responded with bitterness and vengeance when John the Baptist approached Herod and her about their inappropriate relationship. The results were deadly.

While we may respond in healthier ways to criticism or confrontation (one would hope!), it's never easy to hear negative stuff about ourselves. Especially when someone is confronting us about our sin. But when we're being confronted by someone we trust and who loves us, it's important to learn how to accept that kind of confrontation with grace. Those trusted friends are trying to help, not hurt us.

day 336

"On Herod's birthday the daughter of Herodias danced for the guests and pleased Herod so much that he promised with an oath to give her whatever she asked. Prompted by her mother, she said, 'Give me here on a platter the head of John the Baptist.'"

–MATTHEW 14:6–8

Traditionally, Herodias's daughter is known as Salome, even though we don't see her name mentioned in the Bible. And boy, did she follow in her mom's malicious footsteps. This cold-hearted request wasn't directed at John, exactly, but more at his message. Herodias wanted John's message of repentance silenced, and these were the drastic measures she and Salome took to make that happen.

It's hard to tell how much of this wicked deed was Salome's doing and how much was Herodias's. The verse says "prompted by her mother." Does that mean Salome wouldn't have done this if not for her mom's nudging? Did she feel pressured or forced? Or was she totally on board?

It is unfortunately common to find ourselves in situations where we're being nudged to do things we're not comfortable with. Sometimes it helps us to stand firm when we remember that God's opinion is the one that should matter most to us. It's natural to care what other people think. But we need to allow God the final say in our lives. When someone is pressuring you to do something that feels wrong, stand firm! God will strengthen your resolve, if you ask him.

day 337

"A woman in that town who lived a sinful life learned that Jesus was eating at the Pharisee's house, so she came there with an alabaster jar of perfume. As she stood behind him at his feet weeping, she began to wet his feet with her tears. Then she wiped them with her hair, kissed them and poured perfume on them."

–LUKE 7:37–38

Heartbrokenness. It's the only word to describe this woman's attitude as she approaches Jesus. We might wonder what her background was. How did she hear about Jesus? How did she know to come to him for the wholeness she sought? What had she done in her life that branded her as a sinner in the eyes of those surrounding Jesus?

We don't have the answers to these questions. But we do see something so touching, so beautiful, from our savior in this moment. This story shows us that our pasts are irrelevant. The love of Jesus finds us wherever we are, even when we've made mistakes.

Maybe you have some dark mistakes in your past. If so, you're not alone. People with dark pasts have been coming to Jesus for millennia. He doesn't turn away those seeking to turn their lives around. Maybe that message is for you today, but it's also definitely for all of us as we work to show compassion to those who are hurting.

day 336

"When the Pharisee who had invited him saw this, he said to himself, 'If this man were a prophet, he would know who is touching him and what kind of woman she is—that she is a sinner.' Jesus answered him, 'Simon, I have something to tell you.' 'Tell me, teacher,' he said . . . 'You did not give me any water for my feet, but she wet my feet with her tears and wiped them with her hair. You did not give me a kiss, but this woman, from the time I entered, has not stopped kissing my feet. You did not put oil on my head, but she has poured perfume on my feet.'"

–LUKE 7:39–40, 44B–46

This is an interesting contrast. Jesus is dining in the house of a Pharisee, one of the group that would have been considered the most holy, most righteous of his day. And yet he's being attended to by a woman who is identified only as having a sinful lifestyle.

Jesus knew all about the woman's background, of course. But he didn't want to focus on that. Instead, he highlighted to the Pharisee what the woman's actions were *now*, not what her past was like.

Our actions matter. We're not saved by our good behavior, but our actions reveal our faith. When we believe that God is real and when we have faith in his Word, we want to behave accordingly. We want to represent him well and truthfully. This woman with a sinful past was taking her first step toward that, and Jesus received it wholeheartedly.

day 339

"'Therefore, I tell you, her many sins have been forgiven—as her great love has shown. But whoever has been forgiven little loves little.' Then Jesus said to her, 'Your sins are forgiven.' The other guests began to say among themselves, 'Who is this who even forgives sins?' Jesus said to the woman, 'Your faith has saved you; go in peace.'"

—LUKE 7:47-50

Sometimes it's difficult for those who have been through a lot in their lives to feel at home in church. Church can feel like a "perfect" place—one that's holy and sacred. Those who feel marked, whether by their own past sins or by abuse of some kind, sometimes feel like they don't belong.

It's important that we hear the heart of Jesus on this. Jesus did not accept the idea of this woman's sins continuing to stick to her after she'd stepped out in faith. He said she was forgiven. He said she was saved.

We need to bring that heart to church with us. We must remember it for ourselves, surely, and also for anyone else seeking sanctuary in the arms of God. This was the heart of Jesus two thousand years ago, and it's the heart of Jesus now!

day 340

"And a woman was there who had been subject to bleeding for twelve years. She had suffered a great deal under the care of many doctors and had spent all she had, yet instead of getting better she grew worse."

–MARK 5:25–26

Can you imagine what it must have been like to deal with a chronic illness before the days of modern medicine? Even now, it's no picnic. Literally millions of people deal with these issues on a daily basis. Chronic pain, illness, dysfunctions of the body, special needs, impairments . . . these are all realities for many people. Jesus showed compassion for the sick and the disabled.

Do you know someone who suffers from a chronic illness? Chances are, you do. Maybe *you're* the one dealing with this special type of challenge. Know that Jesus sees you and understands your suffering. If you don't deal with a chronic illness, praise God! A healthy body is a tremendous blessing. But remember in prayer those who do deal with chronic conditions. It can be a heavy burden to bear and very wearying for those who live with it daily—and often their family members or caretakers.

day 341

"When she heard about Jesus, she came up behind him in the crowd and touched his cloak, because she thought, 'If I just touch his clothes, I will be healed.'"
—MARK 5:27-28

This is really deep, when you think about it. This woman had been sick for twelve years. She had been to the top doctors in the land. She had tried absolutely everything she could think of to heal her sickness, to no avail. And yet she had heard about Jesus and she had this secret thought—*if I could only touch his clothes, I'll be healed*. Doctors had been completely unsuccessful, but she believed that the mere touch of Jesus would be enough to heal her. Wow.

This may make us long for the days when Jesus was walking around in his human body on Earth. But his presence is still available to us in a spiritual way through the Holy Spirit. And that presence is powerful, just like it was in Jesus's day when this woman believed (correctly!) that merely touching Jesus would heal her body. Being "in God's presence" means we have an increased awareness of him and his power. It means we experience him in a way that's bold and true and authentic. It shocks us into a state of worship   an attitude of praise. That's deep too!

347

day 342

"Immediately her bleeding stopped and she felt in her body that she was freed from her suffering . . . Then the woman, knowing what had happened to her, came and fell at [Jesus's] feet and, trembling with fear, told him the whole truth. He said to her, 'Daughter, your faith has healed you. Go in peace and be freed from your suffering.'"

–MARK 5:29, 33–34

Ah, this is beautiful. Our sick woman's faith that Jesus's touch would heal translated into actual healing for her. After all those years of suffering, her body was whole! Hallelujah!

But we have to be really careful with this. We must both affirm that God absolutely can and does heal (because he still does perform miracles like this!), but we must also acknowledge that even those with faith as deep and true as this sick woman's can suffer illness. Sometimes for their whole lives. Sometimes they even die. We have to be careful that we do not equate this suffering with a lack of faith. Paul mentioned his "thorn in the flesh" that God would not take away in 2 Corinthians 12:7. Job suffered many physical trials, even though it had nothing to do with his faith or lack thereof. Sometimes God allows suffering, and we don't always get to know why.

Have you ever suffered with something—whether physically, spiritually, or emotionally—that God chose not to take away or heal instantaneously? Did you find your faith strengthened through that trial? Take a few moments to express your feelings about it in prayer—even if they're not all pleasant!

----

day 343

> "The teachers of the law and the Pharisees brought in a woman caught in adultery. They made her stand before the group and said to Jesus, 'Teacher, this woman was caught in the act of adultery. In the Law Moses commanded us to stone such women. Now what do you say?' They were using this question as a trap, in order to have a basis for accusing him."
>
> —JOHN 8:3–6A

Jesus went against the grain of his culture to reach out to women.

Compared to the religious leaders of the day, Jesus was downright revolutionary. These Pharisees sought to publicly shame and punish this woman. If their motivation had been to address a spiritual problem in her life, *maybe* we could understand them a little better. But the verse is clear: they dragged this woman out into public solely to trap Jesus. They wanted to attack their enemy, Jesus, and this woman was acceptable collateral damage.

Even when a person has done something wrong, it's important that we treat her with dignity. Finger-pointing and public shaming might make us feel superior, but it has little chance of restoring the person in question to right relationship with God. Instead, let's be like Jesus. Let's treat people with kindness and respect *first* and then follow with important truths, spoken in love.

day 344

"But Jesus bent down and started to write on the ground with his finger. When they kept on questioning him, he straightened up and said to them, 'Let any one of you who is without sin be the first to throw a stone at her.' Again he stooped down and wrote on the ground. At this, those who heard began to go away one at a time, the older ones first, until only Jesus was left, with the woman still standing there."

–JOHN 8:6B–9

This is such a beautiful picture of the heart of Jesus. He knew what was in the minds of the Pharisees. He knew they were seeking to trap him and not at all concerned about this woman or her relationship with God. His heart was to redeem this woman—to save her and not condemn her. Amazing, wild, wonderful grace.

Maybe you have a hard time receiving that grace for yourself. Maybe you feel dark and twisty and irredeemable inside, and you can't imagine Jesus standing in the gap for you, protecting you from your accusers. Or maybe you have a hard time showing this kind of grace to others. Maybe it seems like the world is decaying around you and you're the only one who is getting it right.

If either of those is the case for you right now, you're not alone! Let's take a few moments to pray that our hearts would realign with Jesus's. Let's take a moment to fully grab onto the idea that Jesus's grace is for us and for all those around us, even if they're struggling.

---

day 345

"Jesus straightened up and asked her, 'Woman, where are they? Has no one condemned you?' 'No one, sir,' she said. 'Then neither do I condemn you,' Jesus declared. 'Go now and leave your life of sin.'"

—JOHN 8:10–11

People quote Jesus's words in the preceding verses a lot. "Let anyone who is without sin cast the first stone." Those are powerful, wonderful words. But what many people neglect is this next part. Jesus did not condemn the woman, and he did not stone her to death as the law prescribed. But he *did* tell her to leave her life of sin. There's a difference between offering grace and accepting sin.

This is an excruciatingly difficult balance for us to strike. Some of us just want peace, harmony, no confrontation, and no hurt feelings, so we're more likely to be accepting of others' sins. We don't want to rock the boat. Other people are more given to an uncompromising stance, so we find it easier to call out sin and more difficult to show love and compassion.

But we have to show both kindness *and* correction. One without the other is not a full picture of who Jesus is or the message he brought to Earth. Let's pray that we strike this difficult balance and represent Jesus the way he represented himself—both gracious and holy.

day 346

"As Jesus looked up, he saw the rich putting their gifts into the temple treasury. He also saw a poor widow put in two very small copper coins. 'Truly I tell you,' he said, 'this poor widow has put in more than all the others. All these people gave their gifts out of their wealth; but she out of her poverty put in all she had to live on.'"

–LUKE 21:1–4

Here is another "nameless" woman of the New Testament who is only known by descriptors of her life (poor widow) and what she did (gave two coins). There are many others like her, as Jesus's ministry intersected with the lives of women all the time, and they're all worth reading about.

This widow is a remarkable picture of faith in God's provision. She trusted God to provide for her, so she was willing to give *all* she had. As we see from Jesus's words, the actual monetary value of what she gave was irrelevant. God can use tiny amounts of money—or even no money at all—to do great things. That wasn't the point. The point was that she had so little but she gave *every bit of it*.

That's hard to fathom. Our culture is pretty materialistic. We like our worldly playthings. Can you imagine giving it all over to God if he asked—even the money you had planned to live on? That's crazy, daring, widow-sized faith right there. Even if God isn't asking you to give everything right this second, what is one way you can bring that spirit of generosity and sacrifice before God this week?

---

day 347

"As Jesus and his disciples were on their way, he came to a village where a woman named Martha opened her home to him"

—LUKE 10:38

How cool would it be to be able to say that you were close friends with Jesus during his time on Earth? That's something Martha of Bethany could claim. She shows up in the gospels of Luke and John in a couple different stories.

Martha's name has long been associated with hospitality. We've talked a lot about hospitality and how to bring that spirit with you wherever you go, which is especially important if you're not in a position to entertain in your home. But what are some practical ways to do that?

You can set up a weekly date at a coffee house with a group of friends—to have Bible study, homework time, or just hang-out time. You can plan outings for your friends. They can range from something extravagant like going to an amusement park together, to simple and totally free, like organizing a hike or picnic in the park. You can bring meals (or books or movies!) to those who are sick. If you do have a home space available for entertaining, you can offer to host birthday parties or other celebrations there. What are some of your creative ideas to take your hospitality on the road?

day 348

"She had a sister called Mary, who sat at the Lord's feet listening to what he said."
–LUKE 10:39

If Martha of Bethany has been long associated with hospitality, her sister Mary is connected to the soul that longs for Jesus's words. Mary sat at Jesus's feet, listening, soaking it up, digesting his words and hearing his heart. Mary was a seeker and a learner.

Mary's association may sound preferable to us. That's understandable. Martha's gift was very practical. Mary's was very spiritual. But it's more than okay to be gifted in the practical. If that's you, don't worry! God built you that way, and it's beautiful. But even those of us who are of a practical bent can use a little dash of Mary in our hearts.

What does that mean? Slow down for a minute. Take a breath. Don't allow every moment to be stolen by the drive to do, do, and do some more. Soak it in. Be filled with Jesus. Ponder his words. Turn your hearts toward God in prayer. Even if you have to set a timer to allow yourself this pocket of time to be free (without stressing about it), do it! The practical stuff needs to get done. But we must take moments for our hearts too.

day 349

"But Martha was distracted by all the preparations that had to be made. She came to him and asked, 'Lord, don't you care that my sister has left me to do the work by myself? Tell her to help me!' 'Martha, Martha,' the Lord answered, 'you are worried and upset about many things, but few things are needed—or indeed only one. Mary has chosen what is better, and it will not be taken away from her.'"

–LUKE 10:40–42

Ah, and here we see the downfall of "too much" hospitality. Martha was so concerned with doing everything that needed to be done while she hosted the large group of travelers in her home, she lost sight of the whole point—that *Jesus* was there and he was taking the time to teach them. She would have done well to sit at his feet and listen, just like her "lazy" sister.

The problem wasn't in too much hospitality, of course. The problem was in Martha's attitude. Jesus (gently) rebuked Martha because he knew her heart wasn't in the right place. She cared more about everything going well than she did about hearing Jesus teach. This was a rare opportunity, and Martha had the focus of an event planner, not a disciple.

Let's not get overwhelmed by the practical—or worse, in the temptation to show off. We have the opportunity to sit at the feet of Jesus metaphorically when we listen to his Word, so let's make sure we're present in those moments with our whole hearts.

day 350

"Many Jews had come to Martha and Mary to comfort them in the loss of their brother. When Martha heard that Jesus was coming, she went out to meet him, but Mary stayed at home. 'Lord,' Martha said to Jesus, 'if you had been here, my brother would not have died. But I know that even now God will give you whatever you ask.'"
–JOHN 11:19–22

Martha and Mary have now lost their brother, Lazarus, who was a good friend of Jesus. Martha ran out to meet Jesus to speak with him about it. Now, we may hear a little of that demanding nature Martha sometimes had. But really, this is a cry from an anguished, grieving sister—and it's a cry of faith.

Like the woman who had been bleeding for twelve years, Martha knew—just *knew*—that her brother could have been saved if Jesus had been near. If only Jesus could have prayed. If only Lazarus might have touched him. That's some big faith. But Jesus is in the habit of meeting his seekers and followers at whatever level of faith and challenging it to expand further. Martha said, "If only you'd been here!" and Jesus said, "I didn't even need to be. I can still act."

Does your faith feel small today? Or does it feel big and bold? Wherever you are, Jesus is ready to meet you and challenge you to go beyond what you thought possible.

day 351

"Jesus said to her, 'Your brother will rise again.' Martha answered, 'I know he will rise again in the resurrection at the last day.'"

–JOHN 11:23–24

Can all the Bible-loving, Word-studying ladies among us just take a moment to appreciate Martha here? Her theology was on point. She knew about the resurrection, understood it, and believed in it. You go, Martha!

It's not always the most inspirational thing in the world to talk about sound theology, but it's too important *not* to talk about. While different denominations will interpret the finer points differently sometimes, biblical, orthodox Christianity agrees on the essentials of the Christian faith.

Have you ever taken a few minutes to read your church's statement of faith? In all likelihood, it highlights these essentials, and it may even closely resemble one of the ancient creeds originally drafted by the early church, or perhaps one drawn up more recently during the Reformation of the 1500s and 1600s. Taking the time to dig into this history of church doctrine can help ground you in your beliefs. It may not sound super fun, but you might be surprised!

day 352

"Jesus said to her, 'I am the resurrection and the life. The one who believes in me will live, even though they die; and whoever lives by believing in me will never die. Do you believe this?' 'Yes, Lord,' she replied, 'I believe that you are the Messiah, the Son of God, who is to come into the world.'"

–JOHN 11:25-27

Let's keep it very real: Martha's confession here was a deeper, better, fuller understanding of exactly who Jesus was than many of the disciples had until after Jesus had died and risen again. Martha got it.

It's sad that she's often remembered *only* for her shortcoming—her bad attitude about Mary not helping her. Martha was so much more than that. She was undyingly practical. She was a doer. She maybe cared a little too much about everything going perfectly. But her theology was sound. Her understanding of the Messiah—and her faith in him—was deep and real and true.

People want to put us in a box sometimes, just like they've done to Martha for centuries. It's easy to think of people as one thing—the squeaky-clean church girl, the girl with the sketchy past, the sports girl, the bookworm. But we're all more complex than that and far more nuanced. We can't often control how others choose to define us. But we can make sure we don't pigeonhole people in this way. It's frustrating and unfair, so let's strive to see people for all their many facets!

----

day 353

"When Mary reached the place where Jesus was and saw him, she fell at his feet and said, 'Lord, if you had been here, my brother would not have died.' When Jesus saw her weeping, and the Jews who had come along with her also weeping, he was deeply moved in spirit and troubled. 'Where have you laid him?' he asked. 'Come and see, Lord,' they replied. Jesus wept."

–JOHN 11:32-35

This is one of Jesus's most tender moments recorded in the Bible. That simple verse—*Jesus wept*—is powerful, heartbreaking, and beautiful. Did it particularly move him to see Mary, who had sat at his feet, grieve for her brother? It seems to have. He was a human being, our savior, and perhaps no verse proves it better than this one.

Given that Jesus was so humanly real, with powerful emotions, isn't it strange how we sometimes expect his followers to be stoic? Sometimes Christians are expected to put on a brave face and be bold, accepting, and strong in the face of whatever life throws at us.

Nonsense. God doesn't require that of us. He requires us to trust him. To lean on him. To let him share in our broken-heartedness the way Jesus shared in Mary's. That is the "easy yoke" Jesus puts on us—that we would rely on *his* strength, not our own.

day 354

"Jesus, once more deeply moved, came to the tomb. It was a cave with a stone laid across the entrance. 'Take away the stone,' he said. 'But, Lord,' said Martha, the sister of the dead man, 'by this time there is a bad odor, for he has been there four days.' Then Jesus said, 'Did I not tell you that if you believe, you will see the glory of God?'"

–JOHN 11:38–40

Oh, Martha. How can we not adore Martha? She just had the most amazing profession of faith in Jesus as the Christ, but in the next moment, her concern is back to the practical matter of how decayed the body is and not wanting to expose the crowd to the offensive smell.

We have to love Martha because she's exactly like most of us—a mix of radical, earth-shattering faith and utter, hopeless density. Can't you just see Jesus shaking his head? Oh, Martha. If you believe, you'll see the glory of God. Here it comes!

Jesus says the same thing to us. If we believe, we'll see amazing things. If we believe, we'll draw close to the very presence of the God of the universe. If we believe, we'll see eternity with Jesus. And we believe it—we need him to smack us upside the head with it sometimes too. Let's thank God that he's gentle with those rebukes!

day 355

"Then Mary took [expensive perfume and] poured it on Jesus' feet and wiped his feet with her hair . . . But one of his disciples, Judas Iscariot, who was later to betray him, objected, 'Why wasn't this perfume sold and the money given to the poor? It was worth a year's wages.' He did not say this because he cared about the poor but because he was a thief . . . 'Leave her alone,' Jesus replied. 'It was intended that she should save this perfume for the day of my burial.'"

–JOHN 12:3–7

Mary, our heart-connected, soul-seeking sister, did a beautiful thing here. Her perfume was obviously very valuable. And yet she followed the leading of God and poured it over Jesus's feet as a symbol of his forthcoming death and burial. Mary held nothing back from Jesus.

It's a stark contrast between Mary's heart and Judas's heart in this story. Judas sought to take all he could, even from Jesus's ministry. He betrayed Jesus for money—thirty pieces of silver. It's hard to say exactly how much thirty pieces of silver would be, translated into terms we understand today, but in Jesus's time, it was the going rate for a slave. So, whatever the monetary value, Judas sold Jesus as no more than a slave.

Human nature often wants to lean toward a Judas mentality—to take, take, take—as much as we'd love to be Marys all the time. Let's spend a few minutes in prayer today, asking for more of Mary's generosity in our hearts and less of Judas's greed.

361

day 356

"When Jesus rose early on the first day of the week, he appeared first to Mary Magdalene, out of whom he had driven seven demons."

–MARK 16:9

Mary Magdalene's reputation has gone through a millennia-long game of telephone. Through pop culture references and word-of-mouth discussion about her, she somehow has the reputation of having been a sexually immoral woman or a professional prostitute. But the Bible doesn't say either of these things, only that Jesus cast seven demons from her.

How did her story get so mixed up? It's hard to say. We can only imagine how Mary Magdalene might feel if she were alive today and she could see what the common conception of her is. If you have ever been the subject of an untrue rumor, you can probably relate.

Having your reputation dragged through the mud is awful. There's no getting around it. But, like Mary might if she were alive today, we can rest easy in the knowledge that God always knows the truth. No matter what anyone else's perception of us may be, God knows whether or not we fit the box we're being put in. While it's okay to defend our honor and speak the truth about ourselves, our ultimate comfort comes from the God of truth!

day 357

"Early on the first day of the week, while it was still dark, Mary Magdalene went to the tomb and saw that the stone had been removed from the entrance. So she came running to Simon Peter and the other disciple, the one Jesus loved, and said, 'They have taken the Lord out of the tomb, and we don't know where they have put him!' So Peter and the other disciple started for the tomb."

–JOHN 20:1–3

Mary Magdalene often gets pegged as that "sinful woman." Or perhaps, more generously, that reformed sinful woman. But that wouldn't have been how Jesus or the disciples described her. Here, Mary discovers Jesus's tomb was open and empty. And when she ran to tell Peter and John, they believed her! That's because the disciples respected Mary.

Sometimes it's hard for women to gain respect like this. If we're too mild, we get steamrolled and taken advantage of. If we're too forceful, we get written off as being unpleasant—or worse. So how was it Mary Magdalene managed to gain the respect of these men who followed Jesus?

There are probably many factors, but the crucial foundation is the fact that Mary was hanging out with the right people. These men were followers of Jesus who wanted to honor God. When we hang out with people (men and women!) who are in the habit of being disrespectful and not valuing others, of course we're likely to be treated that way eventually. If we keep solid company, we can give and get respect in equal measure.

day 358

"Now a man named Ananias, together with his wife Sapphira, also sold a piece of property. With his wife's full knowledge he kept back part of the money for himself, but brought the rest and put it at the apostles' feet."

–ACTS 5:1–2

We've skipped ahead in time just a bit to the historical record of the early church found in Acts. Sapphira should have been among our awesome early Christian women, serving alongside her husband. Instead, we have a clear account of their deception. And that's what their sin was. It wasn't that they didn't give the full amount the field sold for. It was the fact that they lied about it. They wanted the glory associated with making a big, generous sacrifice without actually having to make the sacrifice.

In their greed and deception, Ananias and Sapphira misrepresented themselves—but they also misrepresented Jesus. Think about what kind of picture that would have presented to any unbelievers who knew what they had done—a couple who said they followed Jesus but acted untruthfully and greedily. "Hypocrite" would be the accurate word here.

Even if we would never go to these lengths, let's be sure we're presenting an accurate, truthful, real picture of who we are and who Jesus is through our actions. Let's guard against the spirit of Sapphira in our hearts that wants honor without sacrifice.

day 359

"Peter asked her, 'Tell me, is this the price you and Ananias got for the land?' 'Yes,' she said, 'that is the price.' Peter said to her, 'How could you conspire to test the Spirit of the Lord?' . . . At that moment she fell down at his feet and died. Then the young men came in and, finding her dead, carried her out and buried her beside her husband. Great fear seized the whole church and all who heard about these events."

—ACTS 5:8–11

Yikes. Sapphira compounded her sin by repeating it to Peter when he confronted her. She didn't know this yet, but her husband had done the same thing and been struck dead. If she had known, would she have confessed?

It's possible. But it's also possible that Sapphira's arrogance would have prompted her to lie anyway. Her actions revealed a lack of faith that God is who he says he is. We say God is everywhere—that there's no hiding from his presence. We say he's all-powerful and he has the ability to do whatever he wants to. And yet Sapphira and Ananias seemed to believe that, as long as they hid their deed from the disciples, they would be in the clear.

We need to be careful that we don't simply give lip service to ideas we've heard often about God. We must let these truths sink deeply into our hearts so that our confession of faith is real and true. Otherwise, we're in danger of Sapphira's same arrogance.

day 360

"In Joppa there was a disciple named Tabitha (in Greek her name is Dorcas); she was always doing good and helping the poor."

–ACTS 9:36

In the next verses, we learn that Tabitha became sick and died. Then Peter brought her back to life. But before her life became a miracle, she had this said of her: she was always doing good and helping the poor. Before she was a miracle woman, her life was a living, breathing testimony to her faith.

That may sound unattainable—an entire way of life that radiates faith in Jesus as you live it. But this devotional is full of practical advice about small steps we can take toward that kind of living testimonial. There are countless other books—Bible studies, history books, the writings of theologians, and other devotionals—to help us meet this goal too.

Sit for a moment and ponder one thing—just one thing you can change to help you toward this goal. Is it something to add to your life, like serving the hungry in your community? Or is it something God wants you to remove from your life, like a bad habit or an unhealthy attitude? Focus on that one thing for the next week. You'd be surprised the big changes you can make in your living testimony by taking small steps.

day 361

"One of those listening was a woman from the city of Thyatira named Lydia, a dealer in purple cloth. She was a worshiper of God. The Lord opened her heart to respond to Paul's message. When she and the members of her household were baptized, she invited us to her home. 'If you consider me a believer in the Lord,' she said, 'come and stay at my house.' And she persuaded us."

–ACTS 16:14–15

That's a cool tagline: *She was a worshiper of God.* And it's an even cooler description of how it feels to understand the message of Jesus for the first time: *The Lord opened her heart to respond.*

That's the message of Christianity, isn't it? God reaches down to us and gives us new eyes to see and a new heart to understand this crazy, loving thing he did for us when he sent his son to Earth. Lydia was one of *billions* who have heard this message. You are too. When that message touched her heart, she responded in kind and opened up her home to the disciples.

A strong desire to serve is one of the hallmarks of a newly kindled heart for Jesus. Is that the stage you're in right now? Or maybe you've been following Jesus a long time—maybe your whole life!—and that fire has quieted a little. Let's reignite the desire to serve that burned in us when we first came to know Jesus!

_____

_____

_____

_____

day 362

"There he met a Jew named Aquila, a native of Pontus, who had recently come from Italy with his wife Priscilla, because Claudius had ordered all Jews to leave Rome. Paul went to see them. [Later, Paul wrote] 'Greet Priscilla and Aquila, my co-workers in Christ Jesus. They risked their lives for me. Not only I but all the churches of the Gentiles are grateful to them.'"

–ACTS 18:2A; ROMANS 16:3–4

Priscilla and Aquila were some of the apostle Paul's greatest helpers. They often worked alongside him. This couple meant a lot to Paul, and as he said in his own words, he wasn't the only one who was grateful for them! They worked hard, loved boldly, and the church was thankful for them!

Priscilla is almost always mentioned in the same breath as her husband. That's not because she wasn't accomplished on her own (or vice versa). It's because they always worked side by side for the church.

Priscilla and Aquila are a wonderful example of a dynamic team working side by side harmoniously. This is a cool example for working in ministry, whether with a spouse or a friend, but it also applies to other types of work. Community service, your place of employment . . . even group projects for school! Working in groups or with a partner can require an extra dose of patience. But we can accomplish more in unified teams than we ever could on our own.

_____

_____

_____

_____

day 363

"I commend to you our sister Phoebe, a deacon of the church in Cenchreae. I ask you to receive her in the Lord in a way worthy of his people and to give her any help she may need from you, for she has been the benefactor of many people, including me... Greet Andronicus and Junia, my fellow Jews who have been in prison with me. They are outstanding among the apostles, and they were in Christ before I was... Greet Tryphena and Tryphosa, those women who work hard in the Lord. Greet my dear friend Persis, another woman who has worked very hard in the Lord."

—ROMANS 16:1–2, 7, 12

If you have an extra five minutes, go read Romans 16. It's Paul's list of personal greetings as he signs off on his lengthy letter to the Roman church. This is a mere sampling of the names he lists, many of whom are women. Phoebe is listed as a deacon, a word which is only ever translated as someone who serves that specific leadership role in the church. There is Junia, and while there are some alternate suggestions for translation, here the sentence strongly implies she was an apostle—not one of the twelve, of course, but one of the outer ring of apostles leading the church. And then there's Persis, a woman who has worked very hard in the Lord.

These female church servants have one thing in common—they *do work* for Jesus and his church. Their specific types of service varied. But whatever they were called to do, and whatever God put before them, they did it.

day 364

"I am reminded of your sincere faith, which first lived in your grandmother Lois and in your mother Eunice and, I am persuaded, now lives in you also."

–2 TIMOTHY 1:5

It's fitting that our final biblical ladies are Eunice, the mother of Timothy, and Lois, his grandmother. Timothy was Paul's pastor protégé, and Paul's letters to him are full of excellent pastoral advice. But he opens his second letter with a personal note about Timothy's lineage. We know from Acts 16:1 that Eunice was a Jewish believer and Timothy's father was Greek. Both of the maternal figures in Timothy's life poured faithfulness into their boy, and he grew up to have "sincere faith." Eunice and Lois passed it on.

We don't grow in godliness and stretch our faithfulness only for our own wellbeing. That's a great benefit, sure. As we build up the church, we're built up too. But we're also looking to pass along a legacy of faith to others. Maybe we'll pass it along to our actual children and grandchildren. Maybe we'll be like spiritual parents through mentorship. Or maybe our legacy will be written in a book or online, and we won't even meet those who were changed by our words. Each of us will leave something behind—a legacy of the life we lived and what mattered to us most. What is your legacy today?

day 365

> "There is neither Jew nor Gentile, neither slave nor free, nor is there male and female, for you are all one in Christ Jesus."
>
> —GALATIANS 3:28

Paul didn't write these words to erase masculinity or femininity. God created men and women, equally beautiful and reflective of his character, and Paul wasn't trying to undo that. No, he was highlighting a rich truth: whatever the differences between different people groups—different cultures, economic situations, or genders—we are all one in Jesus.

This is an amazing message. Sometimes women are oppressed, especially in certain cultures and eras. We've made great strides toward equality. Words like agency, consent, and empowerment are part of our cultural conversation now. But thousands of years ago, God revealed *his* view: we have always mattered to him, and we have always been a valuable part of his church.

Be empowered, beloved daughter, because you were created to be a change-the-world, make-your-mark woman. We've seen more than fifty different ways this calling played out for biblical women of centuries past. Let's walk in their footsteps and be the women we were created to be!

Adored

365 Devotions for Young Women

In an ever-changing world, we can be certain of one thing: we are beloved by God. *Adored: 365 Devotions for Young Women* tackles tough topics girls face, from bullying and social media to friendships and dating, all the while showing readers how infinitely precious they are in God's sight.

Hardcover 9780310762799

Each day features an easy-to-read, relevant devotion paired with a scripture verse and journaling space to help readers reflect on the day's message. With honest, poignant, and sometimes humorous text, every page will speak to the pressures and changes girls face, giving them real-world applications to find God in their hearts and in their lives. Perfect for everyday use, *Adored* will resonate with girls searching for truth and guidance. Gift givers will love this highly designed book featuring a beautiful, foiled cover, and two color interior pages.

Available in stores and online!

NIV Holy Bible for Girls, Journal Edition

The *NIV Holy Bible for Girls, Journal Edition* is the perfect way to apply Scripture to your everyday life. Designed with the thoughtful writer in mind, a whimsical cover and journaling lines inspire reflection in God's Word. This Bible contains the full text of the best-selling New International Version (NIV) translation.

Hardcover, Turquoise, Elastic Closure: 9780310758969

Features include:
- Lines on each page for journaling and notes
- Thick paper perfect for any writing utensil
- A presentation page for gift giving
- A "How to Use This Bible" page to get started on the right foot
- Ribbon marker
- The complete text of the bestselling New International Version (NIV)

Hardcover Pink, Elastic Closure: 9780310759065

Hardcover Purple, Elastic Closure: 9780310759652

Hardcover Mint, Elastic Closure: 9780310759805

Available in stores and online!

ZONDERVAN®
.com

NIV Beautiful Word Coloring Bible for Girls

Hundreds of Verses to Color

With hundreds of inspiring verses illustrated in detailed, ready-to-color line art, the *NIV Beautiful Word Coloring Bible for Girls* was created just for girls ages 8-12. Thick white paper with lightly ruled lines in the extra-wide margins provides ample space for your own artistic expressions and journaling. The *NIV Beautiful Word Coloring Bible for Girls* is a perfect gift that will become a cherished keepsake full of personalized creative expressions of faith.

Hardcover Pink: 9780310763550

Features of this treasured Bible include:
- Hundreds of verses illustrated in ready-to-color line art
- Thicker white paper for enduring note-taking
- Lined, wide margins for notes, reflections and art
- Full text of the most read, most trusted modern-English Bible; the New International Version (NIV)
- Easy-to-read black letter text in single-column format
- Lays flat in your hand or on your desk
- Ribbon marker
- Beautiful debossed and screen-printed leathersoft over board binding

Hardcover Teal: 9780310763543

Available in stores and online!

Hardcover
Floral:
9780310761082

NIV Beautiful Word Bible for Girls

500 Full-Color Illustrated Verses

Discover God's Word through gorgeous illustrated verses. Crafted on high-quality paper and balanced with inspiring full-color art and blank space for journaling, the NIV Beautiful Word Bible for Girls encourages girls to spend quiet time with God and his Word. This Bible contains 500 illustrated verses to illuminate the rich stories, characters and hope contained within Scripture. It inspires girls to explore new ways to grow their faith, drawing deeper into God's life-changing Word.

Features include:

- 500 full-color illustrated verses
- Wide margins and high-quality paper for notes, journal entries or artwork
- Index of illustrated Scripture passages
- 8-point font
- Single-column text of the New International Version (NIV)

Hardcover Sunburst: 9780310761266

Available in stores and online!